About Island Press

Since 1984, the nonprofit organization Island Press has been stimulating, shaping, and communicating ideas that are essential for solving environmental problems worldwide. With more than 1,000 titles in print and some 30 new releases each year, we are the nation's leading publisher on environmental issues. We identify innovative thinkers and emerging trends in the environmental field. We work with world-renowned experts and authors to develop cross-disciplinary solutions to environmental challenges.

Island Press designs and executes educational campaigns in conjunction with our authors to communicate their critical messages in print, in person, and online using the latest technologies, innovative programs, and the media. Our goal is to reach targeted audiences—scientists, policymakers, environmental advocates, urban planners, the media, and concerned citizens—with information that can be used to create the framework for long-term ecological health and human well-being.

Island Press gratefully acknowledges major support of our work by The Agua Fund, The Andrew W. Mellon Foundation, The Bobolink Foundation, The Curtis and Edith Munson Foundation, Forrest C. and Frances H. Lattner Foundation, The JPB Foundation, The Kresge Foundation, The Oram Foundation, Inc., The Overbrook Foundation, The S.D. Bechtel, Jr. Foundation, The Summit Charitable Foundation, Inc., and many other generous supporters.

The opinions expressed in this book are those of the author(s) and do not necessarily reflect the views of our supporters.

NATURE'S ALLIES

Nature's Allies

Eight Conservationists Who Changed Our World

Larry A. Nielsen

ISLANDPRESS

Washington | Covelo | London

Library of Congress Control Number: 2016946591

Printed on recycled, acid-free paper ⊛

Manufactured in the United States of America
10 9 8 7 6 5 4 3 2 1

Keywords: Island Press, John Muir, Yosemite National Park, Robert Underwood Johnson, Sierra Club, Hetch Hetchy, Ding Darling, Duck Stamp, National Wildlife Refuge System, John Salyer, US Biological Survey, National Wildlife Federation, Aldo Leopold, Sand County Almanac, The Shack, Game Management, Thinking Like a Mountain, Rachel Carson, Under the Sea Wind, The Sea Around Us, The Edge of the Sea, Silent Spring, DDT, Chico Mendes, Extractive reserves, Brazilian rainforest, Rubber-tapping, Deforestation, Billy Frank Jr., Judge Hugo Boldt, Hank Adams, Nisqually Tribe, Treaty of 1854, Northwest Indian Fisheries Commission, Wangari Maathai, Green Belt Movement, Uhuru Park, Nobel Peace Prize, Gro Harlem Brundtland, World Commission on Environment and Development, World Health Organization, Sustainability definition.

To the memory of Joe Florini, as true a conservationist
as those whose stories appear here

Contents

FOREWORD

Conservationist.

What picture does the word bring to mind? For many, and for a long time, it might have suggested a standard image. Likely an older, fair-skinned, well-to-do man, in brown boots and khaki field clothes, toting a field notebook, binoculars, maybe a shotgun. And for a long time that cliché might even have held some truth—though no stereotype can hold up under closer examination of the real human life behind it. But if a generation ago we had a hackneyed idea of what a conservationist should look like and what he does . . . she does not look and act like that anymore.

In these pages Larry Nielsen assembles a conservation portrait gallery, pictures of eight disparate and remarkable lives, lived out in their different places under widely varied circumstances. Collectively they span an arc of history stretching from the modern origins of conservation in the mid-1800s to the verge of our own future, following concerns that range from forests, wildlife, and fisheries to agriculture, climate change, and economic justice. They are women and men, northerners and southerners, rural and urban, indigenous and immigrant, advantaged and challenged, professionals and citizens. They all contributed importantly to a movement that crosses generations, political boundaries, and fields of knowledge. They are elder sisters and brothers in a cause that, more than ever, requires every kind of talent, background, perspective, and voice. And still requires, on occasion, binoculars.

Don't you wish we could gather them together in one place, and hear their voices? John Muir's tale-spinning Scottish brogue. Ding Darling's Midwestern American candor. Aldo Leopold's casual eloquence. Rachel Carson's steel and integrity. Chico Mendes' soft-spoken determination and courage. Billy Frank's persistent, defiant dignity. Wangari Maathai's inspired pragmatism. Gro Harlem Brundtland's seasoned vision. Through their voices we would also hear those of others: the families, cultures, traditions, and institutions that instilled their conservation values.

And don't you wish we could hear them in conversation *together*, trading the quieter stories behind their signature accomplishments, discussing the social cross-currents and political tensions of their times, debating different paths forward? We could, if we wanted, draw lines of connection through these lives: John Muir camping out with Theodore Roosevelt, who put Gifford Pinchot in charge of the US Forest Service; Pinchot's family founding the forestry program at Yale University, where Aldo Leopold studied; Leopold later working with Ding Darling to strengthen the US Bureau of Biological Survey, which became the US Fish and Wildlife Service, where Rachel Carson honed her communication skills . . . and so on and on. Through these individuals and countless others, conservation has grown as an ever-expanding movement, fitfully overcoming its own limitations and forging new connections. But these kindred spirits can meet only in our imagination—and in these pages.

Whether in word or image, it is not an easy task to depict such rich, complicated, and consequential lives as these people led. Larry Nielsen has given us essential portraits, describing not only the facts of their experience, but the contexts in which they made their way. All of them (indeed) changed the world by allowing the world to change them—to excite their intellects and touch their hearts. And they changed the world by reaching the hearts of others, and by linking actions and ideas. A portrait tells a story, and these stories together tell us of people, linked across time, who helped build a movement.

Yet, none of these people acted alone. All emerged themselves from a community. In some cases, a community of place—often a threatened place. In other cases, a community of interest and professional expertise. Or a community bound by a shared sense of responsibility. Each of them, in turn, fostered and expanded these communities. As their work rippled out, all left enduring legacies—among those they influenced and on the land.

And it turns out that, in the long run, these naturalists and hunters and foresters and farmers and scientists and South American rubber tappers and Native American fishers and Kenyan tree planters and international policy-makers all belong to a yet larger community. That community is defined by a common moral commitment to one's neighbors and fellow citizens, to future generations, to other living beings and the complex living systems that support us all. That is not to say that there are no differences of viewpoint or priority or strategy within the conservation community. This collective portrait shows in fact that conservationists have varied motivations, and come in many shades of political persuasion—and they always have. Communities hold together, and progress together, by testing their shared values against changing circumstances. Leaders, including those portrayed here, emerge to help guide that process in lasting and positive ways.

In the 1940s Aldo Leopold wrote, "Conservation, viewed in its entirety, is the slow and laborious unfolding of a new relationship between people and land." The "unfolding" continues. It continues by building on the accomplishments of those who came before; by confronting past shortcomings, taking in new information, expanding ethical horizons, forging new policies, and inventing new techniques; by bringing people together and making common cause with other areas of human need and endeavor.

Fundamental to all these, though, is the obligation to share the stories of the "unfolding" itself. What I especially appreciate about this book is the opportunity it provides for young people to learn a bit more about those who came before, who challenged the status quo and made change happen. Like democracy and justice—tied, in fact, to them—conservation involves continual struggle, regular setbacks, steady advances, and occasional leaps forward. We find our way forward, in part, by carrying with us the stories of those who came before.

Conservationist.

Who do you see when you think ahead another generation? Whoever you see, it is likely that they will look and work in ways quite different from those profiled here. But my guess is that they will, like these eight, love their places deeply. They will value the wild and the beautiful. They will have a gift for working with people. They will be both practical and visionary. They will demonstrate courage and a thirst for justice. They will be curious and creative. And, from time to time, they may well pull out their binoculars.

Curt Meine

Sauk Prairie, Wisconsin

ACKNOWLEDGMENTS

This book has been a career in the making. I am grateful to the many colleagues who have shared their thoughts and perspectives about the project over the past forty years and especially to those who provided specific ideas and insights as the completion of the project drew closer, especially Tom Busiahn (who recommended that I write about Billy Frank Jr.), Erin Sills (who suggested Chico Mendes), and Dan Robison, a continuing source of encouragement and inspiration. My university, North Carolina State University, and my supervisors— Barry Goldfarb, Tom Gower, and Mary Watzin—provided the time, freedom, and encouragement to allow me to complete the book. I thank the wonderful people at Island Press for their belief in the project, and, particularly, Erin Johnson, who shepherded the book from idea to publication. I am indebted to the individuals and organizations that provided illustrations for the book; their names are acknowledged with their photographs. Finally and most importantly, I thank my wife and daughters—Sharon, Jennifer, and Amanda—for their ideas, support, and patience on this and many projects, both those in the past and those yet to come.

Introduction

One accepted the Nobel Peace Prize for her commitment to Kenya's forests; one was murdered for protecting the forests of Brazil. One proclaimed his message in drawings on the front pages of the nation's newspapers; one made his statement in waders on the banks of the Nisqually River. One walked thousands of miles on a lifelong journey of self-discovery; one seldom left her suburban Maryland home. One directed our attention to the natural rhythms of a small Wisconsin farm; one asked us to consider the entire globe as our backyard.

This book profiles the lives of eight great conservationists. A few are well known to people everywhere—ask anyone to name a famous conservationist or environmentalist, and the names of John Muir and Rachel Carson are sure to come up. Some names might ring a bell—Aldo Leopold, Wangari Maathai, and Gro Harlem Brundtland—but the reason might be harder to remember. And the names of Ding Darling, Billy Frank Jr., and Chico Mendes will be new to most readers. My goal is to bring their stories—their highs and lows, their admirable traits and human weaknesses, their triumphs and failures—to all who are interested in making the world a bit better through conservation. Their stories are tributes, of course, but more importantly they are examples of what each of us might be and do on behalf of the sustainability of our world—as an ally to nature.

This book is loosely patterned after another book of short biographies. In 1954, Senator John F. Kennedy was bedridden after back surgery. His back, already weakened and battered throughout his early life, was especially damaged during World War II when the small Navy vessel he captained—PT-109—was rammed and sunk by a larger Japanese ship while the PT boat was on night duty in the Solomon Islands. Kennedy heroically led his surviving crewmen to safety on a small island, where they were rescued several days later. A decade after his wartime injury, Kennedy's back needed extensive surgical repair—and months of recovery time. Kennedy used his time as an invalid to research and coauthor the book *Profiles in Courage*, along with Theodore Sorensen, his colleague and lifelong advisor.[1] Their book tells the stories of eight United States senators who risked their offices and careers to stand up for what they believed—even when those beliefs were unpopular. The authors announce in the preface that they "have attempted to set forth their lives—the ideals they lived for and the principles they fought for, their virtues and their sins, their dreams and their disillusionments, the praise they earned and the abuse they endured."[2] *Profiles in Courage* won the Pulitzer Prize for Biography in 1957. I read the book as a teenager—it was intended for young readers—and found the stories inspirational.

Throughout my career, I have wanted to write a similar book to portray the lives of individuals who have made a difference for our natural environment. Conservation is still a young field—most accounts mark its birth at Teddy Roosevelt's 1908 Governors' Conference on Conservation—and thus our history is still tied closely to the actions and accomplishments of specific persons. And as broadly enacted public policy, both in the developed and developing world, conservation is even younger. In many parts of the world, considerations of conservation are still just beginning to emerge as significant elements of how we govern our lives.

My decision to include lives from a continuum of conservation fame is purposeful. I asked many people to give me suggestions for persons to include. Most rattled off a list of "the usual suspects," like John Muir, Gifford Pinchot, Teddy Roosevelt, and Aldo Leopold. However, once the lives of a few were told (of the more famous, I chose John Muir and Aldo Leopold), the stories of the others seemed redundant, as did those of many of the other prominent leaders of the early conservation movement. Some colleagues suggested names that reach further back in history—George Perkins Marsh, for example—or that evoke a more philosophical tradition, like Emerson and Thoreau. While these names are important as precursors of conservation, I have chosen to stick closer to the actual practice of the field—people who rode the trails, dug the holes, and planted the trees on their way to making a national or international impact. Equally important was moving beyond the mainstream of American conservation to represent a fuller diversity of contributions. Because all people, everywhere, have a role in conservation, three biographies feature stories from Africa, South America, and Europe.

Regardless of how, where, or when these eight individuals lived, they truly did create the concepts of conservation by which we live today. Each was—or is, in the case of Gro Harlem Brundtland—a pioneer in some aspect of conservation, environmentalism, or sustainability. Their accomplishments vary, of course. Some occurred long ago, like John Muir's successful campaign for the establishment of Yosemite National Park. Others are much more recent, like Billy Frank Jr.'s David-and-Goliath campaign to gain recognition for treaties that assured Native American fishing rights. However, as in both those cases, the specific result led to replication of the impact in park after park and fishery after fishery, not only in the United States but also around the world.

Several leaders are known mostly for boiling down the wisdom and experience of a lifetime of work into a signature written volume: Rachel Carson's *Silent Spring* and Aldo Leopold's *A Sand County Almanac* grace the bookshelves of professional and avocational conservationists around the world. In Gro Harlem Brundtland's case, her impact is represented in just twenty-two words—the universally accepted definition of *sustainability*. These accomplishments have no specific action or target, but they inspired new perspectives that have revolutionized public policies, private decisions, and personal attitudes.

Some of these conservation leaders made their mark through sheer hard work. Wangari Maathai huddled on the ground with her fellow Kenyan wives and mothers to plant more than 50 million trees. Chico Mendes tramped the trails of the Amazonian rain forest to support communities of rubber tappers and the trees on which they depend. Because of Maathai and Mendes, forests remain and thrive on the great continents of Africa and South America, under the spotlight of public awareness and the protection of conscientious governments.

And then there is Ding Darling, who defies categorization. A political cartoonist who loved wildlife, Darling used his editorial privilege to tell the story of environmental degradation on the front pages of scores of daily newspapers. Then, in a gesture of monumental humility (and perhaps with an underlying dose of hubris), he went to Washington to do something about it. Less than two years later, the United States had a functioning wildlife refuge system and a mechanism—the duck stamp—that has paid to keep it going.

When I began this project, I wondered what the lives of these eight great conservationists might have had in common. Perhaps, I thought, each was a biologist, educated in the emerging discipline of ecology. Indeed, some of them were: Wangari Maathai earned a doctorate in biology, Gro Harlem Brundtland is a medical doctor, and Rachel Carson and Aldo Leopold each held master's degrees. Ding Darling eventually earned an undergraduate degree, and John Muir gave it the old college try for a couple of years. But Billy Frank Jr. and Chico Mendes seldom saw the inside of a school. So a formal education—especially higher education—doesn't seem to be a requirement to create conservation.

Do wealth and social standing play a dominant role? Gro Harlem Brundtland and Aldo Leopold both came from money and status, but it seems that more fundamental values were at play as well; both grew up in homes dominated by concerns of ethics and integrity rather than worries about getting ahead of the next person. John Muir's family actually threw away its prominent status in Scotland to establish a new, rough-hewn life in Wisconsin; eventually Muir became a wealthy man, but it most certainly was not his primary intention. The others—Ding Darling, Rachel Carson, Wangari Maathai, Billy Frank Jr., and Chico Mendes—were all people of modest means. Although Ding Darling and Rachel Carson became successful, their financial comfort was much more a by-product of their accomplishments than a route to them.

Were they all adventurers who set out to escape from the constraints of everyday life? That describes John Muir to a large extent and Aldo Leopold a bit. But most were ordinary folks living in ordinary surroundings: Wangari Maathai in Nairobi, Ding Darling in his Iowa newspaper office, Rachel Carson in the Washington suburbs, and Gro Harlem Brundtland in downtown Oslo. Billy Frank Jr. and Chico Mendes lived and worked where they were born. Most of these leaders, however, did have a refuge where they could get away—a Florida cottage for Darling and one in Maine for Carson, and a famous little farm for Leopold. John Muir enjoyed a not-so-cozy hideaway that became Yosemite National Park. So, perhaps, having one foot in civilization and another in nature does keep a conservationist motivated and grounded.

Were they all scientists? Far from it. In fact, I consider only one— Aldo Leopold—to be a professional conservationist. Rachel Carson worked as a scientist for the US Fish and Wildlife Service, but had resigned to be a full-time author well before her significant conservation contribution, *Silent Spring*, was even imagined. The others were all amateurs—a cartoonist, medical doctor, union organizer, commercial fisherman. Wangari Maathai was a tree-planter, a sort of modern day Johnny Appleseed. And John Muir just called himself a tramp.

The absence of a stereotypical life pattern shouldn't really be a surprise. Of course their lives followed different paths from different beginnings and with different purposes. Like all of us, these are complex individuals, each of whom had her or his own story. But aside from their demographic differences, I see that three common characteristics flow through each of their lives: passion, persistence, and partnerships.

Passion

All eight were fired from within by a passion to understand, protect, and enhance our environment. For some, the passion started from infancy. Rachel Carson was raised by a mother who believed that nature was the best teacher—and she raised her daughter to be a keen observer of nature. Aldo Leopold spent his youth hunting with his father, but the more important part of every outing was the simple experience of nature. For others, the passion grew with the coming of age. Ding Darling and his brother rode their horses at breakneck speed across the unbroken prairie, immersing themselves in the wonder of their surroundings. John Muir slipped into nature as often as possible in order to escape a repressive home life as a boy in Scotland and a young man in Wisconsin. Gro Harlem Brundtland always enjoyed nature, but gradually she became conscious of its importance as her education broadened. For Wangari Maathai, Chico Mendes, and Billy Frank Jr., however, nature was just where they lived and how their families made their livings.

Yet each came to realize that the relationship between humans and nature needed attention. Wangari Maathai and Ding Darling saw the beauty and bounty of their memories erased by careless destruction of farmland. Chico Mendes rebelled as Amazonian rain forests were cleared and burned for cattle ranches, and he applied a unique form of protest to confront the devastation. Rachel Carson heard the stories of wildlife death caused by the aerial spraying of pesticides, and although she didn't want to get involved, she felt compelled to right the wrongs she was observing. John Muir and Aldo Leopold understood the utilitarian benefits of nature, but they also realized that overuse was worse than underuse; a generation apart from each other, they fought for the protection of lands as parks or wilderness areas. Billy Frank Jr. and other Native American commercial fishermen knew the truth from their personal experience—too much harvest this year means too few fish next year. And Gro Harlem Brundtland grew to understand the links between the human condition and environmental conditions on a worldwide scale as chair of the World Commission on Environment and Development.

Wangari Maathai expressed the need for passion in her Nobel Peace Prize lecture in 2004:

> In the course of history, there comes a time when humanity is called to shift to a new level of consciousness, to reach a higher moral ground. A time when we have to shed our fear and give hope to each other. That time is now.
>
> The Norwegian Nobel Committee has challenged the world to broaden the understanding of peace: there can be no peace without equitable development; and there can be no development without sustainable management of the environment in a democratic and peaceful space.[3]

Persistence

Passion may be necessary for accomplishment, but it is not sufficient. Many lives burn brightly for a short time and then fade as the fuel of passion runs low. Life, as some would say, gets in the way. Each of the lives recounted here, however, also reveals the essence of persistence as a condition of success. By studying a person's entire life—not just their pinnacle achievements, like *A Sand County Almanac* or a Nobel Peace Prize—we can see their struggles, failures, courage, and persistence shining through.

John Muir straddled a world between nature and industrialism as a young man, but when an accident left him temporarily blind, his decision to commit himself to nature, not commerce, was a commitment that would last his entire life. Severe illnesses threatened Rachel Carson's ability to work every day of her adult life, yet she continued the painstaking task of creating *Silent Spring*. Billy Frank Jr. was imprisoned more than fifty times in his struggle to acquire the Indian fishing rights guaranteed in treaties with the US government; he didn't give up, never tiring of the battle and finding some other way to make a living. After years of complaining about how incompetent the federal government was, Ding Darling swallowed his pride and went to work for a man he abhorred—President Franklin Roosevelt—just so he could advance the cause of conservation. Friends warned Chico Mendes and Wangari Maathai again and again to stay away from the dangerous movements they had created, but neither would give up the cause—a cause Mendes paid for with his life. And Gro Harlem Brundtland and Aldo Leopold just kept at it, landing and losing positions, suffering defeats as well as victories, project after project, over lifetimes of accomplishments, large and small, on behalf of us all.

Persistence should make sense to conservationists, because we understand the importance of the slow, patient pace of nature. While the average person is attracted to an individual animal—perhaps an injured bird or a newborn hippo at the zoo—conservationists know that the much more crucial danger is the overharvest of a population and the destruction of habitat. Impacts that occur slowly over time or gradually over vast areas are the real culprits in reducing the sustainability of the earth—and people who spend a lifetime trying to resolve those problems are the true heroes of the environment. Wangari Maathai didn't mount a large, one-time campaign to plant trees in Africa; she spent decades going from one village to another, addressing small gatherings of Kenyan women. And in so doing, she caused 50 million trees to be planted. Rachel Carson didn't rush an incomplete analysis in order to make a publication deadline; instead she plodded steadily through thousands of reports and letters, regularly putting off her editor and publisher, until the story could be told in full. John Muir didn't spend a week in Yosemite Valley and write a flowery travelogue about it; he spent year after year after year hiking by himself to the farthest reaches of the Yosemite ecosystem, eventually forcing a basic shift in the way geologists think about glaciers and their movements.

Billy Frank Jr. talked often about the importance of hanging around, even when the federal and state officials he worked with had gone off to promotions or retirement. Persistence, he knew, was the only thing that would keep his cause on the agenda of agencies, politicians, and the public. As one biographer noted, "He's made himself a credible spokesperson for the resources, and I can't tell you what value that has. He's the guy that's been there the whole time."[4]

Partnerships

The eight biographies in this book are of individuals. But look a bit deeper into their lives and accomplishments, and another quality emerges: most of them worked closely with others to multiply and strengthen their impact. Ding Darling is acknowledged as "the best friend a duck ever had," but his real triumph may have been hiring a young John Salyer to oversee the expansion of our national wildlife refuges. Darling in Washington and Salyer driving the nation's backroads turned into a pair that wouldn't be stopped—and today we have more than 500 wildlife refuges because of their joint efforts. Gro Harlem Brundtland has her name forever attached to the definition of sustainability, but her first act as chair of the newly formed World Commission on Environment and Development was to convince Jim MacNeill, a superb organizer and researcher, to join the team as the full-time director of the commission's work. Billy Frank Jr., the Native American fisherman who specialized in getting arrested, was transformed into a national hero through his partnership with Hank Adams, a legal and communications genius who became Frank's right-hand man.

Photographs of John Muir generally show him alone in the wilderness, his shaggy hair and beard, rough clothes, and walking stick reinforcing the myth of Muir the hermit. Yet Muir was a devoted family man and a gregarious host, the life of the party. Moreover, his signature contribution—the establishment of Yosemite National Park—was a productive partnership between Muir, writing about the marvels of Yosemite, and Robert Underwood Johnson, lobbying the rich, famous, and powerful in New York and Washington to protect the land.

Some partnerships are personal and specific, others are more diffuse. Wangari Maathai, for example, wrote little about specific individuals that helped along the way, but her impact was entirely the product of partnerships. She empowered small groups of rural women to work with her to grow and nurture trees. Rachel Carson relied on her dear friend Dorothy Freeman to restore her fragile emotional balance and spur her creativity. A string of other mentors and collaborators, mostly women, served the same purpose at earlier times in Carson's life.

In other words, none of these eight individuals created conservation by themselves. They were taught, inspired, and prodded by their companions. They walked arm in arm, using their talents and those of their partners to multiply their impact.

What Their Lives Mean for Us

Few of us will ever climb a tree in a windstorm to feel an authentic thrill, or write a series of stories that define an ecological theology, or become the protagonist in a Supreme Court case. We need not be brilliant or wealthy or even particularly virtuous. But each of us can have an impact. Conservation asks only three things of us.

First, we must be passionate. Conservation doesn't come from "business as usual." Accepting the way we do things today will not bring about a better world for tomorrow. Challenging the status quo, discovering ways to live that are more sustainable and more just, becoming, as Mahatma Gandhi said, "the change we want to see"—these are the passions that have the potential to transform and sustain our world.

Second, we must be persistent. Real improvements, those that last through time, don't happen overnight. "Inch by inch and row by row," goes the song by Pete Seeger, "gonna make this garden grow."[5] Nature is resilient, both to our insults and to our attempts at healing. One watch at the wheel will not turn the ship of nature. But a lifetime of care just might.

Third, we must seek partners. Our individual efforts matter, but our combined efforts can be the stuff of legend—indeed, the stuff of biographies like these eight. Being a partner means sometimes working on your own ideas but sometimes working on others' ideas instead. It means sometimes playing the lead, but more often being in the chorus.

Remember that in the web of life, as in the biodiversity of nature, every strand matters.

And with enough passion, persistence, and partnerships, perhaps the next time a book like this is written, it will profile nine lives—including yours.

Figure 1.1 John Muir, 1838–1914. (Reproduced courtesy of the Wisconsin Historical Society, WHS-1946.)

Chapter 1

John Muir

Earth-Planet, Universe

The winds began to freshen, a warning that the balmy California day was about to change. In the Sierra Nevada Mountains, experienced locals were retreating inside to wait out the windstorm about to roar down the Yuba River valley.

One man chose the opposite reaction. Instead of running for cover, he ran for the woods. "For on such occasions nature has always something rare to show us, and the danger to life and limb is hardly greater than one would experience crouching deprecatingly beneath a roof."[1] Trees were breaking all around him, some torn out from the soil by their roots. Branches and leaves flew past as clouds of pollen and bits of moss choked the air. This would be a storm to remember.

Just being out in the storm was not enough, however, so he sought a more authentic spot for observing it: "It occurred to me that it would be a fine thing to climb one of the trees to obtain a wider outlook and get my ear close to the Aeolian music of its topmost needles. . . . Being accustomed to climb trees in making botanical studies, I experienced no difficulty in reaching the top of this one, and never before did I enjoy so noble an exhilaration of motion. . . . I clung with muscles firm braced, like a bobo-link on a reed."[2] He stayed lashed to the trunk for hours, living the pitch and sway of the tree. He closed his eyes at times to focus instead on the sounds of the storm—creaking limbs and scratching branches, the thrashing of leaves. Then he concentrated on the fragrance in the air, released as the plants were shredded by the wind.

Perhaps no one in the history of conservation has been as comfortable in raw nature as this man—John Muir.

As he always did, Muir learned something new in this encounter with wind in the tops of trees. "It never occurred to me until this storm-day, while swinging in the wind, that trees are travelers, in the ordinary sense. They make many journeys, not extensive ones, it is true; but our own little journeys, away and back again, are only little more than tree-wavings—many of them not so much."[3]

John Muir took many journeys with nature in his life, and through his writings he took the American public with him. Eventually he convinced us that keeping some of this nature around, uncorrupted by the utilitarian drive of humanity, was not only a good idea, but maybe the best idea: "Thousands of tired, nerve-shaken, over-civilized people are beginning to find out that going to the mountains is going home; that wilderness is a necessity; and that mountain parks and reservations are useful not only as fountains of timber and irrigating rivers, but as fountains of life."[4]

Destined to Wander

John Muir was born on April 21, 1838, in Dunbar, a thriving harbor town on Scotland's eastern coast. His father, Daniel Muir, was a successful merchant and respected townsman, but he was haunted by two demons. First, he was fiercely independent, bristling under the yoke of convention. He cared little for wealth or reputation, but dreamed of becoming a landowner and farmer, accountable to no one for his livelihood or his lifestyle.

Daniel Muir's second demon was religious extremism. The harsher one's life, he reasoned, the closer one came to God. Hard work and strict discipline were needed to triumph over sin and keep temptation out of reach. Therefore, the Muir home had simple, even miserly meals, no decoration, singing, or laughter, and the bookshelf held little more than the Bible. Daniel Muir disciplined his eight children—and especially Johnnie, the eldest son—with the back of his hand and the crack of the strap.

Johnnie Muir, however, presented his father a formidable challenge. He was all boy, proficient at shooting, eloquent at cussing, and always ready for a boxing match. He was witty, loved to sing and play practical jokes—activities that secretly delighted his mother and siblings when his father was away from home. To escape his father's harshness, Johnnie disappeared regularly, venturing down to the forbidden docks and the seashore. He was always whipped for these and other transgressions, but the whippings never tamed him. His father thought he knew the problem: "The verra Deevil's in that boy."[5]

Johnnie Muir also found relief in the care of his grandfather, who ran the butcher shop across the road and became his daily companion. They walked hand-in-hand through Dunbar, his grandfather teaching him his numbers and letters from the store windows and addresses. Their walks grew longer as Muir got older, extending into the cultivated fields and pastured hills surrounding the town. Every explorer encounters nature in a small way at first, and Muir was no exception. He remembered uncovering a nest occupied by a female field mouse and her young: "No hunter could have been more excited on discovering a bear and her cubs in a wilderness den."[6]

Daniel Muir's dream of becoming a farmer turned real in March of 1849. He packed up Johnnie, now eleven, and two other siblings and boarded a ship bound for North America. The rest of the family stayed behind until these four had secured a farm and built a proper home. When the ship landed in New York, they headed to a new community of Scottish immigrants that was taking root in the rolling landscape of Portage, Wisconsin. Daniel used his life savings to purchase land for a farm bordering a lake that inspired its name: Fountain Lake Farm.

John Muir melted happily into this rural paradise. He experienced freedom that his father had never allowed in Scotland, and nature on the Wisconsin frontier, raw and unconstrained, was a textbook that Muir could appreciate. "Nature streaming into us, wooingly teaching her wonderful glowing lessons . . . every wild lesson a love lesson, not whipped but charmed into us. Oh, that glorious Wisconsin wilderness!"[7]

The Muirs, however, had not come to Wisconsin to revel in nature. They had come to tame it. Although still a boy, John was expected to work like a man—perhaps like two men. In the spring, he was strapped to a mule and he directed a plow from sunup to sundown, Monday through Saturday. In the fall, he harvested crops and carried them to market. As winter came on, the tasks worsened. One of his brothers remembered "the quilts all frozen about our faces in the morning and how awful cold it was to get up in the morning and dress and go down to the kitchen barefooted. . . . And going to Portage with loads of corn—running behind the wagon to keep warm and having to cut frozen bread for our lunch."[8] The farm succeeded, and the family reunited in their new homeland.

While some might have grown weak or sullen under such a burden, John Muir did not. He grew stronger physically and mentally, a lanky bundle of sinew that could endure any hardship. He demanded more of himself than did others, including his father, and he refused any physical limits. Once, while swimming in the farm's lake, he became disoriented and, panicking, he nearly drowned. Outraged at his failing, the next day he rowed back to the center of the lake and dove in repeatedly, swimming to the bottom and back, just to prove he could. "Take that," he said, challenging the lake—and himself—each time he rose to the surface.[9]

Farm life left no time for school, so John Muir educated himself. He learned the trades needed by a frontier farmer, and was soon able to craft tools or equipment and to mend what had broken. He became a proficient hunter and horseman. Reading voraciously from books smuggled into the house from friends and neighbors, he was especially engaged by the tales of explorers crisscrossing the globe in the mid-nineteenth century.

As Muir matured, he gradually became embroiled in an emotional and mental struggle that would mark his entire life. Raised in a religious household, he never questioned that a divine spirit had created the earth. But Muir could not reconcile his father's harsh theology with the concept of a loving and forgiving god. Nor could he accept that God existed in organizations of clerics, churches, and conformist policies. Muir found God in nature, not in cathedrals, as he later wrote about Yosemite: "Nearly all the park is a profound solitude. Yet it is full of charming company, full of God's thoughts, a place of peace and safety amid the most exalted grandeur and eager enthusiastic action, a new song, a place of beginnings abounding in first lessons on life, mountain-building, eternal, invincible, unbreakable order; with sermons in stones, storms, trees, flowers, and animals brimful of humanity."[10]

A Young Man on the Move

Muir's hands and mind were always busy. When the day's work ended, he turned to his avocation: inventor. Muir was always whittling or hammering something to make the farm more efficient or the labor less exhausting. He invented saws, hydrometers, clocks, and thermometers, often encased in wooden cabinets carved into elaborate and bizarre shapes. He even devised an alarm-clock bed that tilted up and threw him on the floor when it was time to start the day.

Neighbors began to pose a serious question: was there a genius or a madman living down the road? Some thought his handiworks were "freaks" and they predicted that he would "come to no good." A close friend of the family, however, was more insightful: "Mark my words, Johnnie Moor will mak' a name for himself some day."[11]

Someday was on the near horizon. Muir's friends argued that the world needed to see his inventions, and they knew where to start— the Wisconsin State Fair. Muir was hesitant, but his friends were adamant, insisting that his inventions were "so out-and-out original. . . ."[12] So, in the summer of 1860 at the age of twenty-two, he packed up his creations and headed to Madison on the first independent journey of his life.

Today, we would say that John Muir "went viral" when the gates to the State Fair opened. Visitors were enthralled by his inventions and by the down-home and passionate way in which he described them. He was an instant success, featured repeatedly on the front pages of the Madison newspaper. The crowds grew daily, and public opinion answered the question that had preoccupied his neighbors: John Muir *was* a genius.

The notoriety was heady, but what captured Muir's imagination lay down the street a short distance—the University of Wisconsin. One walk through campus gave him a new goal: he decided to study science and become a doctor.

When he enrolled in the fall of 1861, he was classified as an "irregular gentleman" because he didn't follow a prescribed curriculum. He originally concentrated on chemistry and ancient languages, a compromise between his interests and his father's. But two specific disciplines attracted Muir most—geology and botany, fields that would be his lifelong passions.

He was irregular in other ways, too. He grew a long beard and long tangled hair, presenting the appearance and demeanor of a simple rural lad. "If I had a beard like yours," remarked one of his friends, "I would set it on fire."[13] His room overflowed with inventions, by then including a mechanical desk that rotated textbooks at fifteen-minute intervals, moving his studies along at a brisk and regular pace. Dried and pressed botanical specimens occupied any remaining spaces.

Almost immediately, Muir fell under the nurturing influence of Mrs. Jeanne Carr, wife of Ezra Carr, professor of science. Mrs. Carr was like many other women who loomed large in Muir's life—educated in both the arts and sciences, a blend of Victorian romanticism and progressive efficiency, socially astute and determined to alter the affairs of both the drawing room and the board room. She guided his academic and intellectual progress at the university, but also influenced many of his personal decisions throughout his life.

Muir returned to the university for a second and a bit of a third year, but that's where his formal education ended. America was in the midst of the Civil War, and although he opposed slavery on moral grounds, he was a confirmed pacifist with no appetite for fighting. So, when President Lincoln began to conscript young men for the war, Muir "skedaddled"—Civil War slang for dodging the draft.

Muir lived in Canada for two years, waiting out the war. He walked wherever he went—one mile or one hundred—beginning the practice for which he became famous. He also began to demonstrate his deep connection to the earth by, for example, describing his discovery of a rare orchid, the *Calypso borealis*: "I never before saw a plant so full of life; so perfectly spiritual, it seemed pure enough for the throne of its Creator. I felt as if I were in the presence of superior beings who loved me and beckoned me to come. I sat down beside them and wept for joy."[14]

In 1866, Muir walked back into the United States. This time he stopped at Indianapolis, where he found employment with a manufacturer of wooden wheels. Muir's wood-working ability and inventiveness impressed the company's owners, and they soon gave him free rein to automate the milling and assembly process and to reorganize the work flow. He was promoted several times and was finally earning a good living. He boarded with a well-regarded family, led local children on Sunday walks in the woods, and enjoyed the city's intellectual and cultural atmosphere. Several young women enjoyed his special attention. His future seemed secure—he would become a successful industrialist, marry well, and raise a family.

But fate intervened. One evening in the spring of 1867, Muir was working late, repairing a belt in the factory's sawmill. The lacing that joined the ends of the belt proved difficult to remove, so he grabbed a sharp, narrow file to pry the lacing loose. He pushed harder, and then harder still. The file slipped out of his hand and flew upward, puncturing his right eye. As he cupped his eye in pain, the vitreous humor—the mass of the eyeball—dropped into his palm, and the eye collapsed. His right eye was instantly sightless. In neurological sympathy, his left eye also shuttered, leaving Muir completely blind.

Muir lay in his darkened bedroom for days, sightless and despairing. He considered blindness the cruelest injury that could befall him: "My days were terrible beyond what I can tell, and my nights were if possible more terrible. Frightful dreams exhausted and terrified me. . . . The sunshine and the winds are working in all the gardens of God, but I—I am lost! . . . I would gladly have died where I stood."[15]

Fortunately, the blindness was temporary. Over the next several months, his eye re-inflated and his eyesight gradually returned to

Figure 1.2 John Muir in Kings Canyon, California, 1902. (Reproduced courtesy of Prints & Photographs Division, Library of Congress, LC-USZ62-52000.)

normal. As he regained strength, he took increasingly longer walks around Indianapolis. "God has to nearly kill us sometimes," he wrote later, "to teach us lessons."[16] Muir's lesson was that he should not squander his life chained to a factory when nature beckoned. "I might have become a millionaire," he said, "but I chose to become a tramp."[17]

And tramp he would. He walked home to Wisconsin and back again to Indianapolis, anxious to move but uncertain of where to go. Finally, he settled on South America in order to retrace the journey of explorer Alexander von Humboldt. But rather than climb onto a steamboat or a train to head south, he walked. He was ready to quit society, unwilling to spend any more time in confined spaces with crowds of other humans. At the age of twenty-nine, without a career or any prospects, he set out "by the wildest, leafiest, and least trodden way" he could find.[18] His pack was nearly empty, most space taken up by a thick botanical taxonomy guide and the notebook in which he would write the story of his journey. The inside front cover bore his name and his version of citizenship: "John Muir, Earth-planet, Universe."

His route took him across the Ohio River at Louisville, then through Kentucky, Tennessee, the far southwest corner of North Carolina, and then southeast through Georgia to Savannah. Each part of the journey was a wilderness revelation as he climbed mountains, descended the coastal plain, and finally stood on the Atlantic shore. His description of one day in the Appalachians reveals the joy of his journey:

> September 12. Awoke drenched with mountain mist, which made a grand show, as it moved away before the hot sun. Passed Montgomery, a shabby village at the head of the east slope of the Cumberland Mountains. . . . Crossed a wide cool stream [Emory River], a branch of the Clinch River. There is nothing more eloquent in nature than a mountain stream, and this is the first I ever saw. Its banks are luxuriantly peopled with rare and lovely flowers and overarching trees, making one of Nature's coolest and most hospitable places.[19]

Muir enjoyed the journey, but he did not dally. His walk occupied September and October of 1867, averaging a stunning twenty miles per day. He slept wherever he could find shelter, sometimes in a friendly home, but more often in a barn or under a tree. He ate little, mostly bread and fruit where he could find it. His encounters with people were generally cordial, for he had nothing of value for anyone to steal. (Others, perhaps, feared him more, an unkempt tramp in ragged clothes walking past their doorstep.)

His walk ended at Cedar Keys, Florida. While there he contracted malaria, but after only a month of bed rest, still weak and suffering occasional relapses, he sailed to Cuba, there to wait for another ship to take him on to South America. Then, however, in another unexplained change in his travel plans, he abandoned Humboldt's path and set out for a new destination: Yosemite Valley.

Neither he nor the world would ever regret the detour.

At Home in California

Long before this journey, Jeanne Carr had put the idea of Yosemite into Muir's head. Carr and Muir corresponded regularly during his temporary blindness, no doubt an attempt by Carr to keep his spirits high. She passed along a magazine description of the Yosemite Valley, encouraging Muir to add it to his travel plans. As usual, he yielded to her influence. South America would have to wait.

Muir landed in San Francisco near the end of March 1868. He left the docks and started walking eastward—out of the city, across the Central Valley, and into the Sierra Nevada Mountains. California immediately seduced him. The environment was gentle and productive, and the footprint of humans still seemed light. "How vividly my own first journey to Yosemite comes to mind," he later wrote. "It was bloom-time of the year over all the lowlands and ranges of the coast; the landscape was fairly drenched with sunshine, the larks were singing, and the hills so covered with flowers that they seemed to be painted. . . ."[20]

He worked as a farm laborer from spring through fall, and with the coming of winter, Muir hired on as a shepherd. He and two borrowed dogs tended a herd of 1,800 sheep that grazed in the mountain valleys. The following spring, Yosemite took possession of Muir. He explored every bit of the region, daring to take outrageous risks, as on the absolute edge of the 2,600-foot-tall Yosemite Falls:

> In tracing the stream for the first time, getting acquainted with the life it lived in the mountains, I was eager to reach the extreme verge to see how it behaves in flowing so far through the air. . . . The last incline down which the stream journeys so gracefully is so steep and smooth one must slip cautiously forward on hands and feet alongside the rushing water, which so near one's head is very exciting. But to gain a perfect view one must go yet farther, over a curving brow to a slight shelf on the extreme brink. This shelf, formed by the flaking off of a fold of the granite, is about three inches wide, just wide enough for a safe rest for one's heels. . . . I concluded not to attempt to go nearer, but did, nevertheless, against reasonable judgment. Noticing some tufts of *Ar-*

temisia in a cleft of rock, I filled my mouth with the leaves, hoping their bitter taste might help to keep caution keen and prevent giddiness; then I reached the little ledge, got my heels well set, and worked side-wise twenty or thirty feet to a point close to the out-plunging current. Here the view is perfectly free down into the heart of the bright irised throng of comet-like streams into which the whole ponderous volume of the fall separates a little below the brow. So glorious a display of pure wildness, acting at close range while one is cut off from all the world beside, is terribly impressive.[21]

Earlier visitors had also been captured by Yosemite, so much so that Yosemite Valley had been designated a state park in 1864, a few years before Muir's arrival. President Lincoln ceded federal ownership of the valley to the California state government with the provision that it be made a park, "upon the express conditions that the premises shall be held for public use, resort, and recreation."[22] Tourism was already booming when Muir arrived, and he readily found work with James Hutchings, proprietor of a ramshackle hotel in the valley.

Muir helped Hutchings repair and improve the hotel, but his major task was to manage Hutchings' sawmill. Muir made the mill operable and improved its efficiency, just as he had done in all his previous jobs. Muir had accepted the work on one condition: that they not cut any living trees, but instead only use trees uprooted from a recent, massive windstorm—a supply of wood Muir estimated would last many years.

When Muir wasn't working, he rambled through the mountains, his destinations unplotted and unscheduled. He taught himself how to climb mountains, just as he had taught himself to rework a sawmill or design a clock. His lanky physique and wiry strength allowed him to spring from boulder to boulder with catlike agility. He shuffled as he walked, almost as though conserving energy for when it was really needed. He wore good shoes, but avoided boots because they were too clumsy. If a climbing maneuver challenged his skill, he stripped to his underwear and shoes to give himself maximum range of movement. He packed light—a blanket, perhaps, and a supply of crackers, oatmeal, and tea. He was immune to hunger, cold, and exhaustion. When a steep descent required him to toss his pack down ahead of him, he wasn't bothered. "The crackers were of course pounded into meal and the bread into mere crumbs, which made some difficulty in fitting into one's mouth, but its nourishment was not impaired thereby, which was the main thing."[23]

Muir lived this way in Yosemite for several years—working only if he needed money, exploring as often as possible. Local folks thought him an oddity, tramping about in unkempt clothing and straggly beard. Muir liked people, to be sure, but they were no match for the allure of a meadow he had never crossed or a mountain he had yet to climb: "I will follow my instincts, be myself for good or ill, and see what will be the upshot. As long as I live, I'll hear waterfalls and birds and winds sing. I'll interpret the rocks, learn the language of flood, storm, and the avalanche. I'll acquaint myself with the glaciers and wild gardens, and get as near the heart of the world as I can. . . . Hunger and cold, getting a living, hard work, poverty, loneliness, need of remuneration, giving up all thought of being known, getting married, etc., made no difference."[24]

Despite this (or perhaps because of it), Muir became known as an expert guide into the mountains, and visitors regularly sought him out. His friendliness and integrity endeared him to everyone he met. He was such a romantic figure that a visiting Scottish countess and author, Therese Yelverton, built a novel—*Zanita*, published in 1872—around the life of Yosemite Valley, casting Muir (called Kenmuir in the book) as the central figure. Biographers have considered her description of the novel's hero to be a true reflection of Muir:

> His bright intelligent eyes revealed no trace of insanity, and his open blue eyes of honest questioning, and glorious auburn hair might have stood as a portrait of the angel Raphael. . . . Truly his garments had the tatterdemalion style of a Mad Tom. The waist of his trousers was eked out with a grass band; a long flowing sedge rush stuck in the solitary button-hole of his shirt, the sleeves of which were ragged and forlorn, and his shoes appeared to have known hard and troublous times. . . . I soon divined that

his refinement was innate, his education collegiate, not only from his scientific treatment of his subject, but his correct English. Kenmuir, I decided in my mind, was a gentleman.[25]

His mentors, especially the Carrs, who had moved to San Francisco by this time, sent a regular stream of their scientific and literary friends to Yosemite, with instructions to seek out John Muir. His most famous earlier visitor was Ralph Waldo Emerson, who came to Yosemite to meet Muir in early 1871. At first shy and tentative before this literary giant, Muir desperately wanted to show Emerson the real Yosemite, away from the crowds and the usual tourist sights. But already frail and held back by timid handlers, Emerson settled for a short tour. Even so, the trip was memorable for both men, and they remained friends for life. In his papers, Emerson kept a list of "my men," those he considered to be his peers and confidants; the last name, penciled by Emerson late in life, was John Muir.

Muir also guided famed geologists Joseph Le Conte of the University of California and Louis Agassiz of Harvard University. Surrounded by his beloved mountains, Muir explained his views that glaciers had carved the narrow canyons and the wide valleys of the region. The two geologists were both intrigued by this theory, but the acknowledged expert on western geology, Josiah Whitney, adamantly disagreed, claiming that Yosemite had been formed by a one-time cataclysm when the ground fell into a massive crater that had formed below it. Muir, though, was so convinced he was right that he wrote his view—his first formal attempt at authorship—into a letter for the *New York Daily Tribune*, the most important newspaper in the nation at the time.

The paper published his article in September 1871, raising the question of Yosemite's formation to a national debate. Whitney counterattacked, claiming that Muir was an uninformed mountaineer, with no academic credentials, whose observations lacked scientific method. Muir was undeterred, however, and continued to write about glaciers for both scientific and popular audiences. His evidence kept growing as his wanderings took him ever deeper into unexplored canyons and crevices in the mountains. There he discovered active glaciers and direct evidence of their erosive activity (he pounded wooden stakes into the ground to measure the progress of glaciers, learning that they moved one inch per day).

Muir not only gained scientific credibility through this debate, he also created a unique literary niche. As he expanded his range of subjects to write more generally about the beauty and grandeur of nature and his experiences as a wilderness explorer, his audience grew. Readers of elite magazines loved nature writings and travelogues, but Muir offered something more. His writing was simple, direct, active, and forceful, lending a manly and untamed quality to his articles. He wrote about California, and later Alaska, capturing the romance of the American frontier and refocusing travel interests away from Europe and toward the West. He also filled his articles with vivid accounts of personal adventures in nature, many of them dangerous. He published profusely in newspapers, and by 1873 he had become the leading contributor to the *Overland Monthly*, the preeminent western literary magazine.

Muir had become an established author and a literary celebrity on both the East and West Coasts, a status that demanded a new lifestyle. He reluctantly gave up his residence in Yosemite and moved to San Francisco, recognizing that he needed a better environment in which to write. His five years living in Yosemite were over, and he would only be a visitor there—a regular visitor, to be sure—for the rest of his life.

His exposure to wilderness did not end with the establishment of a home in San Francisco. Rather, it expanded. His travels took him to the mountains of Nevada, Utah, and Washington, and eventually three times to Alaska. Such broad exposure helped Muir understand that the destruction he had witnessed in Yosemite was not unique. In Yosemite, he had seen grazing denude the meadows, logging remove the forests, and shabby tourism development litter the scenery. Now he saw the pattern repeated elsewhere. Regarding his disgust with sheep grazing in mountain meadows, he wrote: "The grass is eaten so close and trodden until it resembles a corral. . . . Nine-tenths of the whole surface of the Sierra has been swept by the scourge."[26] He wrote to Jeanne Carr, "I have seen a dead river," referring to the sedimentation and toxic impacts of gold mining on local streams in the Sierras.

Seeing the needless destruction of nature gradually converted Muir from a joyous observer of nature to an advocate for its conservation.

Figure 1.3 John Muir is often portrayed as a hermit, but he was a dedicated family man, shown here with his daughters, Helen and Wanda, wife Louisa, and pet dog Stikeen, on the porch of their California home in 1901. (Reproduced courtesy of the US National Park Service.)

Initially, Muir took small steps to use his literary reputation to highlight responsible resource management. He first wrote about the need to preserve forests in 1875, arguing the pragmatic position that forests protected the water resources that Californians needed for agricultural irrigation and direct human use. He advocated the European strategy of replanting forests after logging. He lobbied for a reorganization of the California Geological Survey to make it less academic and more practical, better able to provide the information needed to guide agricultural development and resource conservation.

Muir's dedication to mountaineering, writing, and conservation gradually took a backseat to another passion in his life: companionship. Muir was not the typical hermit, preferring his own company to that of others. He adored his friends in San Francisco and his family back in the Midwest, and he was the life of the party wherever he went. Just as when he was a boy, he still loved to talk, laugh, and make others laugh. A dinner-party companion recalled, "Scarcely would the guests be seated when Muir would begin, as if thinking aloud, pouring forth a stream of reminiscence, description, exposition, all relieved with quiet humor, seasoned with pungent satire, starred and rainbowed with poetic fantasy."[27]

Jeanne Carr never stopped searching for a proper wife for Muir. She found the perfect candidate in Louie (Louisa) Strentzel, the daughter of a successful farmer and rancher. Louie was a proper lady, well educated, but also a lover of nature, especially botany. Carr introduced them in 1874, but it would be five years before Muir, at the time writing prodigiously and climbing the ladder of literary reputation, proposed marriage. Their wedding on April 14, 1880, began a ten-year period when Muir set aside his other interests in order to be husband, father, and son-in-law. He described himself, happily, as "a proper cultivated plant."[28] He gradually took over his father-in-law's agricultural domain, putting his mechanical and organizational skills to work once again. Their family quickly grew to include two daughters, Wanda and Helen, who became the centerpieces of Muir's world. During this time, he traveled seldom and for only short periods, and he wrote nothing.

Louie recognized, however, that Muir needed more than a thriving farm and a loving home life in order to be fulfilled. Farming weighed him down, but nature rejuvenated him. Likewise, the companionship of others—mountaineers, authors, scientists, artists, educators—fed Muir's own creativity. Louie convinced Muir that he needed to re-balance his life, reduce his oversight of the family's lands, and resume his wanderings and writings. He brought family members from the Midwest to run the estate and again took up both his pencil and walking staff. A new era of conservation was about to begin.

The Fight for Conservation

Muir's finest hours often occurred around a campfire. He lit the most important campfire of his life as dusk fell on June 3, 1889. His sole companion was Robert Underwood Johnson, associate editor of the *Century*, a leading eastern literary magazine.[29]

The *Century* published articles by the nation's top writers—including Mark Twain—and often devoted issues to social causes and other special topics. Johnson had come west to recruit authors for a series of articles about gold mining. He also wanted to evaluate Muir as a potential contributor for the magazine. Like Muir, Johnson was a zealous conservationist. He quickly—and correctly—judged Muir as a charismatic leader for the conservation movement and a man who would appeal to the magazine's readership.

The *Century* preached to an evolving middle-class audience known as "mugwumps." Mugwumps were progressives, believing in political and social reform to improve the lives of the masses. They were also independent, not committed to the platforms of any particular political party. They owed their education and financial success to their own hard work, and they rebelled against a social aristocracy of industrial barons and their moneyed families. Although Muir would never describe himself as a mugwump (or as a member of any organized group, whether political, social, or religious), he fit the profile. Johnson knew that Muir's background and character, along with his literary style, could attract his readers to the conservation cause.[30]

That summer, as Muir and Johnson toured Yosemite, they were both appalled by the shabby commercialism of the park and the irresponsibility of the park's managers. Over their campfire, they decided that the broad area surrounding the Yosemite Valley needed federal protection. Specifically, they wanted Yosemite to become the nation's second national park. Their strategy was twofold. Muir was to write a pair of articles for the *Century*, the first describing the features of the region and the second proposing boundaries for a new national park. Johnson was to recruit prominent Americans to write editorials supporting a national park and then to lobby Congress to pass the needed legislation.

Muir's first article, "The Treasures of the Yosemite," appeared in the August 1890 issue of the *Century*. Once again, Muir's prose captivated readers. The article once again blended natural history, flowery language about the grandeur of the landscape, and Muir's daredevil adventures on the mountains. He also made his case for protection of the watershed around the valley:

> Were the importance of our forests at all understood by the people in general, even from an economic standpoint their preservation would call forth the most watchful attention of the Government. At present, however, every kind of destruction is moving on with accelerated speed. . . . Steps are now being taken towards the creation of a national park about the Yosemite, and great is the need, not only for the sake of the adjacent forests, but for the valley itself. For the branching cañons and valleys of the basins of the streams that pour into Yosemite are as closely related to it as are the fingers to the palm of the hand—as the branches, foliage, and flowers of a tree to the trunk. Therefore, very naturally, all the fountain region about Yosemite, with its peaks, cañons, snow fields, glaciers, forests, and streams, should be included in the park to make it an harmonious unit instead of a fragment, great though the fragment be. . . .[31]

The "steps now being taken" were only two—Muir's articles and Johnson's lobbying. At this stage, the campaign to create Yosemite National Park was still just a two-person campaign.

The second article, "Features of the Proposed Yosemite National Park," appeared the next month. This time, the prose was less flowery, the adventures absent, and the message more direct: "Ax and plow, hogs and horses, have long been and are still busy in Yosemite's gardens and groves. All that is accessible and destructible is being rapidly destroyed—more rapidly than in any other Yosemite in the Sierra, though this is the only one that is under the special protection of the Government. And by far the greater part of this destruction of the fineness of wildness is of a kind that can claim no right relationship with that which necessarily follows use."[32]

Johnson had prepared the ground for the planting of Muir's sentiments and proposals, and the result was almost instantaneous. Within a month of the second article's publication, Los Angeles congressman General William Vandever introduced a bill to create the park, with boundaries virtually the same as those proposed by Muir. The bill passed both houses of Congress easily and, on October 1, 1890, President Benjamin Harrison signed Yosemite National Park into existence.

Although Johnson contributed much to the creation of Yosemite, he always credited Muir as the leader of the movement, both for Yosemite and for the overall expansion of protected areas in the United States. "His country men owe him gratitude as the pioneer of our system of national parks," Johnson wrote in a eulogy for Muir. "Muir's writings and enthusiasm were the chief forces that inspired the movement. All the other torches were lighted from his."[33]

And many torches were lit over the next two decades, each expanding the lighted ring of conservation in America.

One torch inspired by Muir was carried by President Harrison's secretary of interior, John W. Noble. Noble favored expanding the national park system, but Congress was not as predictably favorable to parks as Noble wished. In 1891, however, spurred on by Muir's message, Noble devised an alternate way to protect forests. Just before Congress adjourned, Noble and Assistant Land Commissioner Edward Bowers inserted language into a general lands bill that allowed the president to declare "federal forest reserves." On March 2, the bill passed and President Harrison signed it the next day. With Noble's guidance, over the next two years the president established over 13 million acres of reserves, the origin of today's National Forest System.

In contrast to his lifetime practice of avoiding groups, Muir lit another torch when he established a new conservation organization. He had toyed for many years with forming a group to fight for forest preservation, and Robert Underwood Johnson kept encouraging him. Finally, on May 28, 1892, with the participation of faculty from the University of California, Muir presided at the founding of the Sierra Club. He was elected its first president, a position he held for the rest of his life. The club took up the conservation cause immediately, successfully lobbying Congress to defeat a bill to trim the boundary of Yosemite National Park.

In 1896, Muir participated as a consultant to a national forestry commission charged with recommending additional reserves to be set aside by the new president, Grover Cleveland. The report noted the dire

Figure 1.4 Teddy Roosevelt's entourage at the base of the Grizzly Giant (a Sequoia redwood tree), Mariposa Grove, Yosemite National Park, 1903. John Muir is standing just to the right of the president. (Photograph by Joseph Conte; reproduced courtesy of the Yosemite National Park Archives, Museum, and Library.)

condition of many areas and encouraged the president to greatly expand parks, reserves, and national monuments. Cleveland acted swiftly on the commission's advice, establishing 21 million acres of new reserves in early 1897.

Muir's influence as a conservation leader is clearly evident in this episode. Congress was irate that Cleveland had put so much land away, land that was being profitably exploited by the supporters of many congressmen. Some representatives even considered impeaching Cleveland for his actions, and they introduced other legislation to suspend the proposed reservations, revoke previous ones, and forbid future ones. In response, Muir wrote an article summarizing the commission's report for the *Atlantic Monthly* entitled "American Forests." He summed up the conservation argument at the end of the article: "Any fool can destroy trees. They cannot run away; and if they could, they would still be destroyed,—chased and hunted down as long as fun or a dollar could be got out of their bark hides, branching horns, or magnificent bole backbones. . . . Through all the wonderful, eventful centuries since Christ's time—and long before that—God has cared for these trees . . . but he cannot save them from fools,—only Uncle Sam can do that."[34]

As in the campaign for Yosemite, Muir followed up with a second article in the *Atlantic Monthly*, and again his words, passion, and logic captured the public's imagination. Congress surrendered, and all existing and new forest reserves survived intact.

The most famous event in Muir's public life was another camping trip. This time his guest was the recently elected president Theodore Roosevelt. Roosevelt was a committed conservationist, and he scheduled time with Muir in 1903 while on a western tour. Unlike the earlier disappointing visit by Emerson, this meeting was everything Muir had hoped. Roosevelt, as always, was ready for adventure. They spent several days together, riding, hiking, and camping in Yosemite, taking every opportunity to shake the trailing members of Roosevelt's staff. They slept in the open, once awakening covered in a four-inch blanket of fresh snow. "I never before had so interesting, hearty, and manly a companion," Muir wrote. "I fairly fell in love with him."[35] Roosevelt must have felt the same; the day after the camping trip ended, Roosevelt instructed his secretary of interior to greatly expand California's forest reserves.

The fight to preserve Yosemite, however, had been only half won. The valley floor remained under the jurisdiction of the State of California, like a hole in the middle of the surrounding national-park doughnut. Muir and Johnson found this situation unacceptable. So John Muir the author became John Muir the lobbyist. For the six years leading up to 1906, Muir led the effort to unite the entire Yosemite ecosystem into a single park. He wrote about the need for such a measure, and he lobbied the California legislature, often speaking at hearings and meeting privately with influential legislators. The opposition was vocal, accusing Muir of being a rascal, libeler, and plain liar. They called him a hypocrite because he had run a sawmill in Yosemite, exploiting for himself the resources that now he wanted to save from others. For the first and only time in his life, Muir rebuked the slanderers, reminding them that he had used only downed timber, that he had never cut a tree in his life.

The outcome of this campaign remained in doubt until another of Muir's ideas shifted the balance toward returning the land to the US government. Muir believed that men of accomplishment—wealthy and educated—understood the arguments in favor of conservation and could be powerful allies in achieving land protection. With his literary and scientific reputation, Muir had access to the leading persons of his time. One of those was railroad entrepreneur Edward Harriman. Harriman had funded an Alaskan scientific expedition that Muir joined, and they became close friends from then on. As the fight for the unification of Yosemite as a single national park reached its climax, Muir recruited Harriman to the cause. His influence in California and Washington secured the necessary votes. In early 1906, California gave up its ownership of Yosemite Valley, and on June 11, 1906, Congress deposited the lands into Yosemite National Park, making it a whole ecosystem. Muir welcomed the outcome for two reasons— land protection and the end of his lobbying—as he wrote to Johnson: "Yes, my dear Johnson, sound the loud timbrel and let every Yosemite tree and stream rejoice! . . . You don't know how accomplished a lobbyist I've become under your guidance. The fight you planned by that Tuolumne campfire seventeen years ago is at last fairly, gloriously won, every enemy down derry down."[36] In another letter to Johnson, Muir expressed his relief that the campaign had ended: "I am now an experienced lobbyist; my political education is complete; have attended legislature making speeches, explaining, exhorting, praying, persuaded every mother's son of the legislators, newspaper reporters and everybody else who would listen to me. And now that the fight is finished and my education as a politician and lobbyist is finished I am almost finished myself."[37]

John Muir's Legacy

After his wife Louie died in 1905, Muir moved to Arizona with daughter Helen to help her convalesce from respiratory problems. While there, he visited the Petrified Forest and the Grand Canyon. He was appalled by the destruction occurring in the Petrified Forest, as souvenir hunters, both personal and commercial, chipped and sawed away at the fossilized trees. He wrote to President Roosevelt, encouraging him to make both places federal reserves. Almost immediately, Roosevelt set aside the Petrified Forest as a national monument and did the same for the Grand Canyon two years later. Two more torches lit for conservation.

Muir had one more conservation battle to fight. When Muir had argued years earlier that the Sierra Nevada range needed protection because of its ability to provide plentiful, high-quality water, he had been correct. San Francisco needed water, and taking Muir's advice, they looked eastward to the mountains. San Francisco's leaders chose a beautiful valley in Yosemite National Park—the Hetch Hetchy Valley—as the ideal site for a water-supply reservoir.

Muir loved the Hetch Hetchy Valley, considering it a smaller version of Yosemite Valley. Perhaps, he wrote, it was even more stunning and sublime, because the natural features were displayed closer together: "I have always called it the Tuolumne Yosemite, for it is a wonderfully exact counterpart of the great Yosemite, not only in its crystal river and sublime rocks and waterfalls, but in the gardens, groves, and meadows of its flowery, park-like floor."[38]

Muir's efforts to protect Hetch Hetchy replicated those he had exerted for creating and then unifying Yosemite. This struggle was different, however, because the utilitarian cause of providing water to San Francisco resonated with the general public on equal terms with preserving natural beauty. Conservation leaders battled over flooding the valley for a decade, with the balance shifting toward and away from damming with each new president and Congress. The San Francisco earthquake in 1906, however, sounded the death knell for Hetch Hetchy. Fires burned relentlessly throughout the city after the earthquake, convincing the public that a bigger and more reliable water supply was imperative. Eventually, President Woodrow Wilson signed the bill to flood Hetch Hetchy in late 1913. Muir considered this a mortal sin: "Dam Hetch Hetchy! As well dam for water-tanks the people's cathedrals and churches, for no holier temple has ever been consecrated by the heart of man."[39]

Muir was seventy-five years old when Hetch Hetchy Valley was condemned to death. His own death was not far behind. His health had been weakened by chronic respiratory problems, and his spirit, already crushed by the loss of Hetch Hetchy, was extinguished by the onset of World War I. He succumbed on December 24, 1914.

Without question, John Muir is the most prominent figure in the history of American conservation. His name lives on in parks, trails, and forested groves across the western United States, and his image graces the reverse of California's commemorative quarter. The organization that he started and dedicated himself to—the Sierra Club—stands today as one of the world's most influential conservation groups. He wrote nine books in his life-time, mostly anthologies assembled from his journals and magazine articles. Several remain in print today, and they are as fresh and vibrant as when written more than a century ago.

Perhaps what we revere most in John Muir is what we see in him of ourselves. He was a complex man, drawn to opposite poles in many aspects of life. He loved his family and friends and reveled in their companionship, but he also craved the freedom and release of being alone in nature. He was a successful entrepreneur, using the best of innovation and technology to enhance his fortune, but he rebelled against a life dominated by work and money. He never wavered in his belief in a divine presence, but he despaired of organized religions whose rules and practices he saw as unholy at best. He loved individual people, but found that, when formed into groups, they often became greedy and mean.

The most enduring aspect of his personality, however, was his deep understanding of what we need from nature. Nature provides the raw materials of survival—food, wood, water—and the sustainable use of nature's products did not trouble Muir. But nature also provides recreation, solitude, stress release, and spiritual renewal. Muir knew we needed this from nature also, and to assure its availability, we need to set aside lands—preserve them—as parks for all the people, not just the wealthy. And as the crush of population and development threatened to envelop the entire landscape, Muir set himself out to speak for the preservation of the best of the natural world.

Yet he wasn't just a naïve idealist preaching to the trees and birds. As Robert Underwood Johnson, Muir's partner in conservation, wrote in his eulogy: "There has been only one John Muir. He was not a 'dreamer,' but a practical man, a faithful citizen, a scientific observer, a writer of enduring power, with vision, poetry, courage in a contest, a heart of gold, and a spirit pure and fine."[40]

Figure 2.1 Jay Norwood "Ding" Darling, 1876–1962. (Reproduced courtesy of "Ding" Darling Wildlife Society — Friends of the Refuge.)

Chapter 2

Ding Darling

The Best Friend a Duck Ever Had

Newspapers a century ago didn't look like today's newspapers. Photographs were rare, color was nonexistent—and editorial cartoons weren't on the editorial page. In fact, an editorial cartoon was often the paper's most conspicuous item, usually appearing on the front page, above the fold. As Americans poured their first cup of coffee and sat down to breakfast or grabbed a copy of the newspaper on their way to work, their attention focused on the cartoon. The cartoon told a story—the background of a news item, the upshot of a political controversy, an economic or societal concern, or perhaps a tongue-in-cheek commentary on the fashions or entertainment of the day. The front-page cartoon was the window through which Americans looked at their world.

On some mornings, the cartoon warned about the plight of our natural resources. Poor land-use practices washed the fertile soils of the Midwest down the Mississippi River and into the Gulf of Mexico. Over-hunting of waterfowl had reduced duck populations to remnants of their enormous earlier numbers. Meanwhile, human population growth across the globe challenged the capacity of farmers and ranchers to provide the needed food.

A conservation cartoon occupying the front page was not the consequence of a slow news day. Conservation appeared there on purpose, because the foremost editorial cartoonist of the era was an Iowa journalist known throughout the land simply as "Ding." For half a century, Jay Norwood "Ding" Darling reflected the world in cartoons published nearly every day in the *Des Moines Register* and syndicated in scores of newspapers nationwide.[1] And on many mornings, he served the nation a helping of what he cared about most—conservation.

Darling made his living as a cartoonist, but his heart belonged to field and forest, to stream and lake, to clean air and water, to the ability of our earth to support our needs not just for today but forever. He wrote and talked the same way he drew—direct, forceful, and loveable: "Of course you understand that I am not nearly so much interested in the preservation of migratory waterfowl as I am in the management of water resources and the crucial effect of such management on human sustenance. Wild ducks and geese and teeter-assed shore birds are only the delicate indicators of the prognosis for human existence just as sure as God made little green apples."[2] And during a special time of his life, he laid aside his brushes and pens and picked up the gauntlet for conservation in our nation's capital. In the mere span of twenty months, Darling transformed the future US Fish and Wildlife Service from a sleepy bureaucracy into the nation's conservation leader, and he put his stamp—literally and figuratively—on the future of waterfowl management.

Child of the Prairie Frontier

Darling grew up on the edge of the frontier. He was born on October 21, 1876, a few years after the newly completed transcontinental railroad had opened the nation's midsection to the relentless march of civilization. Darling was born in Norwood, Michigan (the source of his middle name), but his family, like much of the country, was restless. His father was a teacher and Protestant preacher, moving often in pursuit of the next available classroom or pulpit, and usually following the now-famous advice of contemporary newspaper publisher Horace Greeley: "Go west, young man, go west."

When Darling was ten, his family put down roots in the frontier community of Sioux City, Iowa. Sioux City sits near the westernmost point of Iowa, across the Missouri River from Nebraska and the Big Sioux River from South Dakota. Developing rapidly in the 1880s like many towns dotting the banks of the Missouri and Mississippi Rivers, it was still a rough frontier town, with plentiful saloons, gambling houses, and other distractions for the wayward appetite. On most days, stern-wheeled riverboats loaded with buffalo hides steamed smoothly down the river to St. Louis; but there were also days when the rain-swollen river just might swallow up whatever the foolish settlers had built on the edge of the bluffs.

Across those rivers lay the unbroken prairie. As the young Jay Darling grew, the nearby frontier lands of Nebraska and South Dakota were his proving ground. He and his brother Frank hiked and camped throughout the region, hunting upland game and waterfowl to fill the dinner pot. He grew comfortable with the hazards of the frontier, from rough-hewn characters to unpredictable and unforgiving weather. Along the way, he also learned to observe and appreciate all of nature: "Those were the days when the Golden Plover came in great flocks and moved across South Dakota, and from early spring until the Prairie chicken sought cover in the fall along the thickets bordering the creeks and marshes, my mind was filled with pictures which have never been erased."[3]

The natural magic of the prairie, however, was approaching its final days. The industrial revolution was in full stride, spawning factories, migration, tenements, and pollution in its wake. Lands were being overused as a consequence, and the observant Darling saw it all. He recalled the devastating impact of returning to Michigan as a young man to represent the family at the funeral of his Uncle John. Darling had spent summers working on his uncle's farm during his teen years. The farm had been a paradise to the young Darling, as he explained in a later interview: "As soon as school was out in the spring I was sent to earn my keep on the farm of my father's brother in southern Michigan. It was a rich little eighty acres, with a crystal clear stream running across one corner, and a few acres of native timber. It was virgin soil, the river was full of fish, the woods abounded with song birds and migratory waterfowl nested in the marshes along the creek."[4]

When he returned for the funeral only a few years later, however,

> . . . it was as if the farm had died with Uncle John. . . . The once-verdant pasture, now barren of grass, was gullied and quite evidently of no further use. A lone crow, which got up from the barnyard and slowly flapped its wings away, was all that was left of the wildlife inhabitants. The well had gone dry and the old orchard was a scraggly wreck of dead limbs and old stumps. . . . This was my first conscious realization of what could happen to land, what could happen to clear running streams, what could happen to bird life and human life when the common laws of Mother Nature were disregarded.[5]

Darling had grown not only into a proficient outdoorsman, but also into a man of varied and useful talents. As a boy he sang in all his father's church choirs, and he became an accomplished mandolin player. During college he played in a band, and he turned his sacred-music upbringing into part-time work. "I could sing in any religion you wanted," he said, "and I made the rounds of all the funerals every week."[6] He purchased a camera during his teen years and learned the ins and outs of photography. In college, he served as photographer, writer, and editor for various school publications.

As it happened, the same love of fun that would be so evident in his cartoons also frequently landed Darling in hot water. He was booted from Yankton College during his freshman year for taking the president's horse and buggy out for the evening—without permission. He transferred to Beloit College in southern Wisconsin, where he became an active student leader in sports, music, and the student press. He didn't pay much attention to classes, however, and continually teetered on the brink of academic suspension.

For his Beloit College yearbook, Darling drew a series of sketches of faculty members and administrators in amusing situations. He signed his drawings "D'ing," a shortened form of Darling. The contraction, he said, was "to make a funnier looking name and in addition to conceal my identity."[7] The signature stuck and, soon losing the apostrophe, became a nationally known brand for his drawings.

The disguised name, however, didn't hide the artist. Darling and his student friends thought his caricatures of Beloit's faculty and administrators were amusing, but the subjects did not. His depiction of the university president dancing the Highland fling in a kilt was the last straw. Darling was suspended for a year, ostensibly for bad grades; the real but unstated reason for his expulsion was outrage over his cartoons.

Darling returned to Beloit and graduated as the nation turned over the calendar to a new century. He aimed to be a doctor, not a reporter or cartoonist. Though he liked to draw, he understood from an early age that art was not an acceptable career for the son of a clergyman. "To my father and mother," Darling said, "artists who drew pictures were classed with wicked playing cards, dancing, and rum."[8] Becoming a doctor, however, required more schooling, which required money—and Darling had none. For the immediate future, becoming a doctor had to take a backseat to earning a living.

On the Front Page

After graduating, Darling returned home to Iowa and took a job as a reporter with the local newspaper, the *Sioux City Journal*. Working for the paper was about as rough as living in the community. One of Darling's jobs was to accompany the authorities every morning as they searched the riverbanks for corpses that had washed up after the previous night's activities. "We would pick up a stiff about once out of three mornings," he remembered, "and it was always good for a story—especially when the corpse could be identified. . . ."[9]

Darling's first published cartoon was unintended. While covering a local trial, Darling was instructed by his editor to photograph one of the arguing attorneys. The attorney was notorious for avoiding photos and ended by chasing the camera-toting Darling out of the courtroom. "The lawyer was close to me as I sailed down the steps in one leap, and the air from his cane breezed across my neck," Darling later recalled. "On the street he was no match for me because my legs were young and his were old, so I soon outdistanced him."[10] Although he escaped, he did so without a photograph. In an attempt to salvage the assignment, Darling drew a caricature of the lawyer that was published in the next day's paper. Readers loved the drawing, and his astute editor assigned Darling to produce a series of humorous but pointed caricatures of local personalities, all of which were equally popular. Soon after, he began drawing the daily editorial cartoon. He didn't stop for half a century.

Most of those fifty years were spent cartooning for the *Des Moines Register and Leader*, which lured Darling away from Sioux City in 1906. His job offer came at a propitious time. Unbeknownst to Darling, he was about to be fired from the *Sioux City Journal* for drawing a cartoon that had greatly offended the leaders of the local school board.

His start in Des Moines was just as troublesome. His first cartoon for the *Register* was a comment on air pollution. It showed a fat monk, labeled Des Moines, smoking a pipe labeled "soft coal" and emitting clouds of black smoke into the air. With a few strokes of his drawing pens, he had alienated the city's industrial leaders and its Roman Catholic citizens. The popularity of his cartoons quickly erased the memory of that first misstep, however, and he soon became a fixture of the Iowa publishing community.[11]

Darling's popularity as a cartoonist owed itself to a number of qualities. He was not a trained artist, and consequently his cartoons displayed a primitive style that connected with readers. He expressed his figures with a minimum of lines, but the visual field packed a high content of information, meaning, and nuance. Later, when a poll of newspaper editors declared Darling the outstanding cartoonist in the country in 1934, one admirer wrote:

Darling, the cartoonist, has a combination of spiritual qualities that makes his work an unalloyed joy. He has wisdom, the wisdom of the humble. He has courage, the courage of unflinching candor. He has a deep and loving kindness that tempers all his work. But the thing that gives him genius is that he sees life wisely, frankly, affectionately, through the perspective of a merry eye. He disarms us with a consummate art, keeps us always smiling, always cheerful. To begin the day with "Ding" makes us happy. And while our hearts are open to lively mirth, he pours in his wisdom, and that day well begun becomes, through the alchemy of "Ding's" genius, something more than a cheerful day.[12]

Darling himself expressed his perspective more directly, just as his drawings did: "Every cartoon should contain a little medicine, a little sugarcoating, and as much humor as the subject will bear."[13]

Whatever the exact recipe of qualities, Darling's cartoons played well wherever they appeared. He won the Pulitzer Prize for editorial cartooning twice—in 1924, when it was only the second Pulitzer ever awarded in that genre, and again in 1943. Within a few years of joining the *Register*, he began receiving offers from big-city papers across the country. He succumbed to one offer in 1911, when he left Des Moines to join the *New York Globe* as their editorial cartoonist. Although Darling enjoyed the celebrity trappings of life in New York, where he met most of the literary, business, and political leaders of the day, he soon tired of the big-city environment. "As for your next-door neighbors," he wrote, "the most you know about them is the odors you get in the hall from their cooking. There is nothing more dreary to me than an endless sea of strange faces, and not a soul among them that knows you or even cares to. A barren prairie without a soul in sight is downright sociability by comparison."[14] Darling abandoned New York within two years, returning to his drawing table at the *Des Moines Register*, which was delighted to have him back.

New York, however, was not done with Darling. The *New York Herald Tribune* began syndicating his cartoons in 1916, eventually reaching well over 100 newspaper markets across the country every day. The national exposure helped vault the *Des Moines Register and Leader* (now just the *Register*) to great financial success and a reputation as being among the nation's top regional newspapers.

Darling was a droll commentator on the plight of the newspaper cartoonist. "Most people think a cartoonist just sits around in his bedroom slippers and lounging robe, waiting for an inspiration," he wrote. "I'm sorry, but that isn't the way it is." He noted that the cartoonist has to put himself "in the kettle, turn on the heat, and boil until enough soup stock has stewed out for serving. Sometimes it's pretty thin broth."[15] Moreover, the cartoonist and the readers often differed on the quality of a cartoon. "My favorite cartoons were not the ones which were the most highly praised by the public," Darling wrote.[16]

Darling's most famous and beloved cartoon, in fact, was a cast-off. News of Theodore Roosevelt's death had reached the *Register*'s office late in the afternoon of January 6, 1919. An editorial cartoon was needed, and Darling went to work facing a short deadline but soon found that his reverence for Roosevelt as a conservationist muted his pen. "I couldn't think of a thing—not anything at all. I looked at the blank sheet of cardboard in front of me in utter despair. . . ." He remembered the last time he had seen Roosevelt, waving good-bye to him on horseback—and that's what he drew. Disgusted with the banality of the drawing, he tossed it on the floor and tried out several other ideas. None was sufficient to express Darling's regard for this extraordinary conservationist and president. Then, he later recalled, "the idea struck me that I might possibly add to that first sketch a trail into the great beyond and allow it to be presumed that Roosevelt was waving good-bye not to me, but to the world." He added background images related to Roosevelt's western and Washington eras—a wagon train and the Capitol building. Darling and the editor agreed that this drawing was far from what was needed but would have to do for the early editions, and that he would draw a more fitting tribute for the day of Roosevelt's funeral. Unfortunately, in his haste, Darling neglected to instruct the pressmen to use the drawing only for the local paper and not forward it to New York. Instead of appearing in just one paper, it appeared in 111 papers across the nation. The next day, readers everywhere were praising the drawing, labeled "The Long, Long Trail." A drawing rescued from the trash pile had expressed the emotions of a nation. Since then, the cartoon has been reprinted more than 25 million times.[17]

Darling's success as a cartoonist made him a wealthy man, with connections to the highest levels of society. He became a friend to six presidents, but his favorite was always Herbert Hoover. They met in 1919, when Darling attended a Des Moines event at which Hoover was speaking. The cartoonist wanted to see Hoover so he could draw him better. "Hoover was the hardest subject to caricature that I ever en-

Figure 2.2 Darling's most famous drawing memorialized the death of President Theodore Roosevelt on January 6, 1919. (Reproduced courtesy of "Ding" Darling Wildlife Society — Friends of the Refuge.)

countered. It is a wonder he ever tolerated me as a friend," wrote Darling later. Hoover, however, more than tolerated Darling. He admired Darling's cartoons for their subject matter, insight, and candor. After becoming president, Hoover often invited Darling to stay at the White House or accompany him on fishing trips. "I got the impression," Darling wrote, "that the calls came when he got fed up with the yes-men around him and wanted conversation with a free-wheeler from the uninhibited Middle West." Today we think of Hoover mostly as the man who led the nation into the Great Depression, but Darling saw him as a great leader who has been inappropriately reviled by history.[18]

In stark contrast to his admiration for Hoover, Darling intensely disliked his successor, Franklin Delano Roosevelt. Darling thought Roosevelt was undisciplined and egomaniacal, a president on his way to becoming a dictator. He thought the policies of the New Deal were destined to destroy the entrepreneurial spirit of the American people, replacing it with a lazy reliance on the welfare state. He abhorred what he saw as profligate spending on inappropriate projects.

The idea that Darling would team up with Roosevelt in support of anything, worthy or not, was unthinkable. But the unthinkable was about to happen.

Conservationist at Heart

Darling's love of conservation began early and never waned. As a boy, he knew the untamed natural spaces of the eastern Great Plains. As a man, he watched them change, and he didn't like it. "All it takes to be a conservationist," he wrote, "is to have been awake and a witness to what has happened to all our continental forests, soils, waters, minerals, and wildlife in the last fifty or seventy-five years and he'll be a conservationist from fright! That's me."[19]

Darling's conservation "fright" was also his call to fight. He regularly used his editorial position to draw cartoons about conservation. A favorite topic was the plight of waterfowl. In the 1920s, waterfowl populations were plummeting, first because of overharvesting and later because of the draining of the Upper Midwest wetlands in which the birds nested. Later, after witnessing the national tragedy of the Dust Bowl, he drew cartoons about the irresponsibility of allowing water tables to fall and soils to wash into rivers and the ocean. He was appalled by the nation's lack of attention to soil. Writing near the end of World War II and comparing the war effort to conservation, he noted that "if an alien aggressor attempts to steal so much as a square inch of our sacred land the whole nation rushes to arms, but there are about 500,000 acres (780 square miles) of our richest land washing away each year—lost forever—and no one, well almost no one, gives it a thought."[20]

Darling first concentrated his conservation leadership in his home state of Iowa. He deplored the usual practice at the time that state legislatures controlled natural resources directly, for example, by setting fishing and hunting regulations, determining where fish and game birds were stocked, or selecting locations for conservation areas. Politics, in Darling's view, was antithetical to conservation, which depended on scientific information and objective analysis rather than public opinion and favoritism. Consequently, he fought hard for—and accomplished—passage of a 1931 Iowa law that created a nonpartisan, five-citizen fish and game commission to oversee the work of the state's professional conservation agency (now the Iowa Department of Natural Resources). The commission was charged with "protecting, propagating, increasing, and preserving the fish, game, fur-bearing animals, and protected birds of the state."[21] This structure quickly became the model for other progressive states to follow and is now the standard across the nation.

Darling was named one of the five original commissioners for the new agency. Among the commission's most innovative projects was a twenty-five-year plan for the combined efforts of the Iowa Fish and Game Commission and the Conservation Department, which managed state parks and recreational areas. The influence of Darling on this plan is in plain sight—in addition to his technical input, he drew eleven cartoons that appeared in the 176-page report. More importantly, the report reflects Darling's view on the importance of natural resources and how to manage them well:

© 1999 J.N. "Ding" Darling Foundation

Figure 2.3 Poor land use, resulting in the destruction of wildlife habitat, was a primary concern of Ding Darling, as shown in this 1937 cartoon. (Reproduced courtesy of "Ding" Darling Wildlife Society — Friends of the Refuge.)

The whole project of providing public recreation for ALL the people of Iowa now stands in the same class of importance as the other great state enterprises, public law and order, public education, public health, and public highways. . . .

We discover, then, that every phase of public recreation to be provided by the state, is dependent upon three major correlative factors—erosion control, the conservation of surface waters, and the conservation of forest and small cover on the land. We also discover that these three are inter-dependent.[22]

A project that had been intended to plan public outdoor recreation had evolved into a comprehensive plan for conservation. Once again, the Darling-led commission had created a model approach that has characterized progressive fisheries and wildlife planning to the present day.

In his oversight role on the commission, Darling realized that the effective operation of a professional and scientific conservation agency needed well-trained personnel. He also realized that an inadequate number of students with the needed skills were graduating from college. With his usual direct assault on any problem, he took a proposal to the president of Iowa State College (now Iowa State University) for an expanded graduate education program. Darling proposed funding the program with a three-way partnership, one-third provided by the Iowa Fish and Game Commission, one-third by the college, and one-third by Darling himself. His pledge was $9,000 over the first three years of the experiment ($9,000 may not seem like a lot today, but it would have bought a 100-acre Iowa farm in 1932). The program was an instant success, and another model for the nation. Today, similar cooperative units operate at forty universities in thirty-eight states and continue to produce most of the nation's masters-level wildlife and fisheries professionals.

Just as his Iowa cartoons led him to a national stage, Darling's Iowa conservation work also led him to the nation's capital. Darling was a longtime friend of Henry Wallace, a prominent farmer and agricultural businessman in Des Moines. Wallace had begun his political life as a Republican (assuring him of Darling's friendship), but became a

Democrat in support of Franklin Roosevelt's New Deal policies. Roosevelt named Wallace his secretary of agriculture in 1933, a job he kept until moving up to become Roosevelt's vice-presidential running mate in 1940.

Roosevelt was a conservationist and sportsman, and he, too, like Darling, was concerned about the fate of the nation's ducks and other waterfowl. In January 1934, Roosevelt convened a three-member "Committee on Wild-Life Restoration." The committee was assigned to look into the work of the US Bureau of the Biological Survey (the future US Fish and Wildlife Service), which was then part of the Department of Agriculture. Darling, no doubt with the backing of Wallace, was appointed to the committee, along with Professor Aldo Leopold of the University of Wisconsin and Thomas Beck, editor of *Collier's* magazine and a member of the Connecticut State Board of Fisheries and Game. The committee conducted sessions with the staff of the Biological Survey, who disappointed them at every turn. The staff couldn't advise the committee on what should be done or what lands were needed, where, or why; the Biological Survey's own background report was worthless. The committee turned instead to the individual states for help, and there they found the wealth of detailed local information they needed.

Working at a flat-out sprint, the committee delivered its report to the president within one month. The report made strong and detailed recommendations about federal purchase of lands for duck nesting habitats in many states and called for $50 million in funding to accomplish the purchases and their management. Committee chair Beck was so disgusted with the Biological Survey that he wanted to dissolve the entire agency and start over; Leopold and Darling were more confident that changes at the top would be enough to free the agency's scientists and professional wildlife managers to do their best.

The leaders of the Biological Survey scoffed at the committee's work. The agency chief ignored the report, even when given a directive by Secretary Wallace to accept and implement the recommendations. Darling observed that one ambitious staff member wrote a rebuttal containing "a somewhat violent criticism of any plan that might be submitted by a magazine editor who got all his ideas from a capitalistic game hog or a cartoonist who was a notorious critic of the New Deal administration."[23]

Because the chief had failed to take the report seriously, Wallace forced him to resign, and his two underlings began a nasty competition to get the top job. Neither succeeded, and the agency reeled in disarray.

Worse, however, was that Roosevelt apparently ignored the report, too. After weeks of waiting for a response, Darling was distraught, unable to understand how the president could neglect a report that Roosevelt himself had requested. Darling returned to Des Moines, even more convinced that the Washington bureaucracy, and particularly that of the Roosevelt administration, was clueless.

The next event surprised everyone, but no one more than Darling. Soon after returning to Iowa, Darling received a phone call from the White House. President Roosevelt was on the line, offering Darling the job as chief of the Biological Survey. The offer seemed ludicrous. The president was handing the keys to the nation's wildlife to one of his most outspoken and prominent critics. And for Darling to accept the offer was equally unthinkable. Nevertheless, it was an offer Darling could not refuse. As Darling confessed to Herbert Hoover, "I see for myself a chance to do a job for conservation. If I wait until a change of administration it will be too late."[24] On March 10, 1934, Ding Darling became the chief of the US Bureau of the Biological Survey.

The Chief

Darling hit Washington like an Iowa thunderstorm. His candor, bravery, and penchant for action roused the Biological Survey from its easy chair. He dismissed most of those in middle-management positions, replacing them with individuals from outside the government whom he knew and respected. He got the agency at work on its tasks, hiring engineers, biologists, law enforcement officers, and others—and then stayed out of their way.

Always an advocate for scientific management, he happily ignored politics when the facts allowed him to do so. He was well aware that duck populations in the United States had fallen by more than 80 percent over the previous decade and that many people considered ducks on their way to extinction. Darling believed they could be saved, but only with immediate and direct action. Consequently, he instituted the most stringent harvesting regulations that the country had ever known, over the objections of hunting groups, arms manufacturers, and the politicians they supported. Darling told Congress that the strict "regulations will stay as long as they are needed to bring back the ducks; and if tougher restrictions will help the cause, we'll find some tougher restrictions."[25]

Lowering the harvest was important, Darling knew, but restoring the birds' habitat was even more crucial. To address that problem, he turned to a young colleague from the Iowa Fish and Game Commission, John Salyer II. Darling gave Salyer the responsibility for running the nation's wildlife refuges. Although Teddy Roosevelt had established the first wildlife refuge in 1903, the few sites that had since been designated existed mostly in name only. Refuges had no assigned managers, no enforcement of their rules, no management plans, and, especially, no funding. Darling told Salyer to develop a waterfowl management program, built around the habitat needs of the birds. The chief had scooped up some government money to buy more refuge land, but it had to be spent fast. Salyer's first task, therefore, was to find the right tracts across the country and buy them up as fast and as cheaply as possible.

Salyer became a conservation legend, well deserving his recognition as "Father of the National Wildlife Refuge System." He jumped behind the wheel of his government sedan and seldom parked it for the next twenty-seven years. He drove 18,000 miles in his first six weeks—averaging more than 400 miles per day—en route to purchasing 600,000 acres of new wildlife habitat in his first year. Together, Darling and Salyer identified, surveyed, and purchased 5 million acres and added fifty-five new refuges during Darling's tenure as chief.

Darling proved to be a master at finding money for the survey's destitute conservation programs. He had extracted promises for funding from Roosevelt before taking his appointment as chief, but those promises were never fulfilled. Whenever Darling asked Roosevelt for a promised $1 million, the president would write out an I.O.U. and tell Darling to take it to the chief of New Deal programs, who consistently ignored Darling. Roosevelt and his colleagues thought this a great joke they were playing on Darling. Undeterred, Darling wandered the halls of government, looking for whatever handouts he could get, using "a straw to suck funds from the other fellow's barrel."[26] In a short time, Darling accumulated $8.5 million from others' barrels, a huge amount for that time and purpose.

Darling's most successful funding, however, would pay back the joke on Roosevelt. One of Darling's ardent supporters was South Dakota senator Peter Norbeck, who had sponsored most of the nation's waterfowl conservation legislation during the previous decade. In 1934, he was getting ready to retire after a long career in the Senate. His fellow senators were happy to support a $1 million budget amendment for wetland restoration as a going-away present for their longtime colleague. The crafty Norbeck, however, had a trick up his sleeve. He spoke with a thick Norwegian accent that was difficult to understand in the best of circumstances, but when he rose to introduce his amendment, he complained about his new dentures and removed them to ease the pain. Although the toothless Norbeck was now totally indecipherable, the Senate unanimously approved his proposal anyhow—without being able to hear that he had changed the $1 million appropriation to $6 million.[27]

When the appropriation reached Roosevelt's desk, he was in a hurry to leave, most fittingly, for a fishing trip. Knowing that the bill was expected to ask for $1 million, he signed without reading the text, and the appropriation became law—allocating $6 million for waterfowl habitat restoration. Later, Roosevelt was livid that he had been bamboozled by Norbeck and Darling. The next time Darling asked for money, Roosevelt responded that he had told a colleague that "this fellow Darling is the only man in history who got an appropriation through Congress, past the budget, and signed by the President without anybody realizing that the Treasury had been raided. . . . Nevertheless, more power to your arm! Go ahead with the six million dollars ($6,000,000) and talk with me about a month hence in regard to additional lands, *if* I have any more money left."[28]

Funding conservation through straws stuck into others' barrels was not sustainable; neither was conning the Congress and the president. So, for several years, activists and legislators had been debating how to fund conservation at a national level. Various schemes were floated, but the one that gained traction was for a federal conservation "stamp," basically a federal license that bird hunters would purchase and whose proceeds would go into wetlands conservation. Gradually, a consensus built for the stamp, but with a modification that it be charged only to waterfowl hunters because all the proceeds were slated for wetland habitat. After several years during which the proposal was shelved because of larger concerns with the economic issues of the Great Depression, the idea finally became law. President Roosevelt signed the Migratory Bird Hunting and Conservation Stamp Act into law on March 16, 1934, less than a week after appointing Ding Darling as chief of the US Biological Survey.

Having an artist as chief came at a good time, because the next job was to decide what a "duck stamp" should look like. Darling met with a representative from Secretary Wallace's office, Hal Sheldon, to discuss ideas for the stamp. They decided the stamp should be rectangular, in landscape format, and, not surprisingly, it should show some ducks. Sheldon asked Darling to make a few preliminary sketches on the spot. Like most Washington executives, the chief kept a supply of freshly laundered shirts in his office for unexpected evening events, and each shirt was wrapped around a sheet of cardboard. Darling pulled out six of the cardboards and quickly sketched some ideas. The best, they thought, was a pair of Mallards landing on water. Darling sent the sketches with Sheldon to review and consider until they next met. When the deadline for sending a design to the engravers approached, Darling asked Sheldon when they were going to get together again to make the final decisions. Sheldon blanched; the design, he said, was already at the engravers—it was the Mallards that Darling had sketched on one of the shirt cardboards. Once again, a makeshift sketch by Darling was destined to become a world standard.[29]

The duck stamp program has become one of the most successful initiatives in the history of conservation. The US Treasury printed over 600,000 copies of Darling's first stamp for the 1934–35 hunting season. Initially the stamps cost $1 each; currently they cost $25. Since 1934, the program has raised $750 million for the purchase of national wildlife refuges that directly benefit waterfowl. The stamp idea has been

Figure 2.4 Ding Darling inspects printing of the first duck stamp in 1934. (Reproduced courtesy of the National Conservation Training Center, US Fish and Wildlife Service.)

copied by all fifty states—not only for waterfowl, but also for many other conservation purposes—and by many nations worldwide. Darling's work as chief of the US Biological Survey on behalf of waterfowl would earn him a most appropriate recognition as "the best friend a duck ever had."[30]

Expansion of the wildlife refuge system and creation of the duck stamp program are the two accomplishments that will always be most associated with Darling. However, the list of his accomplishments as chief is long and varied. He organized game wardens into teams that targeted the places where illegal hunting was concentrated. He expanded the Cooperative Wildlife Research Units from his original Iowa location to eight more across the nation. He helped pass the Pittman-Robertson Act, which taxes hunting equipment and supplies in order to fund conservation. He personally directed the restoration of the Sheldon Antelope Refuge in Nevada, which had been created by Teddy Roosevelt and then virtually abandoned by the agency.

Darling lasted only twenty months as chief. His core differences with Roosevelt and his impatience with the processes of government eventually became too much to bear. Darling's special concern for waterfowl populations often put him on opposite sides from the president. He objected to dams because they inundated wetlands, and he was particularly distrustful of the US Army Corps of Engineers. Roosevelt, however, was encouraging dam construction across the nation in order to provide jobs, water, and hydroelectricity to fight the Great Depression. Regarding a failed effort to restore a drained wetland in South Dakota, Darling later wrote, "That was the bitterest defeat I suffered during my brief period of alleged authority, and whenever I hear anyone boasting of Franklin D. Roosevelt as a conservationist I think of how little the Public knows of the political crimes committed in the name of Conservation."[31]

Darling knew that his effectiveness was wearing thin. "I have trod on so many sore corns in the Government circles that it is beginning to reflect on the functions of the Bureau—seriously," he admitted.[32] On November 15, 1935, he handed in his resignation and headed back to his Des Moines drawing board. Darling's tenure as chief of the US Biological Survey was short, but it was transformative, and he was satisfied with his tenure: "It was to apply the practical principles of conservation to the wasted lands and water resources of the country that I took time out from my daily routine of cartooning. . . . And it has always seemed to me that I accomplished more visible good in that two years than in all the cartoons I made over the fifty years of my active newspaper work."[33]

Always a Conservationist

Darling may have quit his full-time conservation job, but he never quit his conservation work as a citizen. Too much remained to be done, and in Darling's view, Washington wasn't going to do it. Once out of office, Darling became a much more active voice for the plight and possibilities of conservation.

He believed that conservation was weak because it had no coordinated national constituency. Sportsmen and -women tended to be organized around local interests—protecting the lands and waters where they recreated or advocating for better hunting and fishing regulations in their individual states. What conservation needed, Darling thought, was a national organization that could work effectively and efficiently for the common good: "I can think of nothing in the conservation field which promises such beneficial results as a unification—you might call it a 'Clearing House'—of the all too numerous federations, societies, chapters, clubs, and services, each maintaining a staff of paid executives, each owning or renting office headquarters and each spending enormous sums annually in publications for general distribution, and all saying the same thing in just so many words."[34]

While still chief of the Biological Survey, Darling had begun rallying leaders from the sporting industry in support of his vision. At a dinner at the Waldorf-Astoria Hotel in New York, Darling encouraged them to form a new society that would address conservation at the national and continental scale. He also lobbied President Roosevelt to sponsor a large annual meeting of conservation officials and experts to advise the president on conservation issues.

Both ideas took hold almost immediately after Darling left government service. Roosevelt convened the first North American Wildlife Conference in February 1936, with more than 1,500 attendees. The conference has been held annually since then, and has become the continent's most influential gathering of state and provincial conservation officials, along with their federal counterparts and conservation experts from universities and nongovernmental organizations.

At that first conference, led by the guests at Darling's Waldorf-Astoria dinner, the delegates also voted to form the General Wildlife

Federation. Following Darling's plan, the Federation was intended to represent state-level conservation groups, now unified so they could speak with a common voice. The delegates elected Darling as president, a post he retained for several formative years of the Federation. The Federation was quickly endorsed by the states; within months forty-four states had formed state federations as the basis for the national organization. In 1938, the group changed its name to the National Wildlife Federation, as we still know it today.

As soon as he left government employ in 1935, he was back drawing cartoons for the nation's newspapers. He won his second Pulitzer Prize in 1942, this time for a cartoon portraying the wasteful mountains of bureaucratic paperwork generated by the federal government. He retired briefly in 1943, but couldn't stay away: "That Pulitzer Award came darned near being a posthumous award, figuratively speaking, for about six weeks ago I decided that I had drawn cartoons long enough and sent in my resignation. . . . It seemed to me it was time to lay down the shovel and the hoe and hang up the fiddle and the bow like old Uncle Joe, and watch the world go by. I guess I'm not going to be able to get away with it."[35]

He went back to work, much to the delight of his publishers and his readers. As World War II wound down, however, he felt that his style of cartooning was becoming dated. Cartoons were becoming simpler, with fewer words, starker images, and less subtlety. He wrote to colleagues in 1943, "You must know that as cartoons go my style of drawing and my conception of cartoon composition is on the way out. . . ."[36] Darling also believed that the principles he held and illustrated were falling out of favor, and that newspapers were retreating from a position of strength. He lamented that the "vigor of editorial convictions and forceful expression throughout the newspaper world seems to have kept company with the general deterioration of American morale. . . ."[37] Darling finally retired in 1949, after a remarkable fifty years at the drawing table. The volume of his work lies somewhere above 15,000 individual cartoons, a massive portfolio unlikely ever to be surpassed.

His retirement left him even more time to address political and conservation projects. He kept up a storm of correspondence and commentary with public officials, sometimes encouraging, but more often critical. Indeed, his view of the world and the possibilities for its future turned increasingly sour, and he despaired that Americans seemed blind to the realities of modern life as he saw them. He was especially concerned that we couldn't feed a world in which the population continued to expand without control: "The trouble with me is that my convictions run counter to some of the tendencies that are now being broadcast that we should attempt to feed the world. . . . There comes to my mind the old adage that casting your bread upon the water will return it fourfold. The only trouble is that in this feeding of the starving peoples of the world, we get fourfold return of population pressure rather than fourfold return of our bread."[38]

Darling became convinced that education was the only way to get the conservation message across, but that current strategies and programs were losing ground. He contended that conservation education should not be taught as recreation—for example, by amateurs around the campground—but by school teachers as an integrated element in the public school curriculum. He observed that conservation organizations were pumping out hundreds of pamphlets and booklets, an effort largely wasted because the materials didn't suit teachers' needs. "Conservationists are manufacturing rifle ammunition, which does not fit the education shotguns," he said in a 1950 speech. What's more, he thought that whatever information was produced, it needed to be done only once and done well—again through his vision for a conservation clearing house. Continuing his 1950 speech, he noted that conservation groups produced "just 'more of the same.' Books, books, books, largely technical, pamphlets largely specializing in just one branch of Conservation, like soils or Forestry or Wildlife, mailing material on wild flowers and dickey birds. . . ."[39] He remained perplexed—and gravely disappointed—to the end of his life that this idea would not take hold.

Disappointment in his waning years was not restricted to conservation education. He grew increasingly disgruntled with the National Wildlife Federation, believing that it had abandoned its original mission—as a unifying conservation think-tank—to become an uncritical advocate for the US Fish and Wildlife Service. He eventually resigned from the Federation, unwilling to have his name associated with its work. "I had hoped," he wrote, "that the Federation would be the crowning achievement of my devotion to Conservation. It is, instead, my greatest humiliation."[40]

From the beneficial perspective of a long life, however, Darling eventually softened his view about the progress of conservation. He recognized that his old friend Henry Wallace had done well as a New Deal supporter of conservation by mimicking Iowa's innovations: "Then in 1934, '35, and '36, Henry Wallace, who had watched what had been happening to his own state, sought to apply the same principles through the efforts of the Federal government and emergency jobs for the unemployed."[41]

Those principles, which Darling had helped develop and had introduced to the US Biological Survey, had indeed taken hold. The National Wildlife Refuge System continued to prosper under Salyer's leadership, and covered 29 million acres when Salyer retired in 1961; the system now includes more than 550 sites occupying over 150 million acres. The duck stamp program has continued pumping money without interruption into refuges and waterfowl production. Duck populations were coming back, and Darling observed with delight in 1960 that "the season doesn't open for another week but the marshes and lakes are already filling up with Mallards, Teal, and Gadwalls."[42] He eventually reconciled with the National Wildlife Federation and agreed to be honorary cochair, with Walt Disney, of National Wildlife Week in 1962—an event he did not live to attend.

During the final years of Darling's life, awards and recognitions arrived regularly. He received the Iowa Award in 1955, the state's highest citizen recognition; he was only the second recipient (the first, in 1951, was Darling's lifelong friend and fellow Iowa native, Herbert Hoover). In the last decade of his life, he received most of the nation's major conservation awards, including the Audubon Medal and honorary membership in the Boone and Crockett Club. Refuges, lakes, and parks across the country were named for him, including the Ding Darling National Wildlife Refuge on Sanibel Island, named posthumously in his honor in 1967. The Des Moines chapter of the Izaak Walton League carries his name, as does the "Ding Crab," a variety of flowering crabapple tree that was introduced in Des Moines.

Darling died on February 12, 1962, at the age of eighty-six. He had witnessed an extraordinary time, from a boyhood spent at the edge of the wilderness to a place in the elite circles of New York society and

Washington bureaucracy, through two world wars and a great depression. He had also witnessed, and in many ways produced, a massive change in the nation's pursuit of conservation. The span of Darling's life began with the earliest recognition of the need for conservation—protecting lands, regulating hunting and fishing, establishing government agencies—and ended as the postwar generation was coming to grips with a large set of natural-resource issues. Within a year of his death, Rachel Carson published *Silent Spring*, marking the start of the modern environmental movement. Through his "genial, stubborn, lovable, humane, dauntless, graceful charm," as one eulogist put it, every morning his cartoons helped Americans interpret their world.[43]

On the morning after his death, one more Ding Darling cartoon appeared on the front page of the Des Moines *Register*. Ever the man of opinion and action, Darling was not about to let someone else give his farewells for him. His final cartoon showed a messy and crowded studio and a figure exiting through a closing door. It carried these few words: "Bye Now—It's Been Wonderful Knowing You."

Figure 3.1 Rand Aldo Leopold, 1887–1948. (Reproduced courtesy of the Aldo Leopold Foundation, www.aldoleopold.org.)

Chapter 3

Aldo Leopold

A Very Large & Important Sumpin

He rose quietly from his bunk, careful not to disturb others in the predawn darkness. He stirred the embers of the fire, bringing it back to life. When the coffee was ready, he took the entire pot and slipped out the door. Sitting on a nearby bench— one he had fashioned himself from a downed tree—he sipped coffee and listened to the awakening day. He pulled the tiny notebook and knife-sharpened pencil from his shirt pocket and began to record by the light of the stars and moon.

2:45 song sparrow
3:00 "   "
3:05 field sparrow
3:07 song sparrow
3:09 "   " , field sparrow
3:11 field sparrow
3:15 Yellowthroat, field spar.
3:18 Crested Fly field spar. Indigo
       (after which all cut loose)
3:26 meadowlark, towhee . . .[1]

This particular day was May 31, 1946, but it could have been any of hundreds of days that Aldo Leopold spent in the rural simplicity of central Wisconsin. The man who became the prophet of the conservation ethic and the father of wildlife management spent much of his life in the solitary observation of nature. As his powers of observation matured and his understanding of nature deepened, he learned to read a landscape like few others before or since. And he shared his wisdom for all in his posthumously published masterpiece, *A Sand County Almanac.*

Aldo Leopold's life is a story of evolving understanding. He first believed that predators ate too many deer and should be exterminated; he later understood that they were essential parts of the ecosystem. He first believed that utilitarian values of nature were most important; he later understood that nature provided many values, the most precious of which could not be bought or sold. He first believed that wilderness was for hunters who coveted a pioneer experience; he later understood that wilderness was the baseline we needed in order to measure land health.

Had he figured it all out by the end? Were his words in *A Sand County Almanac* the ultimate answer to reconciling human needs and nature's bounty? Hardly. He wrote to a friend, just a month before his death, that he lacked "a completely logical [conservation] philosophy all thought out; in fact on the contrary, I am deeply disturbed and do not myself know the answer to the conflicting needs with which we are faced."[2] Leopold's life was a continuing journey of learning and discovery, a journey from which we have all benefited.

A Boy in the Field

If ever a child was destined to bridge the worlds of nature and human nature, it was Rand Aldo Leopold. Born into a leading family of Burlington, Iowa, on January 11, 1887, he was raised in a wealthy, cultured home overlooking the forested bluffs of the Mississippi River. Aldo, as he was called from birth, was immersed in (and equally delighted by) both field-learning and book-learning.

His father, Carl, was the successful owner of the Leopold Desk Company, which manufactured fine wooden rolltop desks that were sold throughout the country. But Carl's real passion was the field and forest, his chosen tools the shotgun and rifle. In the era before any laws governed the shooting of wild game, he developed his own code of ethics about what, when, and how to hunt. Aldo, his oldest son, was always at his father's side in the field, and early on he absorbed a respect for nature and a strong moral compass to govern its use. Hunting was one skill shared by father and son; careful observation of nature was another. Leopold's younger brother Frederic recalled trips with their father. "He would open up a decaying hollow log to show us the life dwelling inside, such as mice or large insects. . . . We did not need to kill game to have an exciting afternoon in the swamp or field."[3]

When not in the woods, Aldo was in the garden, tending to the vegetables and flowers between the Leopold family home and that of his grandparents. He especially liked birds, so much so that he called himself an "amateur ornithologist." "I like to study birds," he wrote as a boy. "I like the wren best of all birds. . . . I like the wrens best because they do more good than almost any other bird, they sing sweetly, they are very pretty, and very tame."[4]

Leopold's mother, Clara, provided the cultured side of his education. Aldo was his mother's favorite, a fact admitted by his siblings, apparently without rivalry. The house was filled with books and music that supplemented Aldo's outdoor education. Aldo was an excellent student, with special interests in literature and rhetoric. One aspect of a classical education, however, was absent from the Leopold household—religion. They were not church people. Consequently, Aldo remained—as a boy and throughout his life—outside the domain of religious doctrine or practice.

Clara suffered badly from hay fever, so much so that the family escaped Iowa late in every summer for a six-week respite on a tourist island in Lake Huron—another source of joy and outdoor education for Aldo. The trip was an adventure itself, taking a full twenty-four hours— a train to Chicago, a ship to Mackinac Island, and then a smaller boat to their destination on Marquette Island. Aldo was generally seasick on the voyage, much to his dismay. Frederic remembered that he "hated this evidence of physical weakness. We carried dried dog biscuits for our animals, and Aldo found he could eat dog biscuits without getting sick."[5] Once safely at the destination, he had ample opportunity to hunt and fish at will and to improve his woodsmanship. In the manner of

Daniel Boone, he carved this message on the railing of a boardwalk: "Aldo Leopold killed a skunk here on August 20th, 1901."[6]

Leopold began his formal education in earnest when he was seventeen. Following the family tradition, he enrolled at the Lawrenceville Preparatory School in rural New Jersey, one of the oldest and most prestigious boarding schools in the nation. As soon as he arrived on campus, Leopold began taking daily "tramps" through the countryside. As he would do wherever he lived, Leopold observed the landscape thoroughly, making it his own. He drew his own maps of the vicinity, naming places according to what he found there—Fern Woods, Ash Swamp, the Boulders. His fellow students teasingly called him "the naturalist." He deepened his intense interest in birds, but added another love: plants. Equipped with a plant press and a copy of Asa Gray's *Manual of Botany*, Leopold remained a student of both individual plants and the botanic community throughout his life.

Carl Leopold wanted his eldest son to study business in college and then join him at the desk company. That was not for Aldo, however, and his father found it difficult to argue with the outdoor interests he had nurtured in his son: Aldo Leopold was going to become a forester.

Forestry was rapidly developing as a profession at the start of the twentieth century. The United States had begun to protect forest reserves, a trend that John Muir had encouraged under Presidents Benjamin Harrison and Theodore Roosevelt. Roosevelt and his trusted natural-resource advisor, Gifford Pinchot, raised forest protection to a national imperative. Foresters were needed to manage these massive tracts, soon to be called "national forests." If you wanted to become a professional forester at that time, there was only one place to study—Yale.

So that's where Leopold went, starting in 1905. His first year was at the Sheffield Scientific School, an affiliate of Yale where science topics were taught for potential graduate students. The next year, he formally entered the Yale forestry program as a master's candidate. He liked the practical forestry courses best, being out in the field, doing rather than listening. And he had little interest in what happened to the wood after it left the forest, claiming that he "had no ambition to be a Tie-pickler or a timber-tester."[7] Although his excursions into the countryside were now more limited than at Lawrenceville, he took full advantage when he could, riding the New Haven trolley to the end of the line and escaping farther on foot. His approach to nature was changing as well. He had arrived at Lawrenceville a committed hunter, but his zeal wore off through time. He first shot crows whenever he could, but later wrote home that "he had no desire to kill crows or anything else, in spite of favorable conditions."[8] He also matured from a mere observer of nature—which birds he saw or heard, what plants he encountered—to an interpreter of what he saw. His near-daily letters home became less plainly descriptive and instead were filled with what he called "anecdotes and impressions."

> The left hillside is rich brown with scrub oak, the bottom mainly yellow and pinkish Sand Grass, while the right hillside is solid dark and green with many hemlocks. The bottom is a gunshot across, suggesting a great rabbit place. But one walks natural-ly next the hemlocks, for there runs the stream. It is just a big clear brook everywhere else, but in the Valley it feels the spell of strangeness. Swift, dark, and noiseless it glides along the rooty mossy bank and seeks the black shadows that fall from the grim old forest.[9]

His social skills expanded during these years as well. He was naturally shy as a boy, so much so that his mother called him "a born recluse and hermit."[10] College life trumped that tendency, as he joined sports teams, enjoyed several romances, and spent weekends with friends in New York City. He wrote home that he "was enjoying life uproariously," and "had never been so busy, so happy, or so successful."[11] Too successful, it seems, as he landed on probation one semester and needed a firm rebuke from his father to refocus him on his studies.

Forestry at the time was dominated by Gifford Pinchot's utilitar-ian notion that natural resources should be used efficiently and fully—nature's bounty was simply wasted by leaving logs to die on the stump and rot in the woods when they could be used to fuel the nation's prog-ress. Yale taught this approach with evangelical zeal, and Leopold, like his fellow students, was a willing disciple. And, after graduating in February, 1909, the twenty-two-year-old Leopold and all his classmates were snapped up by the United States Forest Service to put that utilitarian training to work.

A Forester by Profession

The newly harvested crop of foresters began their careers with ten weeks of forestry training in the woodlands of eastern Texas. First, they sailed from New York to New Orleans; this time the ship travel suited Leopold better. He wrote home: "In the afternoon we encountered a shoal of porpoises. They were the real treat of the day. They look like a miniature whale, 4 to 5 feet long, with a sharp nose. George how they do swim! They gambol lazily just ahead of the bow, racing with the ship, and every once in a while breaking water with a graceful spring, apparently in pure glee and good spirits. One by one they tired out and gave up the race, but the more enduring ones kept up for over half an hour. I wish I could swim like that!"[12]

The training was relentless, the weather cloying, and the camp conditions harsh. Leopold thrived in this environment, reveling in the immersion in nature. "It is really a very beautiful region," he wrote home to his mother. "If you could see the full moon tonight, sailing high over the towering pine-trees, you would like it too. I had decided again and again, that it is worth all the trouble of the mosquitoes and fleas and snakes and pigs, and more too."[13]

When the assignments came, Leopold found himself headed farther west as assistant forester in the Apache National Forest, straddling the Arizona–New Mexico border. The Apache was one of the more remote national forests; it had been harvested and grazed less than others, and game was still relatively abundant. Escudilla Mountain, just under 11,000 feet tall, dominated the landscape. He climbed the mountain as soon as he could. "There was, in fact, only one place from which you did not see Escudilla on the skyline: that was the top of Escudilla itself. Up there you could not see the mountain, but you could feel it."[14]

He reveled in the expanse of the landscape and the scope of the forestry tasks before him. His fundamental job was to lead a crew into the forest to map an assigned area and inventory its timber resources. He

Figure 3.2 Aldo Leopold on horseback while serving as a forest ranger for the US Forest Service in New Mexico. (Reproduced courtesy of the Aldo Leopold Foundation, www.aldoleopold.org.)

liked the work because, he once recalled, "it deals with big things. Millions of acres, billions of feet of timber, vast amounts of capital—why it's fun to twiddle them around in your fingers, especially when you consider your very modest amount of experience."[15]

Leopold's "modest experience" soon showed. His first summer of timber cruises was a disaster. His leadership was harsh and arrogant; he misread maps; his measurements and data were error-ridden. He botched the work so badly that a review was conducted to determine if he was fit to return for a second year. The review found only that he was inexperienced, not incompetent. He learned from his experience—a lifelong trademark of Aldo Leopold—and the following year's work was carried out successfully.

Once more, he fell in love with the land. The Southwest was a complex, ever-changing landscape, more diverse than others he had experienced. "This land is too complex for its inhabitants to understand; maybe too complex for any competitive economic system to develop successfully."[16] But it was also the most beautiful land he had ever seen: "In the early morning a silvery veil hangs over the far away mesas and mountains—too delicate to be called a mist, too vast to be merely beautiful—it isn't describable, it has to be seen. And all framed in a little Iris-dotted meadow bordered by the tall orange-colored shafts and dark green foliage of the pines, with a little rippling, bubbling spring, half buried in the new green grass. . . ."[17]

It was characteristic of Leopold that once he saw something in nature, he wanted to "own it"—that is, he wished to know it thoroughly, better than a casual visitor or even the owner of the land or grazing permit. "I was made to live on and work on *my own* land. Whether it's a 100-acre farm or a 1,700,000-acre Forest doesn't matter—it's all the same principle, and I don't think I'll ever change my mind about it."[18] As he wrote in a letter somewhat later, "Every one of those little pines is mine, and the great old rock, and the little ferns growing on it—everything even to the sweeping plains that one sees from there, and the purple mountains where the indigo shadows rise at Sunset. It is *all* mine. . . ."[19]

Leopold also loved the game that populated "his" land, and, like others at the time, he despised the predators that acted as though the game were theirs. Exterminating predators was the mantra of resource managers, and he was as sure as others that wolves, coyotes, and foxes were the enemies of hunters. During his first year on the Apache he shot a wolf, an event that lodged forever in Leopold's psyche. The encounter achieved immortality in his essay "Thinking Like a Mountain." Coming upon an old wolf and several pups from above, Leopold and his companion shot into the pack. The old wolf was just injured, and the hunters hurried down the mountain to complete their task. "We reached the old wolf in time to watch a fierce green fire dying in her eyes. I realized then, and have known ever since, that there was something new to me in those eyes—something known only to her and to the mountain. I was young then, and full of trigger-itch; I thought that because fewer wolves meant more deer, that no wolves would mean hunters' paradise. But after seeing the green fire die, I sensed that neither the wolf nor the mountain agreed with such a view."[20]

After erasing the missteps of his first field season, Leopold became well liked and highly regarded by both his bosses and his colleagues. They were impressed by his energy, initiative, and high spirits. (Leopold believed that "a pipe and a sense of humor are two of the essentials for a good Forest Ranger."[21])

Within two years of joining the Forest Service, he was promoted to deputy supervisor of the Carson National Forest, with offices just north of Santa Fe, New Mexico. The Carson was a far different place from the Apache—in fact, it was a mess. Cattle had grazed the forest for generations, and the effects of too many head of cattle, too much greed, and too little oversight were apparent in low grass productivity, eroded hillsides, and parched streams. The existing staff members were lazy and ineffective at best, and perhaps also corrupt. Leopold arrived with a new forest supervisor, chosen for his established ability to turn around a bad situation. Together they cracked the whip, goading the field staff into action, issuing permits with smaller allotments of cattle, and enforcing grazing regulations. Within a few months the forest supervisor was reassigned, leaving Leopold as the acting supervisor of a forest in a state of chaos. Never one to shrink from a challenge or duty, he vowed to persevere. "By God," he wrote home, "the Individual allotment and every other reform we have promised is going to stick—if it takes a six-shooter to do it."[22] Fortunately, the sheep ranchers acquiesced to the new rules without the need for gunplay. Shortly thereafter, "acting" was removed from his title, and Leopold became supervisor of his own forest.

While working on the Carson National Forest, Leopold encountered another treasure that he wished to call his own. Maria Alvira Estella Bergere was the daughter of a prominent Santa Fe family. He described her to his mother as "very dark, her hair has a reddish glint should you ever see it exactly right, she has very beautiful eyes, aquiline nose, and a very fine mouth. Her voice is very low, she is slender and not tall, and dresses extremely well but very simply."[23]

Estella's father was the largest sheep rancher in the United States, and her mother's Hispanic roots were traceable back many generations to Spanish royalty. Consequently, she was a highly eligible young woman, and Leopold faced formidable competition from other suitors eager to win her hand. He was not about to back down. "It's all up with me," he wrote back to his family. "Five minutes after I saw Estella this last time I could have told you what I know now—and that is that I love her."[24] The perseverance that Leopold put into every task worked for him now as well, and he out-courted all his rivals. They were married on October 9, 1912.

Leopold's reign as a forest supervisor was unexpectedly short. Soon after being permanently appointed to the post, he conducted a two-week-long horseback inspection of the forest. He arrived home a gaunt figure, barely able to remain upright in the saddle. He had contracted nephritis, a kidney ailment that often proved fatal at the time. The prescribed treatment for nephritis was bed rest, so the Forest Service put Leopold on a six-week medical leave. He barely improved, however, and under doctor's orders, he and Estella returned to the Leopold family estate in Iowa to continue his convalescence. In total, he required sixteen months to recuperate enough to return to work—but never again to the strenuous job of forest supervisor. "To speak plainly," he told his boss sometime later, "I do not know whether I have twenty days or twenty years ahead of me."[25]

Leopold was not idle while resting in Burlington. He again took advantage of the family library that had fired his intellect as a child. He read extensively in the classics of literature, philosophy, and religion (religion as an academic topic, not a spiritual one), acquiring the breadth of knowledge so evident in his later work.

Leopold rejoined the Forest Service in September 1914. A field job was out of the question, so he was assigned to the regional headquarters in Albuquerque. The regional forester recognized Leopold's interest in the broader values of the forest as well as his ability to write persuasively, and so he created a new position—new for Leopold and for the forest—responsible for fish, game, recreation, and publicity. Leopold was skeptical about the long-term viability of the job. "I don't trust this new job to last," he wrote home, "much less like it. However, I'm so d—— glad to be making a living that I gladly waive the fine questions."[26]

The job did last, and Leopold thrived in it. The range of his responsibilities and opportunities expanded greatly. He and a colleague inspected the dismal state of the lands around the Grand Canyon—the rim was plagued with uncontrolled, cheap, and garish tourist attractions—and together they wrote the first plan for coordinated development of the area. He gained an appreciation for the economic benefits of recreation and the role of abundant fish and wildlife in achieving those benefits. He also understood the need to restore depleted populations. "The breeding stock must be increased," he wrote. "Rare species must be protected and restored. The value of game lies in its variety as well as its abundance."[27] To further that work, he authored a comprehensive handbook on game protection for Forest Service rangers—the first in the history of the agency.

All across the country, sportsmen were organizing themselves into groups for both social and conservation purposes. Leopold took up the charge in New Mexico, with the blessings of his boss. He began organizing "Game Protective Associations" (GPAs), first in Albuquerque and then in the surrounding communities. His skills as an organizer and administrator blossomed in this role. "Extraordinarily persuasive in personal contact, he proved himself a master at appealing to diverse interest groups,"[28] able to unite sportsmen, ranchers, foresters, farmers, businessmen, scientists, and policy-makers in their common interests.

Leopold was still a product of his times, however, and his times were about maximizing the utilitarian value of nature. The renewable resources of the land were to be treated as a crop—nurtured, harvested, or left to be harvested the next time around. This was the principle of scientific forestry, and Leopold saw it as the right principle for the coming field of professional game management. Game was a crop just like trees, and game managers needed to perform tasks to enhance the crop. His views had yet to acquire an ecological basis—he was still thinking in a straight line: what made more game in the short run was also going to work in the long run.

Leopold's perspective entered a new stage of development upon his promotion to chief of operations for the Albuquerque District of the Forest Service, making him second in rank only to the district forester. His main duty was to perform lengthy field inspections of individual forest areas, assessing their status and making recommendations for improvements. These month-long field tours gave Leopold a comprehensive view of the entire region. Two trends troubled him.

The first was erosion. Just as he first saw in the Carson National Forest, overgrazing had started a cascade of problems with soil erosion. Although steps were being taken to reduce grazing to more sustainable levels, more needed to be done—gullies needed to be plugged with brush tangles, streams needed to be stabilized with tree trunks, slopes needed to be planted with willows to hold the soil. He authored a watershed handbook for the Southwest region, filled with practical guidelines for fixing soil erosion. "All civilization is basically dependent upon natural resources," he wrote. "All natural resources, except only subterranean minerals, are soil or derivatives of soil. Farms, ranges, crops and live-stock, forests, irrigation, water, and even water power resolve themselves into questions of soil. Soil is therefore the basic natural resource."[29]

The second problem was the domestication of the landscape. More people meant more cattle, roads, buildings, power lines, and countless other artifacts of modern life. Leopold saw the national forests being sliced by roads and penetrated by development. Recreation was increas-ingly dominated by the automobile. "It is just as unwise to devote 100 percent of the recreational resources of our public parks and forests to motorists," he wrote, "as it would be to devote 100 percent of our city parks to merry-go-rounds. . . . Thrusting more and ever more roads into every little remaining patch of wilderness is sheer stupidity."[30] He reasoned that saving some of the land from development—even natural-resource development—was essential. "It will be much easier to keep wilderness areas than to create them," he wrote. "In fact, the latter al-ternative may be dismissed as impossible."[31]

Leopold also saw wilderness as a manifestation of the American prin-ciples of freedom and democracy. An unspoiled landscape gave people the opportunity to relive the pioneer experience, recreating as they wished and as their forebearers had lived. Of course, that was the kind of activity he himself most enjoyed. He told an audience at the time, "I confess my own leisure to be spent entirely in search of adventure, with-out regard to prudence, profit, self-improvement, learning, or any other serious thing."[32] For Leopold, time spent alone and un-modernized in nature was time well spent.

His interest was professional as well as personal. He reasoned that wilderness was needed as a standard against which to measure our destruction of land and our success in its restoration. He wrote the for-estry profession's first article about wilderness for the November 1921 issue of the *Journal of Forestry*. Leopold used Gifford Pinchot's utilitar-ian idea as the ultimate justification for wilderness: "Pinchot's promise of development has been made good. The process must, of course, continue indefinitely. But it has already gone far enough to raise the question of whether the policy of development . . . should continue to govern in absolutely every instance, or whether the principle of highest use does not itself demand that representative portions of some forests be preserved as wilderness."[33]

While chief of operations, he found an opportunity to act on his belief in the value of wilderness. One of his responsibilities was to inspect the Gila National Forest in New Mexico. Because of the region's rough topography, it had been less impacted by grazing, timber harvest, or development than other forests, and large areas remained roadless. This, he concluded, was the perfect place to demonstrate the value of wilderness as a "product" of the forest. In his assessment report, Leopold included a proposal to make the Gila a wilderness area. His bosses liked the idea and asked Leopold to develop it further. On June 3, 1924, following Leopold's recommendations, the district forester signed into existence the nation's first wilderness area in the Gila National Forest.

Leopold had now reached the tipping point on a journey that had begun with his Yale education. He had moved gradually from the rigid perspective of a professional forester of his time—a focus on growing and harvesting trees—to a more comprehensive interest in all aspects of the forest. The Forest Service, he reasoned, "was entrusted with the protection, and development, through wise use and constructive study of the timber, water, forage, farm, recreative, game, fish, and esthetic resources of the areas under our jurisdiction. . . . I will call these resources, for short, 'The Forest.'"[34]

Leopold had become a leading conservation professional, with a growing national reputation. He was writing prolifically about natural history and conservation for both professional and lay audiences. He was the behind-the-scenes orchestrator of game-management policy and practice in New Mexico. He excelled in his work, and received no fewer than five offers for promotion within the Forest Service, most of which would have taken him to a desk job in Washington, DC. He turned them all down, ostensibly preferring to remain working close to the land. His health restored, he was enjoying an active hunting, camping, and hiking lifestyle in the desert Southwest with his wife and young children, now numbering two sons and two daughters.

Then, one day in the spring of 1924, he inexplicably gave it all up. He accepted the position of assistant director of the Forest Service's Forest Products Laboratory in Madison, Wisconsin. Leopold never explained why he took the job, but the ability to influence the entire agency through its main research facility must have appealed to the broad-minded thinker. There was also a strong hint that the current director was ready to retire and that Leopold would rapidly advance to that position.

Leopold was "a fish out of water" at the lab, according to one colleague.[35] The work—managing the research and conducting public relations for the lab—was not taxing, but neither was it satisfying. The promised retirement of the director did not occur, and the two men regularly sparred over their views of forestry. After four unrewarding years, Leopold put himself on the job market, and in 1928 he resigned from the Forest Service and started a new career in game management, a career that would become immortal.

The Father of Wildlife Management

Leopold pondered several job offers before settling on the least secure and least defined. The Sporting Arms and Ammunition Manufacturers' Institute (SAAMI) had formed in 1926, at the request of the federal government, to set standards for the safe and responsible use of firearms. Along with this task, SAAMI also sought (and still seeks) to promote a healthy environment, including the conservation of wildlife. In the 1920s, the condition of wildlife—game animals, specifically—was desperate. Populations had been wiped out by habitat modification, market hunting, and unrestricted recreational hunting. Knowing that the future of hunting depended on the presence of abundant game, SAAMI decided to document the condition of game across the country and to make recommendations for improvement. They hired Leopold to do this work, giving him a two-year contract from 1928 through 1930.

Leopold was perfect for the job. He was, of course, one of the leading game professionals in the country. But the job also called for three skills that were Leopold's sweet spots. First, the survey required a keen sense of observation and ability to read the land. As his friend and colleague Robert McCabe put it, Leopold "could examine a handful of soil and as it slid through his fingers he comprehended its geological origin, its organic history, its potential for life support and thus its future."[36] Second, the survey involved gathering information from hundreds of strangers who might or might not want to share. Leopold liked people and could relate to them on many levels; he was a great listener, especially eager to hear from people who lived on and worked the land. His daughter Estella remembered her father's manner:

> He was always pleasant and direct, tactful and interesting. When he was speaking with professionals in his field, he used elegant language; . . . with his friends socially he was much the same, but always added an element of good humor . . . with farmers and people in the country, he would often start the conversation by making observations about the weather, then ask the farmer how his farm animals and crops were doing, offer some observations about a pheasant or snipe he had seen while walking to their place, or ask how the native quail were doing this year. Finally, he would get around to asking about the matter of business that brought about his visit. The main business never came first![37]

Third, the survey needed an excellent analyst and writer to produce a final report. Leopold by now was a seasoned veteran with pad and pencil. He did his own writing and editing, working to assure that the message was clear, accurate, and appropriately forceful. His writing "was not that of an inspired genius, but that of any other ordinary fellow trying to put two and two together."[38]

Leopold set to work in a spare office loaned by the University of Wisconsin, in the chemistry department. But most of his time was spent examining the countryside, state by state. Very soon, he realized that a national survey was well beyond the scope of his time or budget. SAAMI and he agreed to narrow the project's scope to the upper Midwest, eight states from Ohio across to Minnesota and down to Missouri. Each state required two weeks to two months of field visits. He began each survey by interviewing game department officials and university faculty, then toured through the state, meeting landowners and local officials and tramping through fields and forests. At the end of the field visit, he returned to the state capital and university, reviewing his impressions with the experts he had consulted earlier. In all, he visited over 300 localities and conferred with more than 600 individuals.[39]

The *Report on a Game Survey of the North Central States* was issued in spring 1931. The 299-page book described conditions of game species by species across the region. It also included sections on research, administration, and education as well as a final recommendation of an appropriate game policy for the region. Leopold's survey revealed that as agriculture became more intensive, habitat for game animals worsened and, consequently, game populations declined: "The physical manifestations of the covert shrinkage are plain to anyone who can look out of a train window: woodlots are grazed clean of reproduction and undergrowth, there is less and less cover on fencerows and drainage channels, hedges are uprooted to make room for metal fences, swamps are increasingly drained or burned to make new pasture or tillage. . . ."[40] At the same time, hunting was increasing in popularity, and more hunting pressure meant even lower game abundance. Leopold also concluded that habitats needed to be improved in order to provide the food, cover, and reproductive sites that animals needed, and that interspersing habitats—creating edges—was an essential tool for improving habitat.

The report was an instant success. One reviewer wrote that "game management in America is going to 'date' from" the report's publication. Leopold was almost single-handedly creating a new field of study and application, earning the now-universal sobriquet of "father of wildlife management."[41] As one biographer reasoned, "One man can hardly establish a profession, but Leopold's stamp has been on the profession so conspicuously from its beginnings around 1930 to the present that the title is perhaps justified."[42]

Simultaneous with his survey work, Leopold was leading the profession in the development of a North American game policy. Until then, game management had concentrated on restrictions of hunting and artificial rearing and then releasing of game for the sake of hunting. The new policy, largely written by Leopold and then endorsed by the profession in 1930, instead emphasized habitat management, restoration of wild populations, and the essential role of the private landowners. The policy also promoted more practical experimentation to replace dogma: "We believe that experiment, not doctrine or philosophy, is the key to an American Game Policy. . . . Timidity, optimism, or unbending insistence on old grooves of thought and action will surely either destroy the remaining resources, or force the adoption of policies which will limit their use to a few."[43]

Leopold may now have become the acknowledged leader of his profession, but he was also out of work. The country was in the depths of the Great Depression, and his contract with SAAMI ended. He advertised himself as a "consulting forester" and cobbled together a few jobs, including leading Civilian Conservation Corps (CCC) groups back into the southwestern national forests. But, as he wrote a friend, "otherwise I am unemployed. Of course I have worlds of things to do, but the question is [how] to get paid for them."[44]

The answer came—permanently—in July 1933, when the University of Wisconsin hired him as "Professor of Game Management." The state of Wisconsin had always been progressive, often leading the nation in new social, economic, and environmental policies. Its flagship university in Madison became the leader again by hiring Leopold as the first wildlife professor in the nation. His task was to help restore the productivity of lands that had been ruined by inappropriate timbering and farming; in his particular case, this task was to be accomplished in part by enhancing the production of game animals. The desired outcomes were utilitarian and financial, so Leopold was appointed to the Department of Agricultural Economics.

A major part of his job was to work with private landowners, a responsibility Leopold coveted. He wanted to teach his ideas "to whomever will listen."[45] From his years with the Forest Service and his recent experience with the CCC (where one crew might one day undo what another crew had done the day before), he was convinced that government was not the savior of conservation. The private landowner, he thought, was a better option. "When the land does well for its owner, and the owner does well by his land—when both end up better by reason of their partnership—then we have conservation."[46] He instructed landowners through

Figure 3.3 Aldo Leopold became the first wildlife professor in the nation when he was hired by the University of Wisconsin in 1933. (Reproduced courtesy of the Aldo Leopold Foundation, www.aldoleopold.org.)

publications, speeches, radio broadcasts, and demonstrations about even the simplest ideas:

> There are many little tricks for increasing the service of woods and vegetation to wildlife. Take the grapevine, for example. A new grape-tangle on or near the ground is usually good for a new covey of quail, provided there be food nearby. How to get a new grape-tangle quickly? Select a tree with a grapevine in its top.

Cut the tree but not the vine, and let it lie. In one season the vine will weave an "umbrella" over the down top which is hawk-proof and nearly manproof—a mighty fortress for bobwhite in even the deepest of snows.[47]

Leopold solidified his position as "father of wildlife management" with the publication of his textbook, *Game Management*, also in 1933. He had been laboring with the idea of a comprehensive book on wildlife for years. With two colleagues from his National Forest days, he had produced the outline and partial draft of a book on game in the desert Southwest, but it never got far. Later, he narrowed the scope to deer management in the Southwest, but the more he learned about deer, the more hesitant he was to write authoritatively about them. His period of unemployment, between the end of the game survey and the start of his university appointment, however, gave him the time, material, and perspective to produce a text.

Game Management mirrored Leopold's perspective and interests as a university professor and wildlife manager. His research was based on empirical observation and field experimentation, not abstract principles or theories. As he explained in the book's preface, "The central thesis of game management is this: game can be restored by the *creative use* of the same tools which have heretofore destroyed it—axe, plow, cow, fire, and gun."[48] *Game Management* was, like the game survey report, an instant success and it remained the profession's core textbook for several decades.

Leopold had found his natural calling as a professor. He and his graduate students—twenty-six in all over the course of his career—occupied a former residence, 424 University Farm Place, on the Wisconsin agricultural campus, adapting the rooms to house his new scientific community. A visitor from Oxford University told him, "[Oxford] is good and sound and grand, but it is not quite *alive* in the way that you have kept your research and your young men."[49] He held evening seminars there every week with graduate students; the gatherings generally ended with a basket of apples or perhaps a plate of cookies baked by Estella. His lectures were always well organized and amply illustrated with his personal drawings and photographs. His teaching voice was pleasant and deep, but "soothing and reassuring, particularly to students and colleagues."[50] He often smoked his pipe while teaching, sitting on the desk and conducting class in an informal and pleasant manner. He built an outstanding wildlife library, mostly with his own funds. "A library," he asserted, "is the most important tool in our field."[51]

His real forte as a teacher, however, revealed itself when he took students into the field. He was expert at reading the landscape, and his goal was to replicate that skill in his students. "The objective," he wrote, "is to teach the student to see the land, to understand what he sees, and enjoy what he understands. . . . Such teaching could well be called land ecology rather than wildlife, and could serve very broad educational purposes."[52] Every plant, every woodlot, every set of animal tracks was fodder for observation and interpretation. A colleague remembered, "You would go out with him, and he'd stretch your brains until they were tired."[53]

It would require a book of its own to summarize the outpouring of research, demonstration projects, and other activities conducted by Leopold during his time as a professor. His energy and commitment were boundless. He oversaw the restoration of the university's arboretum as an ecological preserve. He organized several groups of rural landowners into cooperatives to demonstrate good wildlife management. He wrote profusely in the popular and professional literature, sometimes more than two dozen articles per year. He helped found The Wildlife Society and served as its president from 1939 through 1940. He helped establish the Delta Waterfowl Research Station in Manitoba, Canada. He advised dozens of conservation organizations. He was one of three members of a national committee (along with Ding Darling and Thomas Beck) to develop a plan for restoring the nation's wildlife. He also helped Darling establish the Cooperative Wildlife Research Units, first in Iowa and subsequently throughout the nation.

From Professor to Prophet

Had Leopold remained on the road he was traveling, he would have ended his career as an honored professor in the wildlife profession. But he would have been little known beyond those professional circles. His evolution as a thinker and writer, however, was about to be emboldened by three major events.

First, the Leopolds bought a farm. On a hunting trip west of Madison, Leopold became interested in an abandoned farm in Sauk County, on the banks of the Wisconsin River. The land lay in a transitional zone between prairie and forest, and the forest itself was transitional from northern to southern types. The region had been used heavily and harshly—soils depleted, woodlots cleared, marshes drained, peat burned—and then deserted.

Leopold yearned for a rural refuge to escape the city, a new place that he could call his own. In early 1935, he leased 80 acres and soon thereafter purchased the property; he eventually added more land, growing the farm to 120 acres.[54]

The only structure left on the property was a chicken coop, almost a square about twenty feet on a side. One corner was filled with an immense pile of chicken manure. Together the family shoveled out the manure and set about making the place habitable—or nearly so. It had no kitchen, running water, or toilet, just a hand pump on the front porch; the floor was dirt; and heat came from an ancient fireplace better at producing smoke than warmth. As the Leopolds continued to improve the building, they began to call it "the shack," a name now familiar to millions of readers of *A Sand County Almanac.*

The family gradually warmed to the property. At first they visited only a few weekends during the growing season, but soon it became a regular retreat during all seasons. They built a latrine, nobly named the Parthenon, some distance from the shack. The shack gradually accumulated more comforts—a wooden floor, whitewashed walls, a lengthened chimney that sometimes actually worked, a set of double bunks that would sleep eight in all, and outdoor benches hewn by Leopold himself.

Their real interest, however, was not the shack but the farm that surrounded it. "His first recorded act as a landowner was to plant a food patch for wildlife."[55] Each year they planted hundreds or thousands of trees and other native plants. Success was fleeting, however, and year after year most of the trees died. Undaunted, each year they started again, eventually restoring woods to much of the property. Nina, the oldest daughter, recalled the ordeal:

Dad's selection of sick land as a place for his family outings was perhaps a new concept in recreation. The land our father purchased for $8.00 per acre had been abused, misused, destroyed. It had been carelessly lumbered, carelessly farmed, and carelessly abandoned. . . . Then the marathon began. Over a period of 12 years, we slaved with our father and mother. We gathered seeds of native prairie grasses and flowers from nearby areas; we planted them among the old corn stubble. We planted native pine trees—white, red, and jacks. We planted native hardwoods and forest wildflowers and shrubs. We planted, then carried pails of water. We planted some more. We learned how to nurture, how to care.[56]

One of Leopold's closest colleagues, Bob McCabe, didn't believe that Leopold had bought the farm with any grand scheme to produce "a utopian concept of ecological integrity that came to him in the still of the night."[57] Rather, he had bought the land to recapture a part of the rural life that he enjoyed as a boy, a student, and a forest ranger.

Leopold's personal effort at land restoration evolved with time, as he tried various strategies and observed their success or failure. "The plain lesson is that to be a practitioner of conservation of a piece of land," he wrote, "takes more brains, and a wider range of sympathy, forethought, and experience," than to be any sort of specialized resource manager. "Integration is easy on paper, but a lot more important and more difficult in the field than any of us foresaw."[58] The farm had taught Leopold that the landowner was an essential piece, perhaps the keystone itself, in the arch of conservation.

The second pivotal event in Leopold's evolution was a visit to Germany in the summer of 1935. He was invited as part of a small team to spend three months observing and then commenting on German forestry and resource management. Leopold was dismayed by what he saw. The principles of industrial forestry—grow trees as a crop—had been followed prescriptively in Germany for generations. The countryside grew trees well, but the downside was a landscape that was woefully artificial. A monoculture of spruce had replaced a native forest rich in evergreen and deciduous tree species.

Even worse, however, was the condition of the wildlife. Game and non-game species alike were absent. Deer were the exception—overabundant, present in numbers well beyond the carrying capacity of

Figure 3.4 The small farm that Aldo Leopold and his family restored was the basis of the famous essays collected in *A Sand County Almanac*. Here, he and his wife plant pine trees on the farm. (Reproduced courtesy of the Aldo Leopold Foundation, www.aldoleopold.org.)

the artificial forest. The ravenous deer ate every plant growing in the understory, halting forest regeneration. Consequently, deer feeding had become a necessary standard practice to keep the animals alive, especially during the winter.

Leopold saw this condition as appalling—and he saw it as the endpoint of the road that American resource management was traveling. The tendency to think of forests and farms only as factories for producing wood and food had the potential to deprive citizens of all other values attendant to the land, what he had called "the Forest" in his Forest Service days. He saw that the United States was headed in this way, but he also believed that the direction could be changed. Forest management could and should recognize the other values of land, and he would make it his personal and professional task to carry this message back to his homeland.

The third circumstance that elevated Leopold to a different level of understanding was the emergence of ecology as a science. Leopold was invited to participate in the Metamek Conference on Biological Cycles in Labrador, Canada, in the summer of 1931. About thirty of the world's preeminent animal ecologists were present; most of what was known about animal populations had come from their work. Leopold had gradually become acquainted with the principles of ecology, but now he was immersed. At the conference he met Charles Elton, the acknowledged father of animal ecology, and a lifelong friendship and collaboration began. Elton's work, and that of others at the conference, provided Leopold with the conceptual basis for the natural phenomena he had observed throughout his life.

He relied heavily on the emerging field of animal ecology as he wrote *Game Management* and for his general understanding of the web of relationships among organisms, environment, and humans. For example, by this time Leopold had reversed his view that predators were bad for wildlife. He now understood that eliminating some predators might increase populations somewhat, but eliminating all predation would cause populations to spike, resulting in destruction of the habitat and eventual starvation and population crashes. He now saw wolves as necessary and desirable, not evil and destructive. "The only sure conclusion is that the biota as a whole is useful, and biota includes not only plants and animals, but soils and waters as well."[59]

These three developments—owning and restoring his own farm, observing the sterility of over-managed German forests, and appreciating the concepts of ecology—heavily influenced Leopold's worldview. From then on, conservation was not about producing a crop of deer or turkeys, but about land health. He began to write and speak much more broadly about the concept of land. In a speech to an assemblage of engineers in April 1938, he expressed his summation of the big issue: "We end at what might be called the standard paradox of the twentieth century: our tools are better than we are, and grow better and faster than we do. They suffice to crack the atom, to command the tides. But they do not suffice for the oldest task in human history: to live on a piece of land without spoiling it."[60]

He began referring to his position as "Professor of Wildlife Management," replacing the earlier moniker of "game management." As he shared these ideas with his colleagues, the response was often mixed. Some told him to stick to straight science and management, avoiding the philosophical nature of the bigger questions. As Leopold himself reflected, "To change ideas about what land is for is to change ideas about what anything is for."[61]

His most receptive colleague was P. S. Lovejoy, then retired from the Michigan Department of Conservation. Lovejoy and Leopold had met during the game survey and enjoyed a constant correspondence over the years. The two pondered similar questions, but they took vastly different approaches. Leopold was "orderly, deliberate, relaxed with a touch of formality. Lovejoy was excitable and joyously cantankerous."[62] Lovejoy also employed a unique brand of English—conventional grammar, spelling, and syntax be damned. When Leopold wrote the essay "A Biotic View of Land," he submitted it to Lovejoy for review. Lovejoy resonated with the ideas; he responded, in part, "En route seems like as if you stray into various other slants& now& then into what is mostly (really?) poetry – i e 'more feeling' than thinking.' (Of course & why not? Me too. Could that be because both of us are mammal-critters but recently cephalized & functioning therin not too good & with the 'emotionals' often gumming up 'the rationals' as so often typical of Homo sap. behavior?"[63]

Most importantly, Lovejoy wrote that the essay was "a very large & important Sumpin."[64] Indeed it was. "A Biotic View of Land," published in 1939 in the *Journal of Forestry*, would eventually evolve into "The Land Ethic," the concluding essay in *A Sand County Almanac*. In the essay, Leopold related his understanding of ecology and of humankind as part of it. He defined an elegant concept of the land ethic in his most famous quote: "A thing is right when it tends to preserve the integrity, stability, and beauty of the biotic community. It is wrong when it tends otherwise."[65]

The conservation, philosophical, and literary masterpiece that we recognize in *A Sand County Almanac*, however, had a long and difficult birth. Although Leopold was a prolific writer, his success lay largely in the technical literature or in practical reports for landowners. Writings of a more philosophical or personal nature tended to end up in "the cooler," a bulging folder stored in his desk. The cooler was home to first drafts and partially completed manuscripts. These unfinished works, always written in pencil on yellow sheets with blue lines, might languish for years in the cooler, waiting for Leopold to have the time or inclination to work on them again. As he explained to a graduate student, "Here's where I put my stuff to simmer. It doesn't change in there, but I do. When I get an idea or a new slant or a fresh view, why hell, it's right there where I can grab it. . . . Writing is just as hard for me now as it ever was. . . . Think of it this way. In spite of all the advances of modern science, it still takes seven waters to clean spinach for the pot . . . and for all my writings to this day, it still takes seven editings, sometimes, seventeen, before I let it go off to press."[66]

As World War II took students away and gas rationing allowed fewer trips to the shack, Leopold found more time to focus on the material stacked in the cooler. In 1941, he presented the publishing company Alfred A. Knopf with an idea for a book of essays; Knopf was enthusiastic. For the next three years, Leopold labored over the essays, starting many, being satisfied with few.

In 1944, he sent a completed manuscript to two publishers, Knopf and Macmillan. Both liked the concept, but neither liked it enough to publish it. Macmillan thought the essays were beautiful but would have a limited market; given the shortage of paper and ink due to the war, they turned it down. Knopf thought the collection was unfocused and ranged too broadly; perhaps it should be just nature essays, or just observations from a single place—either Wisconsin or New Mexico, but not both. Leopold was disappointed, but considered the continuing interest of Knopf to be an informal commitment to publish the book if he satisfied their reservations.

He hoped to finish the essay book quickly, but other responsibilities got in the way. In 1943, he had accepted an appointment as a member of the Conservation Commission for the state of Wisconsin. Although many colleagues warned him not to get involved, he believed that everyone had a responsibility to serve their fellow citizens, and this was his way to contribute directly. He became immediately embroiled in a controversy over deer regulations, arguing for more harvests in order to reduce excessive deer populations. The agency head reportedly "hated his guts" because of his questioning of commission policies.[67] Supporters of strict deer regulations and buck-only seasons considered him anathema. One newsletter stated: "Imagine our fine deer herd shot to pieces by a man who rates himself as a Professor and uses a GUESS instead of facts?"[68] He bore it all stoically, understanding that changing the general view of deer management was a long-term project: "An issue may be so clear in outline, so inevitable in logic, so imperative in need, and so universal in importance as to command immediate support from any reasonable person. Yet that collective person, the public, may take a decade to see the argument, and another to acquiesce in an effective program."[69]

In early 1947, he contracted a condition called "tic douloureux," a twitching of the facial nerves around the cheek. The condition was painful and debilitating, often causing Leopold to cancel meetings—sometimes in mid-sentence—and return home for rest. In September he had surgery on his brain, which helped but did not eliminate the problem. His recovery was long and slow, and his sight was permanently impaired. The required rest and long convalescence allowed Leopold to concentrate on the essay book once again.

He completed the text in late 1947. He addressed Knopf's issues by organizing the essays into three distinct parts—the "Sand County Almanac" itself (monthly chapters covering the year on the farm), "Sketches from Here and There" (describing his observations of other places, from Canada to Mexico), and "The Upshot" (the series of essays in which he describes his broader perspective on conservation), all collected under the proposed title of "Great Possessions." Knopf, however, was not satisfied and turned down the book in November. Leopold was angry and discouraged; his son, Luna, took over the process of finding a publisher. Famed wildlife illustrator Charles Schwartz agreed to illustrate the book, adding to its appeal. Luna sent the book to Oxford University Press, which enthusiastically agreed to publish. On April 15, 1948, Leopold and Oxford came to final agreement, with a planned 1949 publication date.

After signing the contract, Aldo, Estella, and their youngest daughter, also named Estella, spent five characteristically wonderful days at the shack. Estella described the time to her sister, Nina, in a letter:

... Monday we three drove in for the pines at Baraboo and walked around the Shack while Daddy showed us the blooming pasque flowers and Hepatica with great pride. We made a special trip to the clay hill, Dad and Mom arm in arm, so Dad could show us a "surprise"—a single *Dentaria* plant he had found. . . . That evening was perfect. We had drinks on the front lawn till the geese started to come back from corn and "leaf" into our marsh. . . . It was heartwarming to watch Dad's enthusiasm over this simple event. He has himself said that a most basic human quality is the ability to appreciate simple things, which can't be eaten or worn or sold. . . .[70]

On the morning of April 21, Leopold was repairing tools at the shack when he noticed smoke rising in the distance. Soon he realized that his neighbor's farm was burning, and the wind was pushing the fire their way. He gathered his wife and daughter and drove over to help fight the fire. He stationed his wife along the road to put out embers that she encountered, sent his daughter back to call the fire department, and set off himself toward the edge of the flames.

In the chaos of fire fighting, no one noticed that Leopold hadn't been seen for some time—ninety minutes, in fact. Sometime later, he was found lying peacefully, his head resting on a clump of grass, dead of a heart attack.

The world acknowledged that, at age sixty-one, Leopold had been taken long before his time. His legacy, however, would not be forgotten. His family and friends worked diligently to edit the essay book into publishable form, now with a new name, *A Sand County Almanac*.

As strange as it might seem now, the book had little immediate impact. It was well regarded in conservation circles, but sold poorly to the general market. As historian Roderick Nash described, "Leopold did not live to see the reviews . . . , but they probably would have disappointed him. Most critics understood the book to be just another collection of charming nature essays. Very few reviewers even recognized the ideas that a later generation would find compelling."[71] In 1970, in the midst of the emerging modern environmental movement, the book was reissued, this time in paperback as well as hard cover. Immediately it was recognized as a classic of ecological conscience. And ever since, *A Sand County Almanac* has been the bible of conservation and its author, Aldo Leopold, has become the prophet for new generations of ecologists, environmentalists, and conservationists.

Figure 4.1 Rachel Louise Carson, 1907–1964. (Reproduced courtesy of the National Conservation Training Center, US Fish and Wildlife Service.)

Chapter 4

Rachel Carson

The Lady Who Started All This

Travel north out of Washington, DC, on New Hampshire Avenue. After passing under the Capitol Beltway, turn left onto Quaint Acres Drive, and then take the next left onto Berwick Road. At 11701 Berwick Road, on a large corner lot, sits a modest brick house much like the others in the neighborhood.

A closer look, however, reveals a small but significant difference between this house and its neighbors. A brass plaque mounted near the front door declares that 11701 Berwick Road is in the National Register of Historic Places. The National Register database states that the historical significance is a person and an event; that the event occurred in 1962; that the area of significance is science and conservation; and that the significant person is Rachel Carson.[1]

In the wraparound study on the back of the house, Rachel Carson, a brave, committed, solitary woman researched and wrote *Silent Spring*, the book that changed our relationship with our natural environment. Racing against the cancer that was consuming her body, she assembled an unassailable scientific record that awakened the country—and the world—to the dangers of broadcast pesticides. William O. Douglas, associate justice of the United States Supreme Court, commenting at the time of publication, called *Silent Spring* the most revolutionary American book since *Uncle Tom's Cabin*. He went further: "This book is the most important chronicle of this century for the human race. The book is a call for immediate action and for effective control of all merchants of poison."[2]

In the half-century since its 1962 publication, *Silent Spring* has come to represent the origin of the modern environmental movement, the tipping point for our pursuit of sustainable lifestyles. Historians, editors, and pundits have listed the book as among the most influential of the twentieth century and Rachel Carson as one of the most influential people of the century. Still others, both then and now, called her a fraud or a sentimental spinster who was attempting to throw civilization back into the Dark Ages. One entomologist wrote that he regarded *Silent Spring* "as science fiction, to be read in the same way that the TV show *Twilight Zone* is to be watched."[3] Carson's message, a sobering warning to the seemingly endless prosperity of early-sixties America, was one that many people were unprepared to hear then—and even now.

Rachel Carson did not set out to change the world. She did not want to write the "poison book." She was an observer of nature, not a crusader. She was a researcher, not a zealot. She was a quiet, reticent woman, not a publicity seeker. Perhaps unfortunately for her, but certainly fortunately for us, her life did not turn out that way.

Born to Be a Writer

Rachel Carson was destined to be a writer. From an early age, words were her best friends. She "read a great deal almost from infancy," she recalled, "and I suppose I must have realized someone wrote the books and thought it would be fun to make up the stories, too."[4] The young Rachel had a natural knack for storytelling. When she was just ten years old, she published her first story in the popular children's periodical *St. Nicholas Magazine*. The next year, the same magazine paid her a little more than $3 for an article; by the age of eleven, Carson would later say, she had become a professional writer.

Rachel's early fascination with words and stories paralleled a second fascination—with nature. Born on May 27, 1907, near Pittsburgh, she

Figure 4.2 As a young girl, Rachel Carson and her mother were often outdoors, developing a bond with nature and with each other that would last a lifetime. (Reproduced courtesy of the Rachel Carson Council.)

grew up among the fields and woods of the rural Pennsylvania landscape. "I can remember no time when I wasn't interested in the out-of-doors and the whole world of nature," she said. "Those interests, I know, I inherited from my mother and have always shared with her."[5]

Her mother, Maria Carson, was Rachel's guide to the world of nature. Maria was an advocate of nature study, an educational movement popular around the turn of the twentieth century that immersed children in nature as their learning environment. Nature study was holistic, encouraging the merger of natural and spiritual interpretations of the world. Carson would later write, "If a child is to keep alive his inborn sense of wonder . . . , he needs the companionship of at least one adult who can share it, rediscovering with him the joy, excitement, and mystery of the world we live in."[6] For Rachel, that companion was her mother. Maria and Rachel spent countless hours together in the outdoors, forming a bond that would make them inseparable throughout their lives.

Given her preoccupation with words and nature, it is no surprise that Rachel Carson was quiet, contemplative, and introspective as a girl and young woman. Maria Carson raised her daughter to look inward to satisfy her emotional and intellectual needs, rather than outward for approval from others. Her self-reliance carried over to college in Pittsburgh, where Carson largely ignored the traditional social life at Pennsylvania College for Women and thoroughly rejected the idea that women attended college to master the skills to become socially gracious wives.

It was without the guidance of social conformity, then, that Carson wrestled with her career direction during her undergraduate years. She entered as an English major, not to be a school teacher—rejecting another expectation for women—but to be a writer. Her love of nature, however, continually lured her toward science and particularly biology. The struggle distressed her, but also set the stage for a career that melded writing and science; consider this 1927 poem, written for an English assignment:

Butterfly poised on a thistle's down.
Lend me your wings for a summer's day.
What care I for a kingly crown?
Butterfly poised on a thistle's down.
When I might wear your gossamer gown
And sit enthroned on an orchid spray.
Butterfly poised on a thistle's down.
Lend me your wings for a summer's day![7]

She eventually took a biology class that was taught by a young, effervescent, and glamorous instructor, Mary Skinker. Carson was mesmerized by the subject and the instructor, who became her friend and mentor for many years. In a bold decision—women weren't cut out for science, the common logic held—she changed her major to biology. Her decision caused a stir on campus; she wrote a friend, "You ought to see the reactions I get. I've gotten bawled out and called all sorts of blankety-blank names so much that it's beginning to get monotonous."[8] Carson, of course, didn't care what others thought. She was determined to become a biologist.

And not just any sort of biologist, but a marine biologist. One evening in her dormitory, during a crashing thunderstorm, she read Alfred, Lord Tennyson's poem "Locksley Hall," containing these closing lines:

Cramming all the blast before it, in its breast a thunderbolt.
Let it fall on Locksley Hall, with rain or hail, or fire or snow;
For the mighty wind arises, roaring seaward, and I go.[9]

She later recalled "that line spoke to something within me, seeming to tell me that my own path led to the sea—which then I had never seen— and that my own destiny was somehow linked with the sea."[10]

When Mary Skinker moved from Pennsylvania College to Johns Hopkins University, she urged Carson to follow. After finishing her undergraduate degree in 1929, Carson moved to Baltimore and enrolled at Johns Hopkins as a graduate student in marine biology. She spent her first summer on the Massachusetts coast working at the Woods Hole Marine Biological Laboratory, then and now one of the world's premier marine research centers. As never before, she was immersed in the aquatic environment: "One can't walk very far in any direction without running into water," she wrote to a friend.[11] Her lifelong fascination with the marine environment had begun, a fascination that eventually brought her fame and fortune.

At the time, however, fame and fortune were distant dreams. Her years as a graduate student were torture. Carson was lonely as a student at Hopkins—before moving there, she had never lived more than a few miles from home or spent more than a few days between visits with her mother. Therefore, after her first year, she moved her family—

parents, brother, sister, and two nieces—to Baltimore so they could be together; living in one house, Carson reasoned, would be cheaper than living in two. Her father worked little during these Depression-era years, however, making Carson's teaching as a graduate student the family's primary source of income. She was also the glue that held an emotionally fragile and illness-prone family together. She struggled to complete her master's thesis and then began doctoral studies. After her father died in 1935 and her sister in 1936, Carson and her mother were left to raise two nieces. Carson's future became crystal clear: she needed to work, not study. She took on more teaching and wrote magazine articles for extra income, forcing her to drop out of the doctoral program, never to return.

The Lure of the Sea

Rachel Carson needed to work, but she also wanted to write—and a lucky circumstance brought both together. By this time, Mary Skinker had moved from Johns Hopkins to work as a scientist for the US Department of Agriculture in Washington, and she encouraged Carson to pursue similar opportunities with the US Bureau of Fisheries (forerunner of the US Fish and Wildlife Service). In 1935, the bureau needed radio scripts written for a series of broadcasts about marine topics called "Romance Under the Water." The bureau's scientists balked at converting their technical expertise into anything resembling "romance"; besides, they hadn't a clue about how to write for the general public. In a meeting arranged by Skinker, Bureau chief Elmer Higgins took a leap of faith. "I've never seen a written word of yours, but I'm going to take a sporting chance," he told Carson, and hired her to write a few scripts.[12] The radio series was an instant success, and Carson became the lead writer, authoring more than fifty scripts as a part-time employee. The next year, Higgins hired Carson full time, one of only two women working in professional positions in the Bureau of Fisheries.

Carson proved to be a rare find—a scientist who could write with accuracy and clarity for a general audience. She was painstakingly thorough in her research, a characteristic that would serve her well in the whirlwind of controversy that lay ahead. However, while a typical scientist would stop writing after recording and discussing the results, that's when Carson's poetic soul took over. She could synthesize the science into a coherent whole and then describe it in a story that captured the imagination of the lay reader. She was the perfect nature writer for the mid-twentieth century, a bridge between the aesthetic appreciation of nature and the scientific wonder of understanding how it worked. Here, for example, she describes the nature of life on the seashore, in her third book, *The Edge of the Sea* (1955):

Only the most hardy and adaptable can survive in a region so mutable, yet the area between the tide lines is crowded with plants and animals. In this difficult world of the shore, life displays its enormous toughness and vitality by occupying almost every conceivable niche. Visibly, it carpets the intertidal rocks, or half hidden, it descends into fissures and crevices, or hides under boulders, or lurks in the wet gloom of sea caves. Invisibly, where the casual observer would say there is no life, it lies deep in the sand, in burrows and tubes and passageways. It tunnels into solid rock and bores into peat and clay. It encrusts weeds or drifting spars or the hard, chitinous shell of a lobster. It exists minutely, as the film of bacteria that spreads over a rock surface or a wharf piling; as spheres of protozoa, small as pinpricks, sparkling at the surface of the sea; and as Lilliputian beings swimming through dark pools that lie between the grains of sand.[13]

Even before hiring her full time, Elmer Higgins gave Carson an assignment that redirected her literary career. Higgins asked her to draft a government brochure about marine fisheries that could be used to inform the public about the bureau's work. When he read her draft, he told Carson that she had failed—she hadn't written a government brochure, she had produced "literature." He sent her back to write a shorter, more direct version, but encouraged her to send the original manuscript to the *Atlantic Monthly*, a leading national literary magazine. The editors immediately accepted "Undersea," impressed with Carson's eloquence and scientific prowess. The article appeared in September 1937 to far-ranging praise by readers, scientists, and nature writers.[14] Carson later said that from this four-page article "everything else followed."[15] Failing at government bureaucratese, she had become a nationally recognized author.

Soon after, Carson began expanding the article into her first book, *Under the Sea Wind*, which appeared in November 1941. Like the *Atlantic Monthly* article, the book was an immediate critical success. Reviewers applauded its combination of beautiful, poetic prose and depth of treatment. Scientists admired it because it presented complex oceanographic topics in engaging ways for the general public—it offered the romance they couldn't produce.

Unfortunately, the public wasn't interested. Carson hoped that the critical acclaim would translate to large sales, ending her nagging financial worries. That hope evaporated one month after the book's publication, when Japan attacked Pearl Harbor on December 7, drawing the United States into World War II. A book about the wonders of the ocean was the last thing on America's mind. *Under the Sea Wind* sold fewer than 2,000 copies, earning Carson a total royalty of $689.17.[16] Book writing, Carson decided, was "a very poor gamble financially."[17]

The war years were tough on Carson. With the commercial failure of the book, Carson turned away from freelance writing. She felt her work for the government was frivolous, including an assignment to write brochures for American wives and mothers about how to cook fish. She was transferred for a year to Chicago, where she felt lonely and out of place.

A new assignment at the end of the war revitalized her spirit. She was tasked with producing a series of publications about selected national wildlife refuges for the general public. To do the needed research, she and her longtime assistant, Shirley Briggs, traveled to refuges across the country—the most traveling that Carson had ever done (or would ever do). Their first journey was to Chincoteague National Wildlife Refuge, newly established on Virginia's barrier islands. Carson and Briggs spent their days in the field and their evenings transcribing notes. Briggs remembered, "We presented quite a spectacle on our return to the hotel of an evening . . . when we came lumbering through, wearing old tennis shoes, usually wet, sloppy and be-smudged pants, various layers of jackets, sou'westers, and toting all manner of cameras, my magnificent tripod, and Ray's binoculars."[18]

These years just after the war were, perhaps, the happiest in Carson's life. Her job with the US Fish and Wildlife Service became increasingly rewarding as she rose in the agency; in essence, she was directing a small publishing business. She worked closely with a dedicated and lively group of colleagues, providing a high level of social interaction. Travel to refuges fed her creative appetite, and the booklets about refuges were praised as "among the best natural histories of the refuges that the service ever produced."[19] Her editorial work also provided her with access to exciting new information. Oceanographic research performed to support naval warfare led to new discoveries about ocean currents, distribution of open-water organisms, sound conductivity, and many other topics. These results expanded her fascination with the sea and deepened her knowledge of its workings, giving her an encyclopedia of novel scientific material.

She also resolved her internal struggle between career goals—scientist or writer. Her true mission, she decided, was to write, specifically to write natural history for the public. Forgetting her own admonition about the perils of book writing, she began working on a second book about the sea. To help the process, she signed with a literary agent, Marie Rodell. Rodell, like Mary Skinker before her, became not only Carson's literary taskmaster, but also for a time her closest confidante. They were as different as night and day—Rodell was outgoing, sophisticated, and stylish while Carson was shy, unworldly, and plain. However, the partnership worked to keep the book project moving, with Rodell prodding and Carson painstakingly drafting and redrafting, organizing and reorganizing. Finally, in 1951, the work, *The Sea Around Us*, appeared in bookstores.

The book earned the same literary praise as her first book, but the commercial result was spectacularly different. The sea had become popular in the wake of such best sellers as Thor Heyerdahl's *Kon Tiki*, relating his adventure of building and sailing a primitive raft across the ocean, and Herman Wouk's *The Caine Mutiny*, the fictional account of a deranged World War II destroyer captain. For Oxford University Press, the main problem was printing copies of *The Sea Around Us* fast enough to keep bookstores in stock—the first printing sold out in two days. The book vaulted up the *New York Times* best-seller list, remaining there for eighty-six weeks, thirty-nine of those as the best-selling nonfiction book in the country.[20] The *New York Times* recognized that "Once or twice in a generation does the world get a physical scientist with literary genius. . . . Miss Carson has written a classic."[21]

Carson was now part of the nation's literary elite, a celebrity and a wealthy author. Awards and recognitions for her and the book rolled in continuously. Her earlier book was re-released in early 1952, this time becoming a best seller alongside *The Sea Around Us*. With these successes, she realized her lifelong dream—to earn her living through writing. Consequently, in 1952 she resigned from the US Fish and Wildlife Service, an outcome about which she was "ecstatic."[22]

Her newfound wealth allowed her one other joy that lasted throughout her life. On an earlier month-long vacation with her mother, she had fallen in love with the Maine coast, where she became enthralled by the forests, the bird life, and the rocky intertidal zone. She also coveted the privacy, noting that "we are so secluded here because of the trees and the contour of the land, that we are not aware of human neighbors."[23] With her royalties, she bought a small stretch of shoreline near Boothbay Harbor and built a cabin right on the shore, where the high tides lapped at her doorstep. Her joy bubbled over in a letter to Rodell: "You have to get down to my low tide rocks if you have to crawl on your hands and knees, or wriggle on your stomach! I found a new part of it last night (on the lowest tide I've seen since we came) that is absolutely the most exciting, as to creatures, I've known anywhere."[24]

In Maine, she met the woman who would become her dearest friend for the rest of her life, Dorothy Freeman. Freeman and her husband, Stanley, introduced themselves when they learned that the famous author had moved nearby. An instant bond formed between the two women. From then on, they were together whenever possible and wrote almost daily when apart. Once again, Carson had found a friend—like Skinker and Rodell—to whom she could freely and completely give her heart, soul, and mind.

Her time on the shore in Maine was the inspiration for her third and final book about the sea, *The Edge of the Sea*, released in 1955. "For the first time," she noted, "I'm writing about something while it is right under my nose, and it gives me a very different feeling about it. . . ."[25]

Figure 4.3 Rachel Carson along with colleague and artist Bob Hines, conducting marine biology research for her third book, *The Edge of the Sea*, in 1952. (Reproduced courtesy of the National Conservation Training Center, US Fish and Wildlife Service.)

The Edge of the Sea traveled the same path as her previous books—critical success and best seller—but it never quite achieved the notoriety of the other two.

The Edge of the Sea exemplifies what made Carson unique as an author and scientist. The book was originally conceived as a guide to the Atlantic shoreline, stimulated by her reverence for the marshlands of the mid-Atlantic coast. But she couldn't bring herself to produce a series of disconnected anecdotes about this species and that, this place and that, as field guides usually do. Instead, her direct experience years earlier in the Florida Keys and now her close association with the Maine shoreline let her see that the Atlantic had three distinct types of shorelines: the northern dominated by tides, the middle dominated by waves, and the southern dominated by currents. This understanding allowed her to draw the physical and biological elements of the seashore together into a unified treatment. She described the shorelines as ecosystems responding to different physical forces and their biological inhabitants as communities of interacting species.

Although now a literary star, she avoided the trappings of fame. Carson was an intensely private person who never sought the spotlight, and although she grew more comfortable and competent as a celebrity, she seems never to have enjoyed the experience. "I'm pleased to have people say nice things about the book, but all this stuff about me seems odd, to say the least," she wrote to a friend.[26] Carson refused most requests for interviews and public appearances, always keeping her personal life totally behind a curtain of privacy.

She was also never a robust woman, and illness was her constant companion. She had a tumor removed from her left breast in 1950, but was misinformed by her doctor that it was benign. She suffered from repeated infections and from shingles, brought on partially by the stress in other parts of her life. Her mother had also become increasingly feeble, requiring Carson to care for her continuously. Although devoted to her mother, she still lamented to Dorothy Freeman, "When I feel, as I do now, the pressure of all the things that seem worth doing in the years that are left, it seems so silly to be spending my time being a nurse and housemaid."[27] In 1956, her niece, a single mother, died, leaving behind a six-year-old son, Roger. Carson became Roger's guardian, a role for which she felt unprepared and that weighed heavily on her time, energy, and emotions.

Carson had also lost her professional direction. With the trilogy of sea books finished, she cast about for other projects. She contracted to write a book on evolution, which never got past the thinking stage. Then followed an idea for a book about ecology, which also waned. She agreed to produce an anthology of writings about nature, imagining it as a grand project; "I'm still groping," she wrote to a friend, "and can't say clearly what I mean but I can see at least sketchily the outlines of perhaps the rest of my 'life's work' in writing, and this seems to be a step in it."[28] Like other projects, the anthology never materialized. Carson needed something to focus on. The choice she finally made changed the world.

The Poison Book

World War II and its aftermath had a profound effect on Carson. She had always believed that nature was omnipotent, confident that "the stream of life would flow on through time in whatever course God had appointed for it . . . without interference from one of the drops of the stream, man."[29] Now, however, she wasn't so sure. The nuclear bombs dropped on Hiroshima and Nagasaki shattered her confidence. Humankind had created devices that could instantaneously change the face of the earth, with radioactive fallout that might blanket the globe for thousands of years. Carson despaired over the direction of modern society.

And then there were the environmental poisons. Carson had always been interested in poisons. While writing a series of articles for the *Baltimore Sun* in 1938, she suggested to the editor that she write about selenium and fluorides in the environment and their negative consequences for livestock, fish, and humans; the editor declined, finding the topic too depressing. During World War II, Carson had learned about federal research examining the impact of the insecticide DDT on fish and wildlife. Based on that knowledge, in 1945 she submitted to *Reader's Digest* a story idea about the perils of DDT; the magazine never even acknowledged her idea.

Most likely, *Reader's Digest* wasn't interested in poisons because the nation wasn't interested. The years after the end of World War II were times of great optimism in the United States. The nation had sacrificed enormously to defeat an evil enemy; now was the time to get back to building happy and prosperous lives. The nation was committed to helping returning veterans and their families with educational opportunities, affordable housing, and the other promises of a thriving middle-class economy—cars, televisions, telephones. The technological advances that had appeared as part of the war effort were now turned to domestic uses, making life more convenient and enjoyable. Chemicals perfected during the war, including DDT, were repurposed into thousands of new products. People were not interested in learning about the negatives of their reemerging optimistic lifestyles; they were interested in enjoying the benefits owed them for their earlier sacrifices. America was celebrating, and it wanted no one to spoil the party.

However, as the 1950s continued, the patina of optimism began to tarnish. The Korean War called America back to reality. The Cold War threatened that whole arsenals of nuclear weapons might be unleashed with the press of a button, causing not only the intended horrible destruction but also the specter of worldwide radioactive fallout. Carson later wrote that "it is a new, and almost a humbling thought, and certainly one born of this atomic age, that man could be working against himself."[30] She was justifiably worried, and, increasingly, so were others.

Because of her fame as a science-based writer, many of those other concerned people began writing to her, seeking her intervention. One issue particularly caught her attention. Carson had learned about a lawsuit that a group of Long Island landowners had filed against the federal government. They were objecting to aerial spraying of their properties with DDT to control gypsy moths, tent caterpillars, and mosquitoes. The case was of great interest to many of Carson's friends whose lands across the Northeast had been sprayed, producing die-offs of birds. The litigants were wealthy, educated individuals who would mount an effective case, using expert witnesses and well-researched positions. Carson knew this was an important case and tracked its progress. She encouraged the editors of the *New Yorker* to commission a story about the case, and she suggested several writers, other than herself, who might be up to the task.

She later wrote that a friend, Olga Huckins, whose land had been a victim of aerial pesticide spraying in Massachusetts, convinced her to work on the issue directly. Huckins had written a letter to the editor of the *Boston Herald* in January 1958, demanding that aerial spraying of poisons be stopped "until all the evidence, biological and scientific, immediate and long-run, of the effects upon wildlife and human beings [was] known."[31] Huckins followed that with a letter to Carson asking her to do something. "Doing something" involved weeks of intensive information gathering and letter writing to federal officials. As Carson learned about the situation, she discovered more pockets of concern among educators, scientists, and conservation leaders. Eventually, she decided to undertake the task of writing a magazine article or two that could be expanded into a short book. As she wrote to Dorothy Freeman, who didn't like Carson getting involved in the disagreeable and depressing "poison book": "You do know, I think, how deeply I believe in the importance of what I am doing. Knowing what I do, there would be no future peace for me if I kept silent. I wish I could feel that you want me to do it. I wish you could feel, as I do, that it is, in the deepest sense, a privilege as well as a duty to have the opportunity to speak out—to many thousands of people—on something so important."[32] She signed a contract to write a book about the poisons in mid-1958, expecting to finish in little more than a year.

She soon discovered, however, that she had misjudged the project completely. The writing would not be quick, nor would it be straight-forward. She began with the expectation that the testimony surrounding the Long Island lawsuit would provide the basic information she needed. Instead she uncovered a complex issue whose tendrils spread in many and unanticipated directions. She had planned to write about insecticides and their impact on wildlife. But many synthetic pesticides were in use—not just DDT, but chlordane, dieldrin, heptachlor, 2,4-D, and others—and reports of their negative impacts were popping up everywhere, exposing their effects on all forms of life. Limiting the focus to insecticides and wildlife was not possible. Her original plan had been for one chapter on human impacts, but the more she learned, the more the book's subject became human public health. Human concerns expanded to four chapters to form the cornerstone of the book.

The greatest time sink, however, was her complete commitment to doing the fundamental research. During her years as a government scientist, she had developed a far-reaching network of scientific and technical colleagues in the research labs of the US Departments of Agriculture and Interior. Similarly, through her nature writing and her growing interest in environmental issues, she had formed correspondence friendships with dozens of dedicated advocates for the control of chemical spraying. Through these contacts, she expanded outward to a much wider range of medical researchers and public health experts. She corresponded with hundreds of individuals, securing their research reports and clinical data and seeking clarification of technical points through letter after letter; she combed federal laboratories and libraries, accumulating obscure reports that might seem trivial by themselves but loomed large when combined with others in her research base. Her

Berwick Road home became filled with filing cabinets and stacks of scientific reports, personal testimonies, and correspondence from researchers across the globe. She wrote to her editor, explaining the delay in finishing the manuscript: "I guess all that sustains me is a serene inner conviction that when, at last, the book is done, it is going to be built on an unshakable foundation. That is so terribly important. Too many people—with the best possible motives—have rushed out statements without adequate support, furnishing the best possible targets for the opposition. That we shall not have to worry about."[33]

Critics later downplayed the validity of her assertions because, they said, she was just a writer, not a real scientist: she didn't have a PhD and had done little or no independent research as a member of the Fish and Wildlife Service. In fact, though, nothing could have been further from the truth. Carson always retained the fundamental qualities of a scientist—the search for truth through a comprehensive examination of the facts and a commitment to find the causal relationships among observations. The task of assembling and tracking this information may seem quaint in the age of electronic indices, abstracts, and databases, but in Carson's time her efforts represented a critical—and incredibly difficult—step in the development of ecological and epidemiological knowledge. She managed to bring together hundreds of disparate studies, building bridges that linked chemicals, basic cellular biology, environmental processes, and organismic health. In a progress report to her publisher, she wrote: "I have a comforting feeling that what I shall now be able to achieve is a synthesis of widely scattered facts, that have not heretofore been considered in relation to each other. It is now possible to build up, step by step, a really damning case against the use of these chemicals as they are now inflicted upon us."[34]

Also, she had to do her work under increasingly difficult conditions. Her mother died in 1958, leaving her mourning for her lifelong companion but also fiercely determined to continue. She wrote to a friend about her mother: "More than anyone else I know, she embodied Albert Schweitzer's 'reverence for life.' And while gentle and compassionate, she could fight fiercely against anything she believed wrong, as in our present Crusade! Knowing how she felt about that will help me to return to it soon, and to carry it through to completion."[35] Meanwhile, her own health problems worsened. She suffered from an ongoing series of infections that weakened her in general, along with arthritis, an ulcer, and a rare malady, iritis, which impaired her vision for months at a time. Her left breast was removed in 1960. It was now clear to Carson that she was succumbing to the cancer that had earlier been misdiagnosed and was steadily destroying her body.

Carson was careful to keep her project as quiet as possible. She knew that her findings and conclusions would be highly critical of both government and industry. She feared that early publicity about the book would lead to immediate attempts to discredit it before she had fully prepared her case. Nevertheless, her widespread correspondence and contacts with scientists caused a heightened awareness of the topic of her next book. She wrote to a colleague: "The news seems to be out on the grapevine, so possibly you have heard, that my current writing project is a book dealing with the basic problem of the effect of chemical insecticides in present use on all living things and on their fundamental ecological relationships. This was something I had not expected to do, but facts that came to my attention last winter disturbed me so deeply that I made the decision to postpone all other commitments and devote myself to what I consider a tremendously important problem."[36] Eventually, her access to government researchers and facilities was cut off, as especially the US Department of Agriculture grew suspicious of what she might be writing.

The government was right to be concerned. Carson had not set out to write an objective, two-sided assessment of the role of synthetic chemicals in modern civilization; she set out to balance the availability of information. She believed that the benefits of chemicals had been well publicized. Manufacturers spent generously to advertise the glorious outcomes of these new chemicals. DuPont Chemical company's slogan—"Better things for better living . . . through chemistry"—exemplified the era. Governmental agencies were similarly enthralled with these chemicals, regarding them as miracles that could rid the landscape of insects and other enemies of agricultural production, forest health, and human comfort. Carson thought people deserved to know the other side of the story as well—the risks of the chemicals themselves, but more importantly the profligate manner in which they were being used.

Massive aerial campaigns sprayed chemicals indiscriminately over the landscape; fogging trucks rolled down city streets and alleys, spraying DDT and other insecticides over whatever lay in their paths, including children eating their lunches at school picnic tables. Carson compiled hundreds of examples of the deaths and serious illnesses of nontarget species, including birds, amphibians, farm animals, pets—and humans.

Her perspective was embodied in her early working title for the book, "Man Against the Earth." But neither she nor her publisher was satisfied with such a sterile title. One chapter in the book was originally titled "Silent Spring," referring to the loss of birds—and their songs—due to aerial pesticide spraying. Eventually, she agreed to *Silent Spring* as the title for the entire book when she read a poem by Keats that included the lines, "The sedge is wither'd from the lake / And no birds sing."[37]

Carson began the book with a fable, the story of a fictional community beset by the impacts of pesticides, including the lack of bird song:

> Along the roads, laurel, viburnum, and alder, great ferns and wildflowers delighted the traveler's eye through much of the year. Even in winter the roadsides were places of beauty, where countless birds came to feed on the berries and on the seed heads of the dried weeds rising above the snow. The countryside was, in fact, famous for the abundance and variety of its bird life, and when the flood of migrants was pouring through in spring and fall people traveled from great distances to observe them. . . .
>
> Then a strange blight crept over the area and everything began to change. . . .
>
> There was a strange stillness. The birds, for example— where had they gone? Many people spoke of them, puzzled and disturbed. The few birds seen anywhere were moribund; they trembled violently and could not fly. It was a spring without voices. On the mornings that had once throbbed with the dawn chorus of robins, catbirds, doves, jays, wrens, and scores of other bird voices there was now no sound; only silence lay over the fields and woods and marsh. . . .
>
> In the gutters under the eaves and between the shingles of the roofs, a white granular powder still showed a few patches;

some weeks before it had fallen like snow upon the roofs and the lawns, the fields and streams.

No witchcraft, no enemy action had silenced the rebirth of new life in this stricken world. The people had done it themselves.[38]

The remainder of the book, however, was not fiction; it was science. Chapters covered the chemistry of pesticides; pesticide fates and transmission in water, soil, and air; impacts on nontarget animals and plants; the indiscriminate assault of aerial spraying; impacts on human health, including especially cancer; development of resistance in target species; the alternative of biological control. Carson fretted that the scientific nature of the book would make it unpopular and hard to read.

In the Wake of *Silent Spring*

She didn't need to fret. As publication time neared, interest in the anticipated book skyrocketed. The *New Yorker* serialized the book in three installments during June and July 1962. *Silent Spring* reached more than 400,000 of the nation's thought-leaders through this outlet. When the book itself was released, on September 27, 1962, it became an instant best seller. Like her sea books, *Silent Spring* took up long-term residence on the *New York Times* best-seller list. President Kennedy referred to the book in a press conference.[39] Magazines and newspapers reviewed the book extensively, book clubs chose it, and school teachers built lessons around it.

The negative furor was also immediate. The chemical and pesticide industry attacked Carson full-force. They couldn't debate the factual content of the book—or its fifty-five pages of references—so they used other tactics. They said it was unfair because it hadn't presented the good with the bad, something Carson fully acknowledged. They misrepresented Carson as being against all pesticide use, when her major objection was the way that they were used. Near the end of the book's second chapter, she wrote, "It is not my contention that chemical insecticides must never be used. I do contend that we have put poisonous and biologically potent chemicals indiscriminately into the hands of persons largely or wholly ignorant of their potentials for harm."[40]

They attacked Rachel Carson the woman. They questioned her politics, discounted her credentials as a scientist, argued that a childless spinster had no reason to be interested in future generations, described her as a sentimental naturalistic writer who yearned to go back to the cave. A reader of the second *New Yorker* installment wrote: "Miss Rachel Carson's reference to the selfishness of insecticide manufacturers probably reflects her Communist sympathies, like a lot of our writers these days.... As for insects, isn't it just like a woman to be scared to death of a few little bugs! As long as we have the H-bomb everything will be O.K. PS. She's probably a peace-nut too."[41] The journal *County Agent and Vo-Ag Teacher* taught its readers "How to Answer Rachel Carson—To Counteract Anti-Pesticide Propaganda." In a later speech, Rachel Carson noted a newspaper article that reported officials in two Pennsylvania county farm bureaus had been enraged by the book; the reporter also noted, "No one in either county farm office who talked to us had read the book, but all disapproved of it heartily."[42]

The agricultural chemical industry was the most disturbed and the most direct in its attacks on Carson. The Monsanto Company issued a pamphlet called "The Desolate Year," which presented its own fable to counter Carson's: "... A cattleman in the Southwest rubbed the back of a big red steer, and his hand found two large lumps under the hide ... gritting his teeth, he placed his thumbs at the sides of one of the lumps and pressed. The hair parted, a small hole opened and stretched. A fat, brown inch-long maggot slowly eased through the hole...."[43]

The industry printed tens of thousands of these pamphlets, sending them to elected officials, agricultural professionals, and anyone else they thought would be receptive to the counter-message. A biochemical researcher, Dr. Robert White-Stevens, became the unofficial spokesperson for the chemical industry. He traveled the country, speaking on radio and television and in person about the disaster that would ensue if "Miss" Carson's perspectives were adopted. White-Stevens was British, his accent adding to his credibility; he spoke with the authority and language of a scientist: "The major claims of Miss Rachel Carson's book *Silent Spring* are gross distortions of the actual facts, completely unsupported by scientific, experimental evidence, and general practical experience in the field. Her suggestion that pesticides are in fact biocides destroying all life is obviously absurd in the light of the fact that without selective biologicals these compounds would be completely useless."[44]

The culminating event in the controversy over *Silent Spring* came on April 3, 1963. The argument had rumbled for nearly a year since the first serialized article. Newspapers, magazines, television, and radio had sought interviews with Carson and had proposed debates between her and the industry; she refused almost all requests. Finally succumbing to the demands for television interviews, she agreed to participate in a program for *CBS Reports*, a television news show similar to today's *60 Minutes*. The one-hour program was narrated by Eric Sevareid, a highly respected journalist who had made his name reporting battlefield news during World War II. The program aired interviews with Carson, White-Stevens, and representatives from the US government; Carson was interviewed twice, the later time at her home because she was too ill to travel to a studio. As the broadcast date approached, CBS received thousands of mimeographed letters, presumed to be a campaign by the chemical industry, asking them to be sure the program was fair. Two food and cleaning supply companies canceled their sponsorship, citing the controversy as not being good for their products; two other sponsors braved the possible consequences. Carson was nervous as the program approached, expressing to her friends that she feared she would look ill or foolish and that the list of interviewees was stacked against her.[45]

Once again, she needn't have worried. Her interview segments were professional, dignified, factual, and sincere. She read excerpts from *Silent Spring* in a calm, clear, determined voice. Government officials appeared inept and uninformed; their standard responses to questions about the dangers of chemicals and their dispersal were, "We just don't know...." Robert White-Stevens, however, dug the grave for the chemical industry. Rather than Carson appearing as a deranged crusader, White-Stevens reserved that role for himself, dressed in a white lab coat and blustering with indignation. His statements mirrored the industry propaganda: "If man were to faithfully follow the teachings of Miss Carson, we would return to the Dark Ages, and the insects and diseases and vermin would once again inherit the earth."[46]

As the program drew to a close, Carson offered the final statement, the ethic that drove her research and writing: "We still talk in terms of

Figure 4.4 On June 4, 1963, Rachel Carson appeared before the US Senate Government Operations Subcommittee to testify about the improper use of pesticides. (Reproduced courtesy of US Library of Congress.)

conquest. We still haven't become mature enough to think of ourselves as only a very tiny part of a vast and incredible universe. Now I truly believe that we in this generation must come to terms with nature, and I think we're challenged, as mankind has never been challenged before, to prove our maturity and our mastery, not of nature but of ourselves."[47] That evening, as more than 10 million Americans watched, the nation came to this conclusion: Rachel Carson was right.

The tide had turned. The next month, on May 15, President Kennedy's Science Advisory Committee issued its long-awaited report, "The Use of Pesticides," concluding that unregulated use of the chemicals was a problem that needed a solution. That morning, the *Christian Science Monitor* headline declared, "Rachel Carson Stands Vindicated." That evening, Eric Sevareid reported that Carson had set out to do two things—inform the public and challenge the government to act; "She accomplished the first months ago," Sevareid said. "Tonight's report by the presidential panel is prima facie evidence that she has accomplished the second."[48]

Three weeks later, Carson was called to testify before Senator Abraham Ribicoff's committee on the matter of pesticides. As she took her seat, Ribicoff repeated what President Lincoln had said upon meeting Harriet Beecher Stowe, author of *Uncle Tom's Cabin*, her novel exposing the evils of slavery, which some credited with triggering the events that led to the Civil War: "You are the lady who started all this."[49]

She did start all this. Her pioneering work on the environmental consequences of broadcast dispersal of chemicals set the stage for the so-called modern environmental movement of the 1960s and '70s. She virtually created a field of science—environmental toxicology—by unifying disparate elements of basic biology, medical research, and environmental management. She argued forcefully that the government should review the impacts of environmental chemicals before approving their sale; new laws promoting clean air, clean water, solid waste disposal, and toxic chemical management were soon to follow—enacted during both Republican and Democratic administrations. She called for the creation of a federal government agency to oversee the environment; the Environmental Protection Agency was formed in 1970. The use of DDT was banned in the United States in 1971. *Silent Spring* has been translated into more than twenty languages and has sold millions of copies; the book remains in print today.[50]

More than a "poison book," *Silent Spring* was also an ecology text. Carson eventually referred to herself as an ecologist, acknowledging her interest not just in natural history, but also in the relationships among organisms and between organisms and their environment. However, Carson went even further in considering the relationships of organisms and natural processes and their linkage with human decisions and actions. She directed our attention to chronic effects as well as acute ones, recognizing that both the intensity and duration of an impact were crucial to its importance. She knew and understood that effects cascaded through an ecosystem, so that more organisms than the direct targets of an environmental change were often affected. Her message was holistic, not reductionist. In an essay about the biological sciences, she wrote:

The scope of biology can be truly defined only in broad terms as the history of the earth and all its life—the past, the present, and the future. Any definition of lesser scope becomes narrow and academic and fails utterly to convey the majestic sweep of the subject in time and space, embracing all that has made man what he is, and holding a foretaste of what he may yet become. For it has dawned upon us in these recent years of the maturing of our science that neither man nor any other living creature may be studied or comprehended apart from the world in which he lives; that such restricted studies as the classification of plants and animals or descriptions of their anatomy and physiology (upon which the early biologists necessarily focused their attention) are but one small facet of a subject so many-sided, so rich in beauty and fascination, so filled with significance that no informed reader can neglect it. . . .[51]

She started all this, and although she did not live long enough to know all that she started, Carson was aware of her impact. She wrote to Dorothy Freeman in early 1964: "I think that you must have no regrets in my behalf. I have had a rich life, full of rewards and satisfactions that come to few, and if it must end now, I can feel that I have achieved most of what I wished to do. That wouldn't have been true two years ago, when I first realized my time was short, and I am so grateful to have had this extra time."[52]

Carson's time after publication of *Silent Spring* was indeed short. The cancer that had been slowly devouring her body advanced, causing numerous other maladies as it progressed. She grew weaker and was increasingly housebound. The same heroic effort that pushed her to complete *Silent Spring* and the same deep understanding of nature that had guided her whole career stayed with her to the end. Just before her death, she wrote again to Dorothy Freeman:

. . . But most of all I shall remember the Monarchs, that unhurried westward drift of one small winged form after another, each drawn by some invisible force. We talked a little about their migration, their life history. Did they return? We thought not; for most, at least, this was the closing journey of their lives.

. . . For the Monarch, that cycle is measured in a known span of months. For ourselves, the measure is something else, the span of which we cannot know. But the thought is the same: when that intangible cycle has run its course it is a natural and not unhappy thing that a life comes to its end.[53]

The intangible cycle ended for Rachel Carson at her Berwick Road home on April 14, 1964, six weeks before her fifty-seventh birthday.

Figure 5.1 Francisco Alves "Chico" Mendes Filho, 1944–1988. (Reproduced courtesy of Denise Zmekhol/ZDFILMS.)

Chapter 5

Chico Mendes

Gandhi of the Amazon

The scene could have been right out of an American Western movie. The normally bustling streets of Xapuri, an outpost town in the far western Amazon region of Brazil, had turned ominously quiet. It was just three days before Christmas in 1988, and the neighborhood should have been bustling with the activity of the season. Instead, friends usually chatting on the street had retreated inside. Children, usually running and laughing with friends, were nowhere to be seen. Traffic was almost absent on the dusty street. Danger was thick in the air.

Inside his home, Chico Mendes and his two bodyguards played dominoes, seemingly unaware of the atmosphere outside his front door. A little before six in the evening, Gomercindo Rodrigues, his friend and closest companion in the union movement, arrived on his motorcycle. Mendes, a skilled card and dominoes player who enjoyed the banter of the gaming table, tried to get Rodrigues involved.

"Oh, Guma, it's great you got here, now we can be partners to beat these dunces. I've already been winning by myself."

But Rodrigues was in no mood for fun. "Chico, I'm worried about what I told you yesterday." His worry was that the menacing gunmen who loitered in the area—a fact of life for Mendes and his activist colleagues in recent years—had disappeared. "I'm going to take a ride around town to see if I find those guys, because I'm very worried."

"Okay, meanwhile I'll take a shower and wait for you to come back to eat, but do come back."

Rodrigues left, and the game continued. Mendes's wife, Ilsamar, was finishing preparations for dinner and encouraging the domino players to conclude their game so they could all eat. Mendes relented, threw a towel over his shoulder, and walked out the back door, heading for the shower at the far end of the yard.

As he stepped out, shotgun blasts exploded from behind the cover of nearby bushes. The massive loads of shot pierced Mendes's right shoulder and chest, many pellets slicing through his lungs, bones, and muscles. The blast knocked him back into the kitchen, and he staggered toward the bedroom, probably trying to see his children one last time. But it was too late. He fell dead into the arms of one bodyguard, massive blood-loss killing him in a matter of minutes.

Ilsamar panicked and ran out the front door, just as Rodrigues was returning from his drive around town. "They shot Chico!" she cried. Rodrigues looked across to the police station, only fifty yards away, where several officers were standing as though they had heard nothing.

"You bastards," he shouted, "aren't you going to do anything?" The police officers stared in his direction, but did not move.[1]

The murder was intended to silence Mendes and to extinguish the movement that he led on behalf of the people and environment of the Amazonian rain forest. It did not work. Mendes's biographer, Andrew Revkin, observed that "when he was gunned down one week after his forty-fourth birthday, everything crystallized: the burning of the forests, the global link created by those rising plumes of greenhouse gases, and the compelling story of a man who had a rare, and crucial, skill set with which to confront ungoverned violence against man and nature."[2] The legacy of Chico Mendes, whom many call "the Gandhi of the Forest," still lives, and, because of him, the future of the Amazon is certainly brighter.

Rubber Tapper

Francisco Alves Mendes Filho was born on December 15, 1944. From his birth, everyone called him Chico. His father and grandfather were rubber tappers, and he grew up to be a rubber tapper himself. His grandfather came to the Amazon around 1900 in the first big migration of Brazilians enticed to leave their homes in pursuit of "white gold."[3]

The white gold was latex, the sticky white sap of certain Amazonian trees. Latex is composed of long, tangled organic molecules that stretch when pulled and return to their original shape when released—an amazing and useful quality. Dozens of tree species in the Amazon contain sap with the properties of latex, but the most productive is the *Hevea brasiliensis*, known simply as the rubber tree. Rubber trees grow large, reaching more than one hundred feet in height and ten feet in circumference, and may live for several hundred years. One estimate is that the Amazon and Orinoco basins together hold 300 million rubber trees. But, like most flora in the rain forest, the rubber tree exists at low densities, usually no more than one tree per acre.[4]

The value of latex was known by the indigenous people long before Europeans slashed their way into the forest. More than 130 distinct Indian tribes lived in the Amazon, at one time totaling more than 6 million in population. Indians coated their utilitarian belongings—bowls, cups, shoes—with latex to make them waterproof.

The massive unknown watershed of the Amazon River intrigued Europeans, and repeated scientific expeditions penetrated the region during the mid-1800s. Of particular interest to these explorers was "an inconspicuous tree whose only distinguishing characteristic is that it bleeds a milky white sap when its soft bark is scratched."[5] Experimentation with latex showed that it could be formed into large flat sheets that retained the qualities of the sap; then the latex could be modified into an array of products—a British raincoat is still called a "Macintosh," named after the man who first embedded a sheet of Brazilian latex between two layers of cloth to make a sewable, waterproof fabric. Latex-based products entered the world market en masse by the 1870s.

With the advent of the tire (latex can be heated with sulfur to make "vulcanized" rubber) and insulation for electric wire (latex does not conduct electricity), demand for latex—now commonly called rubber—skyrocketed. Workers by the thousands were attracted to exploit the Amazon's rubber trees. They migrated mainly from the northeastern Brazilian state of Ceará, where farmers had repeatedly experienced years of devastating droughts that led to bankruptcy and poverty. Promised good jobs and prosperity, they steamed up the Amazon River to Belém and then farther to Manaus, which became the center of rubber trading. By around 1900, when Mendes's grandfather made the journey, 100,000 rubber tappers had passed through Manaus on their way to the far reaches of Amazonia.

A prized location for rubber tapping was the small, isolated state of Acre, the westernmost state of Brazil, bordering Peru on the west and Bolivia on the south. The municipality of Xapuri, where Mendes's family settled, lies just a few miles from Bolivia. Because the soils of Acre were more fertile and less fragile than in other areas of the Amazon basin, rubber trees were abundant and productive. Rubber markets could be reached easily by boat—the region is intersected by a score of rivers deep enough to carry the rubber to Manaus. In 1900, two-thirds of Brazil's rubber production originated in Acre.[6]

The Amazon rubber boom led the Brazilian economy into the twentieth century, but not for long. The market crashed in about a decade. Years before, British explorers had carried rubber seeds back to England and started a breeding program in the Kew Royal Botanic Gardens outside London. Domesticated trees were then shipped to Malaysia, a British colony, and raised on plantations. The plantations thrived, producing abundant supplies of rubber, driving down prices and knocking Brazilian rubber out of the world's markets. Tappers deserted the forest as quickly as they had come, leaving only the most hardy and committed settlers behind.

The rubber industry experienced a short-lived renaissance during World War II. Japan took control of the Pacific in early 1942, cutting off supplies of Malaysian rubber to America. In order to secure a reliable supply of rubber for the war effort, the US government paid Brazil to reinvigorate the rubber industry, promising high salaries and military pensions to men who became "rubber soldiers" by journeying into the Amazon. Fifty thousand answered the call. At the end of the war, however, the industry retreated to its prewar level (and the rubber soldiers never received pensions or any other compensation for their patriotic service).

The rubber tappers who remained were snared in an economic web known as "debt slavery." Rubber tappers were totally dependent on rubber barons, who had claimed the land on which the tappers lived and worked. The rubber barons, often called "colonels of the river-bank,"[7] loaned tappers the money for their upriver journey to Acre and other states, and then, overcharging them, sold them equipment and supplies, on credit, to be paid from their harvest of rubber and Brazil nuts in the coming season. When the tappers sold their crop to the rubber barons, they were underpaid and cheated in various ways because they were illiterate and innumerate. As a result, rubber tappers arrived in debt and typically got further in debt every year, assuring that they would remain in the grips of debt slavery forever.

These were the conditions that greeted Chico Mendes at his birth in 1944. "I am a rubber tapper," Mendes stated as he summarized his career near the end of his life,[8] and that career started early. By the age of five, Chico was hauling firewood and water for the rubber-curing process. At seven, he began sitting in a tree stand at night, helping his partially crippled father hunt for the game that would be tomorrow's dinner. (Mendes claimed that he became an addicted chain-smoker at that age, lighting up continuously to keep ravenous mosquitoes at bay during the long nights.) He never attended school. "My life began just like that of all rubber tappers," he said, "as a virtual slave bound to do the bidding of his master. I started work at nine years old, and like my father before me, instead of learning my ABCs I learned how to extract latex from a rubber tree."[9] By age eleven, he was tapping rubber full time. When he was seventeen, tragedy made him the family's main rubber tapper. His mother died in childbirth (her twentieth birthing), requiring his father to stop tapping to tend their subsistence farm plot; his next-oldest brother died in a hunting accident. With no source of other help, Mendes now tapped rubber six days per week and cared for a family of five siblings and a disabled father. He continued to tap rubber full time until he was twenty-eight years old.

Rubber tapping was exhausting. A Xapuri tapper generally kept three trails within his working area, called a *seringal*. The tapper, or *seringueiro*, worked the trails in sequence, one per day. Each trail had a name that described it, like "Pee Walking" or "Already Hungry" if the trails were unusually long or arduous. The *seringueiro* rose before dawn, downed a bit of breakfast and a glass of coffee, and set off down the trail. Sap flows better when it is cool, so an early start was important. At the first rubber tree, he carved a shallow, slightly angled groove, just deep enough to free the milky sap, but not so deep as to injure the cambium growing beneath the thin bark. The first groove on a tree was cut as high as the tapper could reach, standing on tiptoes. Each day's collection required a new groove, positioned an inch or so below the previous. The tapper hung a small container at the end of the groove or placed it on the ground to catch the sap dripping from the wound. He then hurried on to the next tree, completing the three-to-four-mile-long circuit by midday and returning to his house for lunch.

In the afternoon, he hiked the trail again, collecting the sap in a larger container. In the evening, he cooked the sap over an open smoky fire, turning a spit onto which he slowly poured the sap. The smoke stopped bacteria from growing in the latex. Over several hours, the dripping latex hardened into an oval ball weighing six to eight pounds. Tapping occurred only during the dry season, from about mid-April to mid-November, leaving the five-month wet season for the trees to recover and grow.

During the wet season, the *seringueiro*'s main activity was gathering Brazil nuts. The nuts grow in a coconut-like pod high in the canopy of the Brazil nut tree. Tappers gathered the pods when they fell to the forest floor, then sliced open the top of the pod with razor-sharp machetes to expose the dozen or so nuts, arranged in the pod like the wedges of an orange. Brazil nuts and rubber typically made up equal halves of a family's income.

The work was hard, but the forest produced everything a family needed, and in abundant supply. Jute for rope and quinine for medicine were gathered and processed for trade. Tapper families also hunted for meat—Mendes's favorite meal was fried wild boar and monkey in Brazil-nut sauce—and raised a few acres of subsistence crops—corn, beans, manioc. A typical house was made from native materials as well. Tree trunks provided stilts on which the house was elevated a few feet above the ground, canes comprised the walls, and tree branches sup-

Figure 5.2 Chico Mendes always considered himself a rubber tapper, and he was at home working a rubber trail. He never lost touch with the trees or the people who made their living sustainably by tapping them. (Photograph by Adrian Cowell, reproduced courtesy of Boojie Cowell.)

ported the roof, which was thatched with palm leaves. Mendes loved the life and the forest: "We lived peacefully because we had the forest, and it wasn't threatened; it was part of our lives because it is our mother, we survived from her."[10]

Mendes was a thoughtful child. He had learned to read and figure a little from his father, and undoubtedly he had absorbed his father's distrust of the rubber barons who controlled them. Like his father, he was always interested in politics. Yet he did not stand out in the community. Neighbors at first thought little of him, as one observed: "As a kid, you'd never have thought that Chico could grow into such a man. He used to walk around with his mouth hanging open, and he drooled."[11] All that changed one day when a stranger walked out of the forest into the Mendes' clearing.

"In 1962," Mendes remembered, "someone new passed by our house on the rubber estate where we lived. He was a worker, a rubber tapper, but looked and spoke completely differently from the rest."[12] He was a huge man, burly, with a heavy beard and a voice that boomed through the forest. Mendes's initial reaction was favorable: "This gentleman was very lively, and it was easy to see—even though he was wearing rubber tapper clothes—his way of expressing himself made it obvious that his upbringing was very different."[13]

The stranger's name was Euclides Fernandes Tavora, although he didn't share that information until he had known Mendes for more than a year. He had been raised in eastern Brazil, where he was a member of the elite classes, university educated, and an officer in the Brazilian army. Twice, however, his communistic leanings had caused him to join the losing side in attempted political takeovers of the Brazilian government, and twice he had been imprisoned. Twice also he escaped, the second time across the border to Bolivia. There he joined in the workers' struggle against a repressive government; when another arrest seemed imminent, he snuck back across the border and hid in Acre's dense and remote forests. There he quietly purchased an abandoned rubber estate and learned the basics of rubber tapping.

The way he spoke and the things he said intrigued Mendes, and Tavora seemed to see great possibilities in him. Mendes's father agreed that Tavora could teach the boy to read better, as long as it didn't interfere with his work. Starting immediately and continuing for three years, Mendes trekked three hours to Tavora's *seringal* on Saturday afternoons and trekked home on Sunday evenings.

They had no books, so Mendes took his reading lessons from the newspapers that Tavora stockpiled. Together they poured over the columns, providing Mendes not only reading practice but also a primer in politics, philosophy, and social doctrine. Mendes admitted, "I was so interested in what he had to say that at times I spent the whole night awake, listening to him."[14]

Mendes's education took a radical turn in 1964, after an uprising brought military rule to Brazil. Tavora had "managed to get hold of a radio and I learned how to get the Portuguese-language programs transmitted from abroad."[15] They listened together to the Voice of America, Radio Moscow, and the British Broadcasting Corporation (BBC) and then dissected the different perspectives. The American station recounted how bad the previous regime had been and asserted that the revolt had been a victory for democracy. The Soviet station claimed that the military revolt was an imperial action financed and led by the American CIA and the Catholic Church for their own benefit. The BBC, it seemed, just reported the news. "From that point on," Mendes said, "I became faithful to the BBC of London during those times."[16]

Mendes had learned to read and do math, and he thought and talked confidently about political issues. "Tavora was interested in teaching me other things," he said, "things that would become very important in the future."[17] Tavora also gave him advice on how to make a difference in the world, a path that he believed Mendes would follow. He encouraged Mendes to join in whatever organizations he could, especially unions, even if they were linked to the government. Tavora told him, "What is important is that you get inside and do your work."[18] The effort to help the worker will never die out, he told Mendes, explaining that "we had at least ten, fifteen, twenty years of dictatorship ahead of us but that new unions, new organizations would emerge. Despite the defeats, humiliations and massacres, the roots of the movement were always there. . . . The plants would always germinate again sooner or later, however much they were attacked."[19] And he expressed his faith in Mendes, in the spark that he had seen right from the beginning that caused him to invest so deeply in Mendes's education: "Who knows," he told Mendes, "but someday in your life you might succeed in leading a movement. You can never forget that."[20]

Tavora disappeared from Mendes's life as mysteriously as he had first appeared. In 1965, suffering from severe stomach ailments, he boarded the bus out of Xapuri in search of medical treatment. He never returned, and no reports—of his death or recovery or imprisonment or escape— ever found their way back to the forest. With Tavora gone, Mendes's education stopped abruptly. He remembered: "During the following five years or so I became extremely isolated, because after he disappeared I thought to myself what should I be doing. In this extremely difficult moment of military rule, I couldn't do many things because I was likely to be persecuted."[21]

What he should be doing soon became clear.

Soldier for the Rubber Tappers

In later years, Mendes carried a business card. It read simply, "Francisco Alves Mendes Filho, Unionist."[22] Mendes had found his purpose: he would fight for the rights of rubber tappers.

Rubber tappers certainly needed someone to fight for them. From the beginning, the life of a rubber tapper was an uphill battle. The jungle itself was a big enough obstacle—torrential rains, searing heat, poisonous plants, and stalking jaguars (Mendes was particularly wary of jaguars). The tappers then had to deal with the indigenous Indians. The rubber barons had taught the tappers that the Indians were more like wild animals than humans and that capturing or killing them was necessary to control their *seringal*. For a century, rubber tappers and Indians fought as mortal enemies.

In turn, the rubber barons and their field bosses treated the tappers almost as cruelly as they treated the Indians. The only real law was that imposed by the rubber bosses themselves. If a tapper committed an offense, he might be staked outside the rubber baron's trading post and tortured slowly or even set afire—so others could see and understand who was in charge. "It's just like the American West when it was conquered" was the only excuse a federal police superintendent could make about the lawless conditions.[23]

From the 1960s onward, however, the biggest enemy of the rubber tappers became the Brazilian government and its plans for the Amazon. The revolution of 1964 brought a military dictatorship that lasted until 1985. For the first half of that period, the government was brutally repressive. No rival political parties were allowed, the media was gagged, unions were suppressed, and dissidents were jailed, exiled, or killed. "We had to wait until 1975," Mendes remembered, "at a time when the whole region was under the sway of the landowners, before the first trade unions were formed...."[24]

The word *jungle* comes from a Hindi word meaning "wasteland," an apt description of the Amazon in the minds of the Brazilian military leaders. But they thought development could transform it into something more valuable—farms. The government began a series of programs to convert the rain forest to pastureland. Cattle grazing, they determined, was the future. The regime also made plans to build hydroelectric dams and to open the region to mining. Central to these plans were roads that could open up the interior forests. One major road, BR-364, snaked its way northwestward from São Paulo all the way to Acre, a 3,000-mile stretch, replacing the long, arduous river journey with a somewhat less arduous direct route into the rain forest (originally, the road was unpaved for most of its length and, during the rainy season, became a thousand-mile ribbon of mud holes). In 1971, the road reached Rio Branco, the capital of Acre, and consequently Acre was named a regional hub for development.

The development program changed the landscape of Amazonia, including Acre. The majority of land in Acre had been designated as *terra devoluta*—public lands that belonged to the nation and could be used by anyone. To kick-start settlement, the government sold or gave away the land as fast as possible, under a slogan "land without people for people without land."[25] In contradiction to the slogan, most land ended up in the hands of wealthy landowners who received generous incentives—low-interest loans, tax write-offs, even free land—to settle the region. Soon, half of Acre was owned by ten people. The other half was being bought by hopeful citizens lured into a land-speculation frenzy that hoisted prices by 100 times in a few years. Forests were converted to pasture at a rapid pace, particularly along BR-364 and the associated spur roads that penetrated the forest like ribs on a fish's backbone.[26]

When ranchers arrived to claim their prizes, they expected to find the promised "land without people." Instead, they were shocked to find the land inhabited by rubber tappers who had lived and worked in the forest for generations. The ranchers' plans for raising cattle and the tappers' tradition of sustainably using the trees were incompatible, so the ranchers used any means, legal or illegal, to drive the tappers away. Mendes remembered that "from 1970 until 1975 or '76, all our comrades who lived along the margin of the road . . . were expelled, using the most violent means possible. Their shacks were burned down, gunmen would show up on their lands, their animals were killed."[27]

Mendes was appalled by what was happening. "Progress," he lamented, "means cattle, devastation, expulsion of the rubber tappers, genocide of the rubber tappers in Amazonia."[28] Mendes had begun writing letters to the Brazilian president as early as 1966, explaining the unprincipled exploitation of the rubber tappers and asking, politely, for schools, medical care, and other basic elements of human life. He was still tapping rubber full time, but he also trekked across the region, observing conditions, listening to his fellow tappers, and explaining his wish to organize them into a union. In 1971, he moved to Xapuri and began teaching in a government school, focusing first on adults who needed to be able to read and do simple math so they wouldn't be cheated by the rubber buyers.

Mendes married in early 1969, but the marriage lasted only a few years. He was seldom home, instead traveling the countryside to promote the interests of the rubber tappers. He did not involve his family in his work, stating firmly, "My work is not play."[29] His second wife, Ilsamar, whom he married in the early 1980s, later lamented, "Chico never should have had a family. . . . He used to say that although he'd like to give his family more, his heart was with the *seringueiros*."[30]

The rubber tappers found another ally at this time in the Catholic Church. Catholic priests and leaders throughout South America met in 1968 and adopted a "liberation theology" that directed the church to help the poor. Bishop Moacyr Grechi of Acre endorsed this theology fully, setting up "base communities" for delivering both religious and social services to the local poor. Mendes served as a "monitor" in this effort, helping to connect the needs of the people with the church. This activity also furthered Mendes's education, as the progressive priests explored with him the connections among poverty, environment, politics, and the economy.

Government repression began to soften in the mid-1970s, under pressure from both inside and outside the country. The Catholic Church became more aggressive in support of rural peoples and land reform. Unions were allowed to expand to more industries and more locations. The government-backed Confederation of Rural Workers' Unions began organizing in the state of Acre, which had no unions at the time. The first union was established in Brasileia, a town thirty-five miles down the road from Xapuri. Mendes didn't hesitate. "When I heard that the first union was to be founded in Brasileia, I remembered Euclides' advice and went straight there, without waiting for an invitation."[31] With the skills and knowledge taught to him by Tavora and the priests, Mendes was welcomed to the union and was then quickly elected its secretary. "From that point on," he stated, "I began discussions with our comrades on how we might resist the large-scale deforestation, the destruction of our forest, and expulsion of our comrades. . . ."[32]

A major strategy for resistance became the *empate*—Portuguese for "standoff." When ranchers wanted to clear a piece of forest, they hired laborers, often former rubber tappers, to cut down the trees with chain saws and set them on fire. The action was illegal, even if the rancher held a legitimate title. Under Brazilian law, a person who worked on the land had the right to continue using the land and to defend that use, by force if necessary, as long as the defense was made immediately. During an *empate*, a group of rubber tappers—usually dozens, but sometimes hundreds—would gather at the clearing site and confront the loggers. "Comrades," they would say, "you are cutting down the trees, and you know that without the forest we can't live, we don't have our work, our families will go without food. Comrades, you're on the wrong side, but we're here to say there isn't going to be any more deforestation."[33] The loggers generally gave up peacefully and headed back to town, not wanting to stand between the tappers and ranchers. Mendes said, "I remember, in March 1976, we planned the first *empate*. . . . Sixty men organized themselves and spent three days entrenched there and stopped the destruction of 24,500 acres of virgin forest."[34] Mendes claimed that between then and 1985, he led forty-five *empates* in all—some successful, some not—that saved 1.2 million acres of forest from destruction.

Although Mendes did not invent the *empate* by himself (as some of his admirers claim), the character of the action was an extension of his demeanor. "*Ave Maria*," remembered Ilsamar, "he was such a sweet, decent man, no matter how tired or worried he was. . . . There was always that immense love."[35] *Empates* were always peaceful, a requirement in Mendes's philosophy. He never carried a weapon and never acted in anger. The loggers were respected: they were workers, like the rubber tappers, but had made a bad decision to take a job clearing the forest. They were never injured, persecuted, or robbed. Controlling mobs like this is not an easy task, but Mendes was always in charge. "He was," according to a comrade, "a modest and unpretentious man, but nevertheless a natural leader."[36]

In 1977, he returned to Xapuri to set up a union there, the second in Acre. Mendes continued his habit of walking the forest, often alone but sometimes in company with the local priest. He contacted rubber tap-

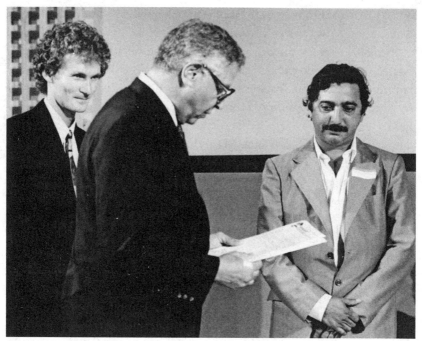

Figure 5.3 Chico Mendes received the United Nations Environment Programme's Global 500 Award in 1987. On the left is Steve Schwartzman of the Environmental Defense Fund. (Photograph by Adrian Cowell, reproduced courtesy of Boojie Cowell.)

pers, person by person and tract by tract, until he had won over the entire municipality. His brother remembered Chico as a man who "never got mad at anybody. And he never got a thing for himself. It was always for the *seringueiro*."[37] He had great appeal to the average worker, as one colleague observed: "Overweight, smoking heavily, friendly and talkative from the beginning, he seemed quite an ordinary sort of guy, reminding me of a small-town mayor, perhaps. . . ."[38] Within a year, the union numbered 30,000 members, and Mendes was universally recognized as their leader. Ilsamar remembered that "the rubber tappers saw Chico as their father."[39]

The union activists were thorns in the side of developers, and Mendes had the sharpest point. "He was to the ranchers of the Amazon what Cesar Chavez was to the citrus kings of California, what Lech Walesa was to the shipyard managers of Gdansk."[40] Ranchers created lists of potential assassination targets, including Mendes and others.

In Brazil, the target of an assassination is always told in advance—the *anuncio*. This is not a warning, but a statement of fact, designed to multiply the terror felt by the target. Mendes's friend and colleague Wilson de Souza Pinheiro, who headed the Brasileia union, received his *anuncio* in early 1980—and was shot to death at his union offices later in the year. Mendes had been deep in the forest talking with rural workers when this happened, or he would have been gunned down, too. Thousands of tappers attended the funeral and demanded that the police make an arrest within a week—everyone knew who the murderer was. Mendes tried to calm them down, to avoid violence, but this time his pleas for pacifism went unheeded. When the deadline passed without an arrest, a group of tappers took matters in their own hands, firing more than thirty bullets into the assassin.

Pinheiro's death ushered in a new era of violence. Mendes went underground for several months after the murder, moving regularly from location to location in the forest. He was arrested briefly later in the year on suspicion of being a communist agitator, but was eventually cleared. *Empates* were now dealt with more forcefully by the government. Mendes remembered: "On at least four occasions, we were arrested and forced to lie on the ground, with them beating us. They threw our bodies, covered in blood, into a lorry but we all sang hymns. We got to the police station, perhaps more than a hundred people, but they didn't have enough room to keep us there and we had to stand up in the corridors. In the end they had to let us go free."[41]

Little by little, though, the unions were making progress. An important project of Mendes's group was *Projecto Seringueiro*, designed to bring education and medical care to the region's tappers. By this time, Mendes had begun to get the attention of outsiders, including Mary Allegretti, a Brazilian anthropologist, and Tony Gross, a representative of the British relief agency Oxfam. With Allegretti's help and Oxfam's financial support, Mendes's union opened its first school in 1981. The school educated adults at first, in order to give them literacy and numeracy skills to confront the rubber traders, but it soon shifted to children's education. By 1984, they had opened six more schools around Xapuri and a total of twenty others across Acre. Mendes was rightfully proud of the schools, stating: "We believe that all our advances, the fight against the destruction of the forest, the organizing of the cooperative and the strengthening of our union, were all possible thanks to the education program."[42]

Ranchers and government leaders often accused Mendes and the unions of being against progress. The future, as they saw it, required the Amazon region to adopt a more modern approach to life, based on paved roads, cheap electricity, and, most of all, cattle ranching. Unfortunately, this model left behind the people who had lived in the Amazon for more than a century—the rubber tappers. Mendes was not against development, but he advocated an alternative based on sustainable use of the forest, rather than its conversion to other land uses he knew were unsustainable. He saw the future of the Amazon, and Brazil, in the gentle exploitation of the land by hunters, gatherers, and small farmers. "You have already seen," he told anyone who would listen, "that until today our struggle has been to preserve the forest, because it is in this forest that we have our whole survival. There are centuries of existence in this jungle, this forest, in which the man of the forest lives and has never plundered."[43]

But he needed help to carry his message to more people. He was about to find that help in a most unlikely place.

The Making of an Environmentalist

"I became an ecologist long before I had ever heard the word," Mendes said.[44] As a lifetime denizen of the rain forest, he had learned how the landscape worked. He knew that trees could only be tapped in ways that would allow them to live and prosper—if not, their sustainable yield would disappear. He appeared to be one with the forest and the trees. A companion described watching him on a tapping trek: "He would talk to the trees, jingling their cups to ask them which would give the most milk, and they would answer by shaking their leaves."[45] Most importantly, however, he understood that the individual rubber tapper and the occasional *empate* could not assure the future protection of the forest.

Opportunities for faster progress looked promising in early 1985. The military regime was defeated in a democratic election, and the new government understood that massive land reform was needed. By this time, Mendes's friend, Mary Allegretti, had established herself as an important spokesperson for the Amazon and especially for the rights of the indigenous people there, the Indians. She had formed a civil society organization, one of Brazil's first, to address the Indians' issues. As she worked with the government on the land reform legislation, she was shocked to see that little mention of the Amazon was included and only Indian needs, not rubber tappers', were being addressed. She wrote Mendes with the bad news that the proposed laws ignored the tappers' interests, but her most important message was: "They don't know you exist."[46]

It was time for rubber tappers to make their presence felt. At Allegretti's suggestion, she and Mendes organized a nationwide meeting of tappers for October 1985 in the capital city of Brasilia. The government could hardly ignore them if they showed up en masse. The strategy worked. In all, 130 representatives of rubber tappers attended the meeting, along with a gallery of reporters, academics, government officials, and other leaders from Brazil and beyond. The tappers told stories, sang songs, and described their lifestyles and hardships. They explained that many had come to the jungle as patriots to support the Allies in World War II—and then had been abandoned. They told how they had been exploited as "debt slaves" to the landowners and their foremen. They wrote a set of sixty-two demands that presented their position. The final item represented a subtle but clear change in the future of Amazonian activism: "We demand to be recognized as [the] genuine defenders of the forest."[47]

The most important practical outcome, however, was the origin of the idea for "extractive reserves." Until then, Mendes and his comrades had been arguing that the forest needed to be protected, but they didn't know how. Mendes observed, "Well, someone would ask, 'You are fighting to defend the forest, but what is it that you want to do with this forest?' And many times we would become a little taken aback, encountering difficulty in making a response."[48] Mendes had actually developed an idea a year earlier, at a national meeting of rural unions. The government was proposing to allocate small tracts to farmers of up to 250 acres, but Mendes knew this was too small an area to support a family through rubber tapping. He suggested a much larger, 700-acre allocation for tappers, calling this a "special rural module."[49] His idea was rejected as too radical, but it came up again at the rubber tappers' meeting; the proposed allocation was now called an extractive reserve and modeled after reserves provided for indigenous tribes. "The extractive reserve is a form of land reform, discovered by ourselves," observed Mendes.[50] He explained the idea this way: "We accepted that the Amazon could not be turned into some kind of sanctuary that nobody could touch. On the other hand, we knew it was important to stop the deforestation that is threatening the Amazon and all human life on the planet. . . . What do we mean by an extractive reserve? We mean the land is under public ownership but the rubber tappers and other workers that live on the land should have the right to live and work there."[51]

Using the forest this way—tapping rubber, gathering Brazil nuts, hunting for food, and growing subsistence crops in small patches—made good economic sense as well. The annual economic return from grazing cattle in converted forestland was small and it dwindled each year as the soil became exhausted; in a few years, the pastures were worthless. The harvest of forest crops was more valuable, however, and sustainable. Studies had shown that cattle ranching earned about $15 per acre annually at best, while sustainable extraction earned over $70 per acre per year.[52] Mendes believed that the difference was much greater, arguing that he "could prove the income from one hectare of forest is twenty times greater than when the forest is cleared and given over to cattle."[53]

Another group of observers at the Brasilia meeting had also taken note of the rubber tappers' movement and, especially, of Chico Mendes. Adrian Cowell, a veteran videographer who had spent years chronicling the changes in the Amazon region, had come to film the event. After watching Mendes at the meeting, Cowell realized that Mendes was the only person smart and capable enough to elevate the movement to a global issue—and he spent the next three years filming Mendes's life.

Also present was Steven Schwartzman of the Environmental Defense Fund, an American nonprofit organization. Schwartzman was a leading advocate for rain forest conservation and for coercing the World Bank and the Inter-American Development Bank to stop investing in forest-destroying projects. He had previously met Allegretti in Washington, DC, and was intrigued by the possibility of partnering with the rubber tappers. With her encouragement, he flew to Brasilia to observe the meeting—and his intrigue turned to commitment. As Goma Rodrigues said, "Suddenly the discovery of extractive reserves was like the discovery of gunpowder to the environmentalists."[54]

Of course, the movement to conserve the Amazon basin needed more than the indignation of rich environmentalists from the first world. It needed Chico Mendes, a representative of the local interests for saving the forests. With the idea of extractive reserves and the persona of Mendes, the conservation message took on a different meaning—not only was the Amazon itself in peril, but so were the lives of the people who lived and worked there, following lifestyles that stretched back a century. Schwartzman wrote later, "The answer, as Chico himself saw, is that the living forest has to be worth more than cut-down, dead forest if people—rubber tappers or ranchers—are going to want to protect it over the long run."[55]

Was Mendes willing to take on the environmental mission? Absolutely. Mendes had always appreciated the connection between his fundamental interest—rubber tappers—and the preservation of the rain forest. Gradually, he recognized that his work on behalf of rubber tappers had a bigger meaning, and he stated that "the Amazon's destruction represents genocide for the peoples of the forest with negative consequences for the entire planet, for the whole world."[56] He had just not known that there was an international audience for the idea. "Our biggest assets," he now understood, "are the international environment lobby and the international press."[57]

Mendes had never been wedded to a particular philosophy in any part of his life. He was a "conciliator" according to Goma Rodrigues, able—and willing—to build alliances where others could not.[58] He united the Indians and rubber tappers, who had been in conflict for more than a century. He readily acknowledged that "the Indians were always the legitimate owners of the Amazon."[59] He insisted, "We are not enemies of one another. We should be together today to fight together to defend our Amazonia."[60] His early companion in organizing rubber tappers, Father Dom Moacyr, described a practical Mendes: "Chico was flexible, not rigid in his positions. He was never fanatical. It was a very localized, organized struggle, and it evolved from the struggle for land to the struggle for nature...."[61]

Were environmentalists like Schwartzman willing to join forces with a local movement for human rights and with its unlikely leader? Absolutely. As Schwartzman said about Mendes, "His charisma was in his convictions. Only after talking with him about the history of the struggle did I realize what an incredibly courageous man he was, and the importance of what he was doing."[62] Not only did Mendes put an engaging human face on the campaign, the reality was that environmental progress occurred in Latin America only when connected to the efforts of local people to improve their economic and social conditions. Although this might bother some environmental zealots, the linkage was essential. As stated by veteran Latin American observer Helen Collinson, "Latin Americans' concern for the environment is motivated by basic and immediate material interests.... The predominance of material motivations may mean that Latin American communities' relationship with their environments are not always as ecologically pure as environmentalists in the North might wish."[63]

Mendes became the common international spokesperson for both the environmental and rural worker movements in the Amazon. With the help of Schwartzman in March 1987, Mendes flew to Miami, where the members of the Inter-American Development Bank were meeting. Travel beyond the borders of the Amazon was new to Mendes, and he was poorly prepared to make the trip. He had no suitable clothes and no money to buy any. He was rescued by a local convent that distributed donated clothing to the poor; they found a grey suit that vaguely fit his unusual physique. At US customs in Miami, he was detained because he had no money. He told them that he "hadn't brought any dollars because I wasn't going to do any sightseeing. I wasn't on a tourist trip. I was going at the invitation of environmental groups to represent the rubber tappers of Acre and Amazonia."[64] When he got to the meeting, however, he didn't have an official invitation from the Bank, and couldn't enter. Adrian Cowell, the filmmaker, smuggled him inside with fake press credentials.

At the meeting, he stood out in his rumpled charity-store suit among the guests in tailored black-tie. But he talked to everyone who would listen. "The result was very good...," he remembered. "I went to see the executive directors of the Bank of Japan, the Bank of America, the Bank of England, the Bank of Sweden. . . ."[65] Assistance for road development in the Amazon needed to stop, he told them, because it was destroying the forest and destroying the people who depended on the forest. The Brazilian representative at the meeting fumed, but the message hit home with two crucial allies—staff members from the offices of US senators Bob Kasten of Wisconsin and Daniel Inouye of Hawaii, the Senate's leaders on foreign affairs. With their encouragement, Mendes and Schwartzman immediately flew to Washington to meet with Senator Kasten, who had grown increasingly frustrated by the development banks.

The trip was a success. "Chico went over well, a little like Kit Carson or Davy Crockett, the straight-shooting homespun backwoodsman, coming to the capital and telling what it's like on the frontier."[66] As Mendes reported, "All of a sudden, I discovered that my denunciations had important repercussions. The environmental groups had taken them seriously, and the World Bank's own commission had also taken them very seriously."[67] Within days, the Senate told the Inter-American Development Bank the United States would suspend their road-building projects in the Amazon unless their earlier promises of environmental protection were implemented. Eventually, the projects were stopped until $58 million was put up for environmental projects. Soon afterward, the World Bank announced that it would adopt extractive reserves as a primary part of its development projects.

Mendes had now reached the world stage. In 1987, his American colleagues nominated him for two global environmental awards, not just to honor their deserving friend but also to provide him a platform to carry his message further (forged press credentials weren't going to work forever). He received both awards—the UN Environment Programme's Global 500 Award and the Better World Society's Protection of the Environment Medal. He traveled again to the United States and later to England to accept the awards. In England, he was especially appreciated because he embodied the spirit of labor movements of British workers in the 1920s. He accepted both awards, not for himself, but on behalf of the workers—the rubber tappers of Brazil. His brief acceptance of the Better World Society award demonstrated his position:

I am a rubber tapper. My people have lived in the forest for 130 years using its resources without destroying it. The Amazon is the greatest biological resource in the world. We appeal to the American people to continue to require responsible environmental policies and practices of these institutions. Help us to confront these multinational corporations, including American ones, who are increasing deforestation through logging. Together we can preserve the forest and make it productive, securing this immense treasure for the future of all these our children.[68]

He was instantly and lovingly embraced by his international audiences. He exuded the attractive combination of humility and passion, his interest not in himself, but in his cause. The director of the Better World Society described him this way: "My first impression of Chico was that he was a very quiet, humble, soft-spoken guy, who did not fit the mold of a charismatic. But when he stood in front of 700 people in the Grand Ballroom and got his arms pumping, it was clear that he had the ability to light people up. . . ."[69]

In Brazil, however, the message that Mendes delivered to the world was not popular with the rich and powerful. Brazilian officials, ranchers, and other large landowners denounced him as being anti-development. The delays and changes in development projects that he caused were said to be making Brazil poor and backward. The political party that represented ranchers scoffed at his environmental awards: "That was not a medal," they said. "That was a rattle to put on a donkey's neck."[70] Death threats became more frequent and ominous, and six times he escaped from foiled assassination attempts. Friends begged Mendes to leave the forest. But he would not. "I would be a coward to do this," he said. "My blood is the same blood as that of these people suffering here. I can't run. There's something inside me that cannot leave here. This is the place where I will finish my mission."[71]

The protection of the forest and the forest workers, however, could not be ignored any longer. In 1987, fires raged across the Amazon— 170,000 separate fires by one estimate—as ranchers cleared more forest and maintained the pastures they had created earlier. By early 1988, an area twice the size of California had been cleared. Satellite images were becoming available, making the devastation visible immediately and globally. The spring of 1988 saw record rainfall, and in the absence of the forests that normally held both water and soil, floods raged through the state of Acre and elsewhere. Reporters from around the world came to see what was happening—and to interview Chico Mendes. "Our river, the Acre River, the principal river in our region, is today in danger of disappearing as a direct consequence of the deforestation," he told them.[72] The situation finally captured the attention of the Brazilian people. Newspapers and talk shows started covering both the environment and the rubber tappers. A university began teaching about tappers. And, consequently, the government began to listen. In June 1988, the Rio de Janeiro City Council gave Mendes the keys to the city, and he and the leader of the nation's Indian tribes led a parade through the city.

The extractive reserve idea was adopted by the World Bank and the Brazilian government. The first reserve was established in early 1988. Mendes considered this only a partial victory because the land was already in public ownership and, therefore, not immediately in peril. What Mendes wanted was for land titles to be bought back by the government from private landowners (a process called "disappropriation") and designated as extractive reserves. Landowners, naturally, resisted the idea.

The use of disappropriation reached the boiling point at the homestead called Seringal Cachoeira, where Mendes had grown up and worked as a rubber tapper. The land had been recently purchased by a rancher, Darly Alves da Silva, known for murder, drug smuggling, and other violent crimes elsewhere in Brazil. He had raised his two sons, Darci and Oloci, to follow in his footsteps. Alves began to log the homestead, but Mendes organized a major *empate* that stopped his efforts for a short time. Alves's men began walking the streets of Xapuri brandishing their weapons and threatening citizens. On June 18, a leader of the rubber tappers was gunned down in the streets of Xapuri. The government could no longer ignore the violence. Within two days of the shooting, government officials came to Acre and established the first extractive reserves by the act of disappropriation, taking away Alves's lands and those of two other ranchers.

Darly acquiesced in public, but secretly he seethed over the loss. He promised, "Chico won't live out the year. No one has ever bested me."[73]

Figure 5.4 The memory of Chico Mendes has remained a motivating force in the efforts to halt deforestation in the Amazon rain forest. One leader carrying on his work is Marina Silva, shown here, who served as Brazil's minister of the environment during 2003–2008.

Mendes celebrated his forty-fourth birthday on December 15, but the celebration was muted. He was convinced that he would not live until Christmas. He was right. On the evening of December 22, Darci Alves and another gunman hid in the bushes outside Mendes's home. At 5:45 p.m., Mendes was dead.

The murder of Chico Mendes might have been intended to stop the movement to protect the forest and its workers, but the effect was exactly opposite. Unlike the hundreds of assassinations that had occurred without notice in the Amazon—his murder was the ninetieth of rural activists in 1988—Mendes's death became world news. Four thousand people attended his funeral on Christmas Day, and thousands more made a pilgrimage to his home in subsequent weeks. Unlike in previous cases, both the gunman and his father were arrested, tried, and convicted of murder; they were imprisoned for several years before escaping and disappearing into the Bolivian wilderness.

The extractive reserve whose disappropriation led to his death was eventually named in his honor—the Reserva Extrativista Chico Mendes.

Brazil now has eighty-five extractive reserves covering 44 million acres.[74] Do extractive reserves work? Gomercindo Rodrigues has answered yes: "At the boundaries of the Chico Mendes Extractive Reserve, up to the place where the reserve begins, everything has been destroyed. But when you cross the barrier, you start to see forests. The extractive reserve has helped preserve the forest."[75] In 1988, fewer than 125 acres were cleared in Xapuri municipality, and deforestation across Brazil has slowed dramatically, as the government replaced its policy for forest clearing with one for forest protection.

And Chico Mendes himself became an instant symbol of the struggle of common people against tyranny—both human and environmental. "I see him as a kind of worldwide folk hero," said Al Gore, "an ecological folk hero."[76] Brazilian President Luiz Inácio Lula da Silva declared Mendes a national hero in 2004, naming him the "Patron of the Brazilian Environment."[77] Environmental institutes and other significant places have been named after him as well. Marina Silva, former Brazilian minister of the environment, 2014 Brazilian presidential candidate, and a fellow *empate* activist with Mendes, remembered him this way: "Today the historic accomplishment of Chico Mendes, with his tactful style and democratic behavior, is obvious. He organized a resistance movement that established pioneering links between environmentalists and unionists, Indians and extractivists, political parties and civic organizations, Amazonian people and the world."[78]

Figure 6.1 Billy Frank Jr., 1931–2014. (Reproduced courtesy of the Northwest Indian Fisheries Commission.)

Chapter 6

Billy Frank Jr.

The Getting-Arrested Guy

Pacific salmon are tough and persistent fish. They begin life as energy-rich eggs maturing in the gravel of a western river, as far as hundreds of miles upstream of the Pacific Ocean. After months in the gravel, the young salmon hatch and begin a grueling journey downstream. They careen over dams and through power turbines, navigate polluted and silty waters, avoid predators attacking from the water and air. The lucky survivors hit salt water and spend the next several years eating, growing, and avoiding their natural enemies in the open ocean. Then, at the trigger of some ancestral signal, they head back home, enduring a gauntlet of nets and traps set for them by commercial fishermen.

The survivors enter freshwater and proceed upstream through another set of fishermen, this time attacking with seductive baits and lures. They encounter dams again, but this time they must somehow climb over them. They fast along the way, so with each obstacle, they have less muscle and less energy to win the engagement. Yet the species persist. And each year, exhausted individuals reach their destinations and spawn a new generation that joins a continuous history of countless generations flowing back across millions of years.

The Native American Indian is like the salmon, also tough and persistent. Just as the obstacles standing in the way of salmon have multiplied over the past 150 years, so have those confronting Indians. They have endured the relentless march of colonists pushing westward. Sometimes the colonists have attacked the Indians directly with guns and swords, sometimes indirectly with disease and temptations, sometimes covertly with treaties and laws and well-meaning protective programs. Yet, the Indians persist.

In the Pacific Northwest of the United States, a comparison between the fates of salmon and Indians is more than analogy. Indians and salmon are woven together in an unbroken fabric of culture, economy, and spirituality. In the second half of the twentieth century, that fabric has been held together by a number of brave and resourceful Indians. One name stands out among the many leaders—that of Billy Frank Jr. He is revered for his tenacity and his diplomacy, for evolving from an Indian fisherman known for being arrested to a statesman known for being the champion of the salmon.

An Indian and a Fisherman

According to one calendar, Billy Frank Jr. came into this world on March 9, 1931, the only child of Willie and Angeline Frank. His father Willie was the last pureblood member of the Nisqually tribe; his mother was descended from the Squaxin Island tribe. Billy's exact birthplace is not recorded, but it was surely somewhere near the place he would call home for most of his life, Frank's Landing, on the shore of the Nisqually River, a few miles southeast of Olympia, Washington.[1]

By another calendar, however, Billy Frank Jr. has always lived and will always live. He is part of an Indian consciousness that extends backward and forward across unbroken generations. According to friend and colleague Charles Wilkinson, Frank "is best understood as a plainspoken bearer of traditions, a messenger, passing along messages from his father, from his grandfather, from those further back, from all Indian people, really. They are messages about ourselves, about the natural world, about societies past, about this society, and about societies to come."[2]

Frank's role in the conservation of Pacific salmon has been to be just such a messenger. His welcome column on the Northwest Indian Fisheries Commission website illustrated the point. "Webs, nets, networks—these are not new tools to us," he wrote. "The twenty treaty tribes of western Washington have used these tools for thousands of years. This electronic river we now all share provides a wonderful opportunity to get to know one another. Come, let us show you a little of what we are about."[3]

Frank immersed himself in learning "what we are about" from his earliest years. A keen observer of nature from the first, he studied the life of the river and the prairie around it. He grew to love and know his river from its origin on the flanks of Tahoma (known as Mount Rainier to most of us) to its mouth in the far southern end of Puget Sound. "Our river isn't like the Puyallup River," Frank observed, referring to a parallel stream a few miles north of his home. "Our river moves across that valley and back and forth. One year you'll have a place to set net and the next you won't. . . ."[4] "I have been blessed with a strong sense of place for my home, the Nisqually River. I know my place, my home. It's where I feel the best."[5]

He lived as an Indian, and he learned the Indian traditions. He knew which plants to pick for medicine—prince's pine for stomach ailments, for example—and where and when to pick them. He developed a functional theology, direct from his father. "The Creator gave us everything we have," he asserted. "That was his belief, and Mom and all of us. The Creator put that salmon there for us to survive. And all the shellfish, and this clean water, and our medicines, and all of our food, our animals. We respected all of them. We took their life because it was given to us for our life."[6]

Billy Frank Jr. reveled in a family that defied a simple family tree. Angeline was married twice and Willie once before settling into the partnership that would last to the end of their very long lives—104 years for Willie and 95 for Angeline. The family, therefore, included stepbrothers, stepsisters, cousins, nephews, and nieces that filled Billy's life with companionship. He was especially fond of his sister Maiselle, who became his lifelong ally in the defense of Indian culture and tradition.

Most of all, Billy revered his father. "My dad—he took me wherever he went," Billy recalled.[7] Whether Willie, who was known as Gramps to his entire community, was chairing a Nisqually Tribal meeting or poling a canoe down the river, Billy was in tow, absorbing his father's demeanor and wisdom. Willie taught his son to be prepared and to be patient. "My dad always told me to prepare for the salmon coming back. . . . He told me about a guy cutting a net in the dark and stabbing himself in the stomach. 'Don't be like that,' he told me."[8]

Billy's father was, first and foremost, a fisherman. Willie Frank fished for three-quarters of a century, repeating the experiences of his father and those before him. "Indians were living in paradise before the white man came. . . . Nisqually were living a perfect life," Willie said in a 1971 documentary film.[9] He and the other Nisqually caught salmon on the river in traditional ways, using fish traps that spanned the river and interrupted adult fish migrating up to spawning grounds. Later, they also used gill nets, composed of an open mesh that grabbed fish by their gills as they attempted to swim through the almost invisible nets. Frank recalled those days:

> I can picture Dad. Maybe he'd take fifty salmon. Then he'd go over to a gravel bar, lay the fish down, and butcher them right there. His dad and granddad taught him. . . . Then you take the fillets and weave three cedar sticks through them crossways. The stick up near the gills comes out on both sides so you can hang the fish on poles in the smokehouse. But you don't hang them up the first day. They'd drop off the sticks. So, you let them drip and dry out a little, overnight. Then Dad would get his fire going in the smokehouse the next morning. He'd hang the fish on poles across the eaves of the smokehouse.[10]

Billy Frank Jr., like his father, grew up to be a fisherman. As a boy, he worked odd jobs, picking crops for local farmers, for example, but in the fall he always returned to the river to spread his gill nets. He caught his first salmon at age eleven. He learned from his father, and he learned well. "When you set a gill net," he said, "you have got to have a backwater coming back up the river. . . . You can't just set a net out in swift water and expect to catch any fish."[11] He knew the right conditions to catch fish, when the river might have "just sent down the big winter freshet that gets the salmon going every year,"[12] and where an overhanging tree might provide a refuge from the sun and current.

Those were the perfect conditions that Billy, fourteen years old, found on the river one December morning in 1945. He had started to fish at night, to avoid the prying eyes of game wardens who stalked the riverbank in search of Indians who, they claimed, were fishing illegally. Billy had set his gill net overnight in just the right place, and under the cover of predawn darkness, he returned to claim a harvest of steelhead and chum salmon. He retrieved his catch and, as his father had taught him, began to butcher the fish on a gravel bar.

Suddenly, flashlights glared out at Billy through the darkness, blinding him. Two game wardens closed in on him. They called out to Billy, "You're under arrest."

Billy ran, but the wardens soon caught up to the boy, burdened in his escape by bulky hip waders. As he struggled with the men, Billy shouted, "Leave me alone, goddamn it! I fish here! *I live here!*"[13]

Trouble began for Billy Frank Jr. on that cold morning in 1945, but the stage had been set on a similar December day ninety-one years earlier.

The Treaty of Medicine Creek

A century before Billy Frank Jr.'s first arrest, the land that became the state of Washington was just coming into focus for Americans. For the first few decades of the nineteenth century, this area had been jointly colonized and administered by America and Britain. Most settlers during this period were British, however, and the commerce of the region was dominated by the Hudsons Bay Company, operating on behalf of the British monarchy. Headquarters for the company was a rough village, Fort Nisqually, near the mouth of the Nisqually River.[14]

For the first white settlers who called this place home, it was, as Willie Frank described it a century later, a paradise. The climate was mild, fish and game were abundant, the soils of the prairie deltas were deep and productive, and the forest yielded high-quality wood for many purposes.

Glaciers and snowpack on Mount Rainier melted slowly in the spring and summer, feeding the short coastal rivers with a reliable supply of cold, clean water.

The native residents, of course, knew their home was paradise. They had lived there forever—at least 10,000 years, according to archeologists—in a benign environment that required no migration, expansion, tribal rivalry, or conquest. They had evolved a lifestyle supported by fishing, farming, and forest resources, with strong artistic, cultural, and spiritual practices. Tribes were many and small—Nisqually, Puyallup, and eighteen others are recognized today within the region—typically split into a series of small villages dotted along a riverbank or lakeshore.[15]

Paradise began to change when England and the United States chose to separate their interests. The nations divided the territories along the 49th parallel north in 1846, with the United States taking the southern portion, designated the Oregon Territory. British interest in the region declined, and the influx of "Bostons," as Indians called American settlers, began soon after. Immigration was encouraged by the Donation Land Act of 1850, which allowed white men over the age of eighteen to claim 320 acres in the Oregon Territory for free, if they settled there.

US law, however, also required that title could not be given to settlers until a treaty had been signed with the resident natives, ceding their control of the lands to the US government. Such treaties had not been accomplished in the Oregon Territory, so homesteaders were acting illegally. The Indians objected, and conflicts arose. When representatives of the homesteaders went back to Washington to seek help, they noted the territory "is alive with Indians, who keep up a most provoking and unceasing broil about the lands which they say the 'Bostons' are holding without a proper and legitimate right and title."[16]

To solve this problem, US authorities decided to divide the huge and unwieldy Oregon Territory into two pieces. The new territory to the north was to be called the Washington Territory, and it needed its own government, including a governor. The post was not attractive to most government careerists—it meant living in uncivilized country, populated with potentially hostile Indians, thousands of miles from the seat of power; succeed and no one would notice, fail and perhaps die. One man took this as a challenge, however, and he petitioned newly elected President Franklin Pierce for the job. At the age of thirty-five, Isaac Ingalls Stevens became the first governor of the Washington Territory.

Stevens was a military man who had graduated first in his class at West Point. He served with distinction in the Mexican–American War in the late 1840s. He was self-confident, decisive, brave—and, most of all, ambitious. His biographer labeled him a "young man in a hurry."[17] Stevens arrived in late 1853 and established his territorial government in Olympia, Washington. He had one crucial task as the new governor: sign treaties with the Indians.

Stevens' first treaty negotiation began with his closest neighbors, the members of the Nisqually, Puyallup, and Squaxin Island tribes. More than 600 members of the three tribes assembled with government officials for a tribal council on December 25, 1854. They convened on the banks of Medicine Creek, a traditional gathering place of the Nisqually people. Because the tribes lacked written language, the content of the treaty was recited orally so that all tribal members could hear and understand. Throughout Christmas day and into the next, Stevens talked and the Indians listened. On December 26, in what is now seen as a rushed process, sixty-two Indians signed the treaty for the assembled tribes. Governor Stevens signed for the United States.

The treaty was similar in most ways to others. The three tribes ceded 2.5 million acres of their homelands; each tribe retained ownership of 1,280 acres as their "reservation." The treaty included several other conditions that gave the US government the upper hand if its needs changed in the future.

One portion of the 1854 treaty is particularly important. Article 3 reads, in its entirety, as follows:

> The right of taking fish, at all usual and accustomed grounds and stations, is further secured to said Indians in common with all the citizens of the Territory, and of erecting temporary houses for the purpose of curing, together with the privilege of hunting, gathering roots and berries, and pasturing their horses on open and unclaimed lands; Provided, however, that they shall not take shellfish from any beds staked or cultivated by citizens, and that

Figure 6.2 Billy Frank Jr. was first and foremost and always a fisherman on the Nisqually River. (Reproduced courtesy of the Northwest Indian Fisheries Commission.)

they shall alter all stallions not intended for breeding-horses, and shall keep up and confine the latter.[18]

The first twenty-eight words of Article 3 are the important ones. They allow Indians to retain their opportunity to fish where they had always fished, without limit. These words, understood differently by Indians and state officials, have been at the center of a century of imprisonment, conflict, violence, debate, and court proceedings. Indians held that they could fish where and how they had always fished, whether on their reservation or not, and without restrictions. Once fisheries management began in the first decades of the twentieth century, however, the state of Washington insisted that their rules for conserving fish stocks—regulation of fishing seasons, equipment, and catch—applied to everyone, Indians and non-Indians alike.

Indian fishing, therefore, found itself in the crosshairs. Willie Frank was first brought into custody on charges of unlawful fishing in 1916. As the years passed and the conflicts escalated, Willie was known to shout at the government officials who chased him, "I've got a treaty. . . . The Treaty of Medicine Creek in 1854 with my people. . . . I'm Willie Frank, Nisqually Allottee No. 89."[19] Willie persisted in his demands to be allowed to fish until, in 1937, a federal court issued an injunction that prevented state officials from taking action against him and other Nisqually fishermen. The confrontations cooled down after that, while the country focused on escaping from the Depression and winning a world war. After the war, however, attention again turned to the issues of Indian fishing, and from then on, the focus was a new generation of Indians, personified by Billy Frank Jr.

The Getting-Arrested Guy

Perhaps the conflict between Indian and non-Indian fishermen would never have reached a crisis had Pacific salmon remained abundant and widespread. But that wasn't to be. After World War II, Pacific salmon felt the full brunt of a prosperous and growing nation.

Dams may be bad news for salmon, blocking their migrations, but America began building dams with all its might. Construction of big dams—those taller than fifty feet—began at the turn of the twentieth century and accelerated in the 1950s, largely to provide the electricity and water to fuel a booming economy. Home building also surged after the war. Returning soldiers expected to realize the American dream of owning a home to accommodate their growing families, and the nation was eager to help. One strategy was to increase timber harvest on the large national forests that blanketed Oregon and Washington; private forest owners were also eager to oblige. Loggers harvested trees right to the banks of the streams, unrestrained by the environmental laws that today require streamside buffers. Consequently, sunlight reached the streams directly, raising water temperatures dramatically, and sediment washed freely into the streams, suffocating salmon eggs and young fish. Much later, Frank told the now-familiar tale of habitat degradation:

> As tribal people we have told stories for a long time, and we have to keep telling our stories, . . . because they are the stories of all of us. They document the story of environmental change resulting from increased population growth, polluted stormwater runoff, climate change, urban growth, and the diking, filling, and armoring of our rivers, estuaries, and shorelines. These factors have, over time, led to a transformation of the landscape that degrades the ecosystem functions necessary to provide the clear, cool, free-flowing water that salmon need.[20]

Fishermen caught fewer salmon each season, and Indians caught the blame. After all, Indians could ignore the state's rules and regulations, whether on their reservations or not. Indians put up fences made of tree branches that blocked streams, seemingly preventing almost every migrating fish from reaching their spawning grounds. This was bad enough for commercial species, like chum salmon, but was unconscionable when the target was steelhead trout, a salmonid classified as a recreational species. "The Game Department people thought that it was basically blasphemous for anyone to be catching steelhead with nets and selling them," recalled Indian attorney Tom Keefe.[21] Data later showed that Indians caught only a small fraction of the total, but facts were not important—finding someone to blame was.

In response, the state conservation agencies ramped up their enforcement. For game wardens, sworn to uphold the laws of the state, enforcement "was a holy crusade and they would give no quarter. They saw these Indians as renegades who were flouting state conservation laws, sensible and valuable laws that had been adopted for good reasons. They saw this lawless Indian conduct as a main reason the runs had crashed."[22]

Billy Frank Jr. grew up in the midst of this ongoing battle. He lived at Frank's Landing, which had become the epicenter of most of the conflicts between enforcement agents and Indian fishermen. He quit school after the ninth grade so that he could contribute to the family income. In the spring and summer he did heavy construction work on roads and sewer systems, and, of course, he fished in the fall and winter. The family made their income from selling fish at Frank's Landing, as well as sneaking in cigarettes, firecrackers, and alcohol from neighboring states and selling them on the black market. Billy was regularly hassled by enforcement agents and occasionally arrested.

In 1952, he accomplished one of his dreams by joining the US Marine Corps. "I took real pride in that, the discipline, the hard training. I was in good physical condition, always have been," he said.[23] He served a two-year hitch as a military policeman at Camp Pendleton, California. "Billy is a patriot," recalled a friend. "He was ready to go to Korea and put his life on the line."[24] During his military service, he married his first wife, Norma McCloud.

Far from home, the couple began drinking heavily, an affliction that dogged Frank for more than twenty years. Back at Frank's Landing after his tour ended in 1954, he worked as a lineman, constructing power lines throughout the region. He was often away from home for months on end, the loneliness and tedium feeding his need for alcohol. His addiction plagued him until his sister Maiselle convinced him to enter a treatment facility in 1974. He never touched alcohol again.[25]

Frank was regularly arrested for fishing during these years. No one knows how many times he was arrested, although most sources say more than fifty times. "I lived on the river and I fished on the river. So, they'd take me to jail and nobody would know I went to jail," Frank recalled.[26] "It was nearly a daily event to get hassled by those guys. It was a good day if you didn't get arrested. After a while, I didn't even bother to tell people at the Landing because they already knew; 'If we don't come back home, call C. J. Johnson.' He was the bail bondsman."[27]

Arrests were troublesome, but the Indians didn't usually stay in jail long. "When we first started going to jail, they put us in with all the other people that was in jail. . . . They'd always ask us: 'What are you guys in for?' 'We're in for fishing.' 'Fishing? What the hell are they doing? We're here for robbing a bank and killing somebody.'"[28] When Frank didn't come home, family members typically pawned some fishing equipment and went back to the courthouse to bail him out.

The real problem was confiscation. Wardens often seized the catch when they arrested the fishermen, and even worse, they took away nets and sometimes boats and motors. "We were fighting for our life," Frank recounted. "We fished. We sold our fish. We ate fish. That was what we did. You go down there and there ain't no fish. There ain't no boats. There ain't nothing."[29] Without their catch, their winter food supply was gone. Without their fishing equipment, the Indians' livelihood was gone. "So that really pisses you off, you know? So you do whatever you got to do."[30]

The confrontations about treaty fishing rights were episodic, occurring mostly during the late fall and winter when the fish ran, and retreating into the background during the rest of the year when families turned to other ways of supporting themselves. When there was trouble, though, it often centered around Billy Frank's home: "But during the runs, Frank's Landing was hyperactive, white hot. The surveillance was continuous. There were scores of raids, many of them—preserved both in front-page photographs and a great amount of film footage—ugly, heartrending brawls. In time, the banks of the Nisqually merged with the schoolhouse steps of Little Rock, the bridge at Selma, and the back of the bus in Montgomery."[31]

The emerging role of Billy Frank Jr. during these years is hard to pin down, but it was crucial to the struggle for Indian fishing rights. Whenever something was happening, Frank was generally there—in a canoe, on the riverbank, and, then, in jail. "I was not a policy guy. I was a getting-arrested guy," he admitted.[32]

While others might turn sullen or discouraged, however, Frank was different. He was a natural diplomat, making friends wherever he went. Frank loved people, all kinds of people. He greeted people with a smile, a firm handshake, and often a hug. Frank's sons described him as resilient in the face of trouble, letting insults and criticism bounce off and always searching for a better way forward. His youngest son, Willie, said, "It doesn't matter how people treat him. He's always going to treat them with respect."[33]

Washington governor Dan Evans remembered that "Billy was the guy who very quickly started to say, 'This isn't working. We've got to find a better way.'"[34] In 1963, Frank gained a partner in the cause of fishing rights, and together they did find that better way.

Hank Adams and Judge Boldt

For Americans alive at the time, November 22, 1963, is unforgettable—the day that President John F. Kennedy was assassinated. For Hank Adams, an Assiniboine-Sioux Indian from eastern Montana, it was particularly memorable. That day, Adams, a college sophomore with limitless academic potential, walked off the campus of the University of Washington in dismay and disbelief. He never looked back. From then on, he devoted himself, directly and completely, to improving the lives of Native Americans.[35]

When Adams walked off the Seattle campus, he walked into the offices of the National Indian Youth Council, a radical group promoting Indian rights. He became a special-projects director, organizing events to showcase the plight of Indians across the country. He focused on Indian fishing. Adams brought a new weapon to the cause—the media. With a background in law and policy, skills in communications and networking, and a fearless sense of duty, Adams moved the issue from the banks of the Nisqually River and the local jail to the nation's front pages and living rooms.

Adams made certain that Indian fishing rights stayed in the national consciousness. At Adams's urging, actor and civil rights activist Marlon Brando came to support Indians in the early spring of 1964. Brando, who later turned down an Academy Award in protest over Indian treatment, went fishing. He got in a boat, and then he remembered that "someone gave us a big salmon we were supposed to have taken out of the river illegally and, sure enough, a game warden soon arrived and arrested us."[36] All this time, the television cameras rolled, and the nation learned about the "fishing wars."

Adams's media campaign never waned. He convinced television journalist Charles Kuralt to cover Indian fishing on his CBS national broadcast. African American comedian Dick Gregory and his wife were regular supporters—and regular arrestees. Adams provided the impetus for a documentary, *As Long as the Rivers Run*, by filmmaker Carol Burns.[37] Along with confrontations with game wardens and poignant statements by Indians (Maiselle Bridges, Billy Frank's sister, says, "In 1964, we decided we wasn't going to move any-more"), the documentary shows Indian women clinging to their fishing nets, being dragged out of the water and up the bank by game wardens.

The time was ripe for America to rise up against this kind of treatment of Indians. The 1960s and early 1970s was an era of awakening across the nation, as the country addressed segregation, women's rights, poverty, the Vietnam War, and issues of free speech and personal freedom. Indian issues expanded far from just fishing rights, and the unfair treatment of Indians caught the attention of socially conscious youth. "Perhaps most important, the cause of the Nisqually and other Northwest tribes had acquired a dignity, a moral content that was understood and appreciated by a great many Americans."[38]

Hank Adams was usually in the background, pulling the strings, and his role was instrumental. "When Hank came into the fishing rights struggle, the Indians were disheartened, disorganized, and certainly demoralized. In the decade in which he has been active, the situation has completely reversed," wrote Vine Deloria, another Indian leader of the time.[39] He has been called the "most important Indian" for his dogged and effective work on behalf of Indian rights and communities.[40] His friends consider him a genius, even a "mad genius." Syndicated newspaper columnist Jack Anderson warned the nation not to be fooled by Adams's gentle demeanor. "He speaks softly, too, as the Sioux once trod. . . . His gentle manner, nonetheless, was but the moss on a character of granite."[41]

For his efforts, Adams was hounded by the FBI and, some suspect, by the CIA. "His phone had so many clicks on it, it sounded like music."[42] He was once shot in the abdomen while protecting a friend's nets. The shooter was never apprehended, but Adams knew his foe. "I can't identify him, but hell, I've seen him before, in a thousand taverns, in a thousand churches, on a thousand juries."[43] Yet Adams never shrank from the task before him. "His primary occupation was explaining Indian history and treaty rights to Indian people and anyone else who'd listen," wrote another admirer.[44]

Billy Frank Jr. said, "Hank shoots for the stars, and that's what he's been doing his whole lifetime. We're just tagging along."[45] Once Frank and Adams got together, they were virtually inseparable, speaking daily, the two as close as brothers. The combination of Adams's analytic, legal,

Figure 6.3 Billy Frank Jr. and Hank Adams (right) made an unstoppable team that changed the course of Native American fishing rights. (Reproduced courtesy of the Northwest Indian Fisheries Commission.)

and communication skills with Frank's fishing heritage and diplomacy changed the way Indian fishing rights were pursued.[46]

With Billy Frank Jr. in front of the cameras and Hank Adams behind them, the stakes rose and the game changed. A series of high-profile court cases, assisted by the legal strategy of Hank Adams, began to establish binding precedents on Indian fishing. The US Supreme Court ruled in 1968 that Frank's earlier arrests for fishing on the Nisqually and the arrests of other Indians for fishing on the Puyallup were legitimate. But the court also reasoned that the state could only regulate Indian catches as long as the purpose was conservation, not discrimination against Indians. Indians knew that the state was discriminating against them—Indians took only a few fish, long after commercial and recreational fishermen had filled their nets—and so they remained undeterred in their fishing and their demands for justice.

The next case, filed in 1968 and decided in 1969, reversed the field. Richard Sohappy, a highly decorated Indian soldier on leave from his second tour in Vietnam, was arrested for illegal fishing on the Columbia River. The federal court found this time that the state was at fault for failure to recognize the treaty rights of Indian fishermen; the judge further declared that the Indians deserved a "fair share" of the fish catch, although he didn't define what a fair share was.

Meanwhile, the fight for fishing rights continued on the riverbank. Indians kept fishing, sometimes under the cover of darkness, sometimes in the bright sunlight of the media. Adams once estimated that the state of Washington conducted at least thirty major operations against Indian fishermen during the late 1960s.

In one poignant demonstration, Billy Frank Jr. and his fellow fishermen hoisted an American flag on the pole at Frank's Landing. The flag had once covered the coffin of Frank's brother-in-law, who had died in battle during World War II. "Our people have fought and died for the United States and we have an agreement with it to fish these grounds. We plan to do so . . . and this flag will give us courage," stated Indian organizer Janet McCloud.[47] But they flew the flag upside down—"a signal of dire distress in instances of extreme danger to life or property."[48]

The defining confrontation occurred on September 9, 1970. Indians had set up camp on a small patch of land on the Puyallup River, near Tacoma. As the salmon began their upstream migration, the Indians set their nets, as they had done for millennia. A large crowd gathered— supporters from across the Pacific Northwest—to defend the Indian nets from state and local police. "We are fishing! We're armed and prepared to defend our rights with our lives!" shouted Billy Frank's sister, Maiselle Bridges.[49]

"The State of Washington came down on us that day, just like they had done many times before, to stop us from exercising our treaty right to fish," Frank wrote later.[50] This day the conflict escalated beyond the usual. Guns fired. Fire bombs exploded. A railroad bridge burned. Tear gas engulfed the Indians. "It felt like someone put a lighter up to your face," recalled Frank's niece Alison.[51] Police attacked, and Indians fought back. More than sixty people were jailed.

"But someone else got gassed that day, too," recalled Frank. "His name was Stan Pitkin, the US attorney for western Washington. He was part of the crowd that gathered that day to watch the event unfold."[52] Pitkin didn't like what he saw. Nine days later, on September 18, on behalf of the United States government and in support of Billy Frank Jr. and his fellow Indian fishermen, Pitkin filed suit against the State of Washington for ignoring the Treaty of Medicine Creek. "A lot of people were getting shot at, and Stan Pitkin . . . said, 'We need to do something to stop this.'"[53]

George Hugo Boldt, a federal district court judge for western Washington, was assigned to the case of *United States v. State of Washington* in 1970. "He was a slight, gray-haired man who wore a bow tie."[54] He was known as a strict but fair judge who was willing to take on the tough cases but brooked no foolishness in his courtroom. In the beginning, opinions differed on whether Boldt was an asset or a liability to Indian interests. He was not Indian, and he had no experience in Indian law. Hank Adams initially tried to have Boldt removed from the case, fearing that his background and demeanor would make him unsympathetic to the Indians' position. Fortunately for the Indians, Adams failed.

The suit was filed in 1970, but suffered years of delay by legal maneuvering. The delays gave Boldt time to dig deep into Indian history and law, reading "all the great decisions on Indians and fishing rights. Over and over again, all the great minds who dealt with the problem of Indians put in their opinions that we were taking away from the Indians their rightful heritage."[55]

The trial itself lasted only three weeks in the fall of 1973, with more than fifty witnesses resulting in 4,600 pages of transcripts.[56] Billy Frank Jr. testified, as did his father, then ninety-five years old. Frank appreciated the way Boldt conducted the trial, stating: "That judge listened to all of us. He let us tell our stories, right there in federal court." A prominent law professor observed, "He educated himself and came to what he believed was the truth. He was strong-minded enough that he would apply simple justice."[57]

Boldt issued his 208-page ruling on Valentine's Day in 1974. He ruled from a fundamental commitment to the validity of the treaties and a moral persuasion about their interpretation. Relying on legal precedents going back nearly a century, he reasoned that treaties should always be read as Indian signers would have understood them and that interpretations should never disadvantage the Indians. Boldt wrote in his decision: "And we (the court) have said we will construe a treaty with the Indians as (they) understood it and as justice and reason demand. . . ."[58]

The specifics of Boldt's decision sent tremors through the fishing world. Yes, the treaties were intact and operable for all the tribes of western Washington. Yes, the Indians had the right to fish where they always had fished, and they could use whatever methods they wished. No, the State of Washington did not have authority to regulate their fishing, because federal law superseded state law. Yes, he would define the Indians' "fair share" of the catch: half of the total catch of the salmon runs on the rivers they fished; not the 5 percent they were currently catching, but 50 percent. And most importantly for the future of the salmon, yes, the Indians had equal authority, with the state, to manage the fisheries. The victory was complete—treaty rights and Indians had won, the state had lost.

State fisheries officials and non-Indian fishermen were livid. They burned Boldt in effigy. The state refused to enforce the decisions. An official of the US Fish and Wildlife Service reportedly said, "My God, we've got to appeal!" But then his assistant reminded him, "Wait a minute, you can't appeal. You won!"[59] The state could appeal, however, and it did. But in each case—once in a federal court of appeals and twice at the US Supreme Court—the judges agreed with Boldt completely. Now, without question, the Boldt decision was the law of the land. Billy Frank Jr. understood that this "is one of the biggest decisions of our time—in US history, in world history."[60]

From Activist to Statesman

The Boldt decision changed Billy Frank Jr.'s life. Hostilities didn't stop immediately, but there was now a bigger need for Frank. He spent less time on the river and more time in meeting rooms. He stopped drinking and getting arrested. His personality—persistent and friendly, bent on partnership rather than conflict—made him the leading advocate for Indian fishing and for the conservation of salmon.

Hank Adams believed that the most important part of the Boldt decision was not the allocation of 50 percent of the catch to Indians, but rather the responsibility given to the Indians to co-manage the fishery. He summed up the situation this way: "We refuse to be treated as just another class or classification of fishermen who happen to be Indian. If the State must deal with us, let them deal with us in our collective sovereign capacity, as Nations of Indian People; and let us maintain our relationship to the fishery resources in that capacity. Only in that capacity can we maintain our responsibilities to resources and all our people for all time; only in that capacity can we fulfill our contract with our children, born and unborn, our own contract to their future."[61] In that statement, Adams outlined the connection that transformed the justice of honoring fishing treaties from a civil rights issue into a conservation issue. Billy Frank Jr. described it a bit more directly: "I've been talking a lot lately about the connection between salmon, habitat, and treaty rights. That connection is pretty simple. No habitat equals no salmon; no salmon equals no treaty rights; and no treaty rights equals a breach of contract between the tribes and US government."[62]

The responsibility for co-management meant that the Indians needed to get organized. In order to implement that responsibility, President Nixon issued an executive order in 1974 establishing the Northwest Indian Fisheries Commission. (Hank Adams drafted the order for Nixon.) The commission's constitution makes clear its purpose and approach: "We, the Indians of the Pacific Northwest, recognize that our fisheries are a basic and important natural resource and of vital concern to the Indians of this state, and that the conservation of this natural resource is dependent upon effective and progressive management. We further believe that by unity of action, we can best accomplish these things, not only for the benefit of our own people but for all of the people of the Pacific Northwest."[63]

Except for a short interval in the late 1970s, Billy Frank Jr. served as chairman of the commission for more than thirty years. In that position, his influence grew regularly. Adams observed that the leaders of the day "started to know him personally in their own sphere of activity or in their boardrooms, as in the cases of banks, or in the cases of Rayonier or Weyerhaeuser, and in the government offices at the highest levels in the Congress. And knowing him on a personal, face-to-face level, they discovered they liked him."[64]

Frank understood that the time had come for change. "The fighting, that is, the fish-ins and demonstrations, is over now," he told a reporter at the time. "Now we have to sit down and be reasonable. The State is a reality we must deal with for the sake of the people and the resource."[65] He took on the title of "fishery manager" for his tribe, and he and Hank Adams wrote the first fishery plan for the Nisqually River.

Fishery management became essential to following the law. The need to allocate half the catch to Indians meant that the state and the commission had to know how many salmon were available for capture. To know that, they needed to model the fish populations and the rates of harvest. And because of this need for active co-management, the conservation profession probably knows more about Pacific salmon fisheries than any significant fishery in the world. Research, monitoring, and real-time regulation have become standard practice in the Pacific Northwest and a case study for other fisheries around the country and world.

Frank said that the tribes needed to work with the state, and, eventually, the state realized that it needed to work with the Indians. In 1982, Bill Wilkerson was promoted to director of fisheries and began a journey of reconciliation. "I've been to court seventy-eight times. We won three of them. . . . So, I personally think it's kind of ridiculous, this process that we've been sucked into, or nailed ourselves into," Wilkerson explained to the governor.[66] In 1984, the State of Washington and the Indians began—sincerely—to implement the intent of the Boldt decision.

Each spring, the two responsible groups gathered together to forge a harvest agreement. Wilkerson credited Frank with their success. "Billy was just the glue in a lot of ways. He kept the tribes coming to those discussions. . . . I made sure that my . . . staff was in the room. We just kept working on it. We didn't get to leave until we had agreement on the season."[67] The meetings have now been institutionalized as the "North of Falcon process." Frank explained why it works: "While the process for setting salmon seasons through NOF is highly complex, the rules for getting there are simple: Be polite and try to meet each other's needs while protecting weak and ESA-listed salmon stocks and ensuring that enough adult salmon escape harvest to sustain the next generation."[68] The State of Washington agrees, explaining that the process's "guiding principle is that much more can be done to strengthen, preserve, and restore salmon and steelhead resources by working together in a cooperative manner."[69]

Figure 6.4 As the years went on, Billy Frank Jr. became the leading national spokesperson for Native American fishing rights—and for the conservation of the fish upon which those rights depend. (Reproduced courtesy of the Northwest Indian Fisheries Commission.)

Frank and Wilkerson also knew that salmon would never recover unless a bilateral harvest agreement was made between the United States and Canada. Once again, Billy Frank Jr. proved to be the difference in getting a deal. "He was so respected in the Canadian delegation because they had a tribal delegation. He was Billy Frank to those people, one of the top tribal leaders in North America," recounted Wilkerson.[70] The Pacific Salmon Treaty was signed by President Reagan and Prime Minister Mulroney in March 1985.

The next issue was timber harvesting. Commercial forestry was big business in the Pacific Northwest, and logging had proceeded with little regulation. Frank and Wilkerson worked together again, this time with representatives of the timber industry. "Six months and sixty meetings later, the Timber, Fish, and Wildlife Agreement was announced on February 17, 1987. The new pact over the use of Washington's tree-covered landscape struck a balance among competing interests and spurred an historic shift in how Washington managed its natural resources."[71]

Frank always believed that a fish hatchery was necessary to help restore the salmon runs and to provide fish for harvest. An analysis by the US Fish and Wildlife Service revealed that the best place for a hatchery was on a tributary of the Nisqually, Clear Creek, a few miles upstream from Frank's Landing. The trouble was that the site sat in the midst of Fort Lewis, the sprawling army post that has bordered the Nisqually River since 1919. Skeptics said the army would never give up the land, but Frank found a way. A persistent and natural negotiator, he persuaded the army to trade the land for the hatchery in exchange for two small Indian holdings within the base. Fort Lewis ceded the land, and Congress appropriated money to build the hatchery, which opened in 1991; today, a local utility pays the annual operating expenses, and Fort Lewis maintains the access.

Frank's ability to work with Fort Lewis epitomized his ability to work with anyone, anywhere:

> You have to understand their mission. The army's mission is to train troops, not to cut trees. We've had long talks with their generals and colonels about their mission and ours. Now they're an ally. The army is a much better land manager than the Forest Service.
>
> You can deal with the army. The commanding general is the boss. It's not like the governor or the president or the secretary of interior. When I talk to those guys, I don't know who the hell's in charge. But when I go across the river to Fort Lewis, I know who's in charge. When he tells his soldiers, "Don't drive any more tanks across Muck Creek," or "Don't poison that lake anymore," or "Let those Indian people collect their medicines"— that's what's going to happen. Boy, that is powerful. When you've gotten a handshake with the general—boy! It's been very positive over the past twenty years.[72]

Frank had his detractors, of course, and some think the spotlight shone too brightly on him while ignoring the impacts of others. And indeed, the spotlight did shine on Frank. As the *New York Times* would later report in its obituary of Billy Frank, "Mr. Frank was transformed from an outlaw to a voice of wisdom and authority, a national figure recruited to serve on boards and commissions."[73]

He was friends of every president since Carter, and he has been likened in his impact and demeanor to Barack Obama. He received the American Indian Distinguished Service Award in 1989, the Martin Luther King Jr. Distinguished Service Award for Humanitarian Achievement in 1990, the Albert Schweitzer Award for Humanitarianism in 1992, and the inaugural American Indian Visionary Award in 2004.[74] Hawaii Senator Daniel Inouye nominated him for the Nobel Peace Prize in 2010.[75]

Despite all this, Billy Frank's first and continuing passion was always the restoration and management of Pacific salmon. "You know, you have to give a lifetime to what I'm talking about. You can't be here today and gone tomorrow," Frank said. "The directors of the federal government, the directors of the State of Washington, they've retired. And I've watched them. I went to their retirement ceremonies. They've all left. They've left us with poisons. Us tribes, we can't leave."[76]

Billy Frank Jr. died unexpectedly and quietly on May 5, 2014. But he didn't leave us. As he had written sometime earlier, "We're the advocates for the salmon, the animals, the birds, the water. We're the advocates for the food chain. We're an advocate for all of society. So what you do is, you do what you can for your lifetime. Then that'll go on to another lifetime. Then another lifetime. Then another."[77]

Nor did the awards stop, even with his death. In 2015, President Obama awarded Billy Frank Jr. the Medal of Freedom, America's highest honor for civilians. Among the scores of remembrances about Billy Frank Jr., from presidents, governors, senators, and other leaders, this tribute, from Jeff Shaw of the North Carolina Justice Center, rings particularly true:

> If you care about the US Constitution, you should care about Billy Frank. If you're concerned with honoring oaths and the dignity of keeping your word, you should be glad he lived. If you fight for social justice in any capacity, you had a fellow traveler. If you're concerned about the fate of the planet we're leaving to our children, you owe him a debt.
>
> And if you have a beating heart in your chest, as God is my witness, you would have loved him.[78]

Figure 7.1 Wangari Muta Maathai, 1940–2011. (Photograph: © Martin Rowe.)

Chapter 7

Wangari Maathai

The Green Crusader

he trumpet fanfare rang out loudly on December 10, 2004, in the Oslo City Hall. Guests in the crowded chamber stood to applaud the procession of dignitaries as they walked to the front of the room. Ole Danbolt Mjøs, longtime chair of the Nobel Committee, approached the podium.

"The Norwegian Nobel Committee has decided to award the Nobel Peace Prize for 2004 to Wangari Maathai for her contribution to sustainable development, democracy, and peace."

After the cheering subsided—it rang much longer and more joyously than usual—Mjøs explained the committee's choice. "Peace on earth depends on our ability to secure our living environment. Maathai stands at the front of the fight to promote ecologically viable social, economic, and cultural development in Kenya and Africa. She has taken a holistic approach to sustainable development that embraces democracy, human rights, and women's rights in particular. She thinks globally and acts locally."[1]

Wangari Maathai beamed in a gold-colored gown that, like the woman herself, blended traditional and modern styles. Her selection as the Peace Prize recipient was historic. She was the first African woman to receive the prize. And the first African honoree not involved directly in defusing armed conflict. And the first person to be awarded the prize for commitment to the environment. And, most important, the first recognition that a peaceful and just world is only possible if that world is also sustainable.

Beyond these remarkable firsts, Maathai herself was also an unlikely Nobel Laureate. She had lived and worked for most of her life in Kenya, laboring among rural women in village after village of her native land. Her organization, the Green Belt Movement, was small and independent, never part of government, never part of any large, multinational organizations that tend to get attention in the nonprofit world. She was "not an economist, a social scientist, or a political theorist"; she was a biologist.[2]

All she had done, it seems, was plant trees. First a few trees, then many trees—50 million trees in Kenya and uncounted millions more in other African countries. Those trees began to heal the earth around them and the communities that tended them. In time, as she stated in her Nobel lecture, "The tree became a symbol for the democratic struggle in Kenya. . . . The tree also became a symbol for peace and conflict resolution. . . ."[3]

When asked how people everywhere might honor her recognition as a Nobel Peace Prize Laureate, her reply was simple—and expected: "Plant a tree."[4] This request, one she had made countless times before, barely hinted at the unstoppable force embodied in a remarkable woman who planted trees.

Child of the Soil

Wangari Muta was born on April 1, 1940, the eldest daughter of a typical Kikuyu family living in the highlands of south-central Kenya. She grew up in the village of Ihithe, near the provincial capital of Nyeri. Her parents were farmers, a heritage that stretched back into prehistory. This region of Kenya was a cornucopia, providing amply for the nutritional needs of the local Kikuyu people. The climate was temperate, with plentiful rainfall and clean-flowing streams. "Hunger was virtually unknown," Maathai remembered. "The soil was rich, dark red-brown, and moist."[5] Farmers grew food mostly for their own use, taking advantage of the diversity of fruits and vegetables that sprang naturally from the land.

The Kikuyu, the largest ethnic group in Kenya, understood the connection between their livelihood and the land. Symbols of reverence to nature surrounded them. Mount Kenya, the second-highest peak in Africa and sacred to the Kikuyu, loomed in the near distance. They built their homes so that the doors opened to greet the mountain. As a girl, Maathai thought the world ended at the top of the two ridges that rose above her home, and that God lived at the top of them. The giant fig tree near the village was also sacred; ceremonies took place under its broad canopy, and villagers approached it only barefooted. "My mother told me very clearly when I was a child that I was never to collect twigs for firewood from around the fig tree near our homestead since, she said, it was 'a tree of God.'"[6]

The traditional first meal of a newborn baby was not breast milk, Maathai recalled, but a special juice that blended local products: "green bananas, blue-purple sugarcane, sweet potatoes, and a fattened lamb, all fruits of the land." That meal made her not only a child of her parents, but also a literal "child of my native soil."[7]

Such customs and beliefs, however, had undergone radical change in Kenya and across Africa in the late nineteenth and early twentieth centuries. Maathai's grandparents had been illiterate, their heritage transmitted in stories told and retold around the cooking fire. Her parents, however, grew up in an entirely different world. By the early 1900s, missionaries from Britain and other European countries had blanketed the region, bringing Christianity, literacy, and modern lifestyles. Her parents were of the first generation to convert to Christianity; in addition to being Kikuyu, they were also called *athomi*, or people who could read. Maathai observed: "It must have seemed like a new form of magic that overshadowed what Kikuyus had known until then. Reading and writing fascinated them and they embraced it with a passion."[8]

British occupation also disrupted the communal economy. Imposing foreign concepts of land titles and individual ownership, colonists stole the land from the native peoples. They supplanted subsistence agriculture with plantations of tea and other crops for export, employing the disenfranchised native Africans as wage-earning laborers. "A nearly complete transformation of the local culture into one akin to that of Europe had taken place in the generation before I was born," Maathai recalled.[9] Her father, like many others, moved away from the family in order to work on plantations and in urban areas. Maathai's family was lucky. Her father, well known and well regarded locally, became a mechanic for a sympathetic British landowner. Their relationship eventually led to a gift of farmland assuring that the family would always stay just a step ahead of poverty.

Kikuyu fathers remained aloof from their families, but mothers were close to their daughters, especially the eldest. "When you are the first girl in a Kikuyu family, you become almost like the second woman of the house. You do what your mother does and you are always with her. The two of you become almost like one. As far back as I can remember, my mother and I were always together and always talking. She was my anchor in life."[10]

Because women did most of the family-oriented farming, Maathai also spent many hours in the fields, enchanted by her experiences. "At that time," she remembered, "nothing in life was more pleasant than to be asked to take the animals into the fields."[11] She reveled in nature and "loved listening to the birds around our homestead and learning their names."[12] In her own small garden, she said, "When my beans produced flowers, I loved seeing the bees and the butterflies. . . ."[13]

Her family moved several times during her youth as they were buffeted by the changing economy and colonial rules about where and how native Kenyans could live. The family finally settled in the market town of Nyeri, a day's journey from the capital city, Nairobi, when Wangari was eight years old. One of her brothers asked her mother, "How come Wangari doesn't go to school like the rest of us?" After a moment's reflection, her mother answered, "There's no reason why not."[14] And so Wangari became a student—a lifelong avocation. "When I finally learned to read and write, I never stopped."[15]

She progressed from elementary to middle grades, boarding at a Catholic school in Nyeri. By the age of twelve, she had been thoroughly immersed in European culture. Her home life of farming, food preparation, dancing, singing, and storytelling was replaced by a school life of books, studying, prayer, and sports. She dressed in European clothes, spoke only English (because using a native language was cause for punishment), accepted Christianity, and was christened with a Western name, Mary Josephine.

Most girls finished middle school and returned home, but Wangari, who graduated at the top of her class, received a position at Loreto Girls' High School in Limuru. Loreto was the only Catholic high school for girls in Kenya, and the privilege of attending was not lost on her. "Even though I was a good student, I was more hardworking than naturally bright," she conceded.[16] The hard work paid off, and she again graduated at the head of her class. Most girls leaving high school became teachers or nurses, but that wasn't for her. With a will and a determination that would never waver, she said, "I am not going to be either of those. I'm going to Makerere University."[17] She loved science and was determined to become a scientist. Her desire for a university education would be fulfilled, but not as she expected.

During her school years, Kenya—and much of Africa—was immersed in a struggle for independence. The European nations that had claimed and subdivided Africa were slowly relinquishing their control. In Kenya, the path to independence began with the Mau Mau Rebellion, a civil uprising that erupted in 1952 and led to devastating armed conflict between the Kikuyu, who led the Mau Mau, and the British. By the end of a decade of brutal conflict, independence was assured—and nation-building could begin.

In the United States, experts on foreign affairs realized that this nation-building would require educated and responsible native leaders, and that the emerging governments needed to see America, not the Soviet Union, as their friend and mentor. Among those far-sighted Americans was Senator John F. Kennedy. "Education," he said, "is, in truth, the only key to African independence and progress."[18] He became aware of a program that was paying to bring bright Kenyan students to the United States for a university education. When the program appeared to be in jeopardy for lack of funding, Kennedy convinced his family to fund the flights—the "Kennedy Airlift," it has been

Figure 7.2 Wangari Maathai consults with rural Kenyan women about planting trees as part of the Green Belt Movement in 1983. (UN Photo/ Jackie Curtis.)

called—and cover educational expenses for hundreds of East African students.

Wangari Maathai was one of these fortunate students. "I was in the right place at the right time," she recalled.[19] She and her classmates landed in New York City in September, 1960, awestruck by the high-rise buildings, escalators, and elevators. ("Going to New York City was like landing on the moon," she later wrote.[20]) From there, the students dispersed to schools around the country. Maathai and a few others boarded a Greyhound bus bound for Atchison, Kansas, where they enrolled at Mount St. Scholastica College for girls.

She loved her time at college and in the United States. Her teachers were both kind and resourceful; her classmates and the town residents were friendly to their new African neighbors. Although the liberal ways of America were a shock at first, she grew to embrace them. She liked American styles that flattered her tall, slender figure. "By the time we graduated," she admitted, "we were fully Americanized."[21]

Being Americanized meant challenging much of what she had experienced as a child in Kenya. She learned to "listen and learn, to think critically and analytically, and to ask questions."[22] She observed that dancing with a boy or holding a boy's hand, forbidden back home, were allowed in the United States, even in the presence of nuns. An open and informal lifestyle coexisted with religious practices in the United States, and she couldn't understand why Kenyans had to choose one or the other.

She continued her study of science, majoring in biology. During summers, she interned at a medical laboratory in Kansas City, preparing tissue samples. Encouraged by her teachers, she entered a master's program at the University of Pittsburgh, completing her degree, again in biology, in 1965. Her advanced degree attracted the attention of officials from the University of Nairobi who were scouring the United States to find Kenyan university graduates for positions back home. Maathai was offered a position as a research assistant; she accepted the offer and happily planned her return to Kenya as the calendar turned over to 1966.

She was a different woman now than the young student who had ventured to the United States almost six years earlier. She was independent and confident, now a blend of her rural Kenyan heritage and her modern education. She abandoned her Westernized name and became Wangari Muta again. "When I left the United States, I was taking back to Kenya five and a half years of higher education, as well as a belief that I should work hard, help the poor, and watch out for the weak and vulnerable."[23]

Kenya was also a different place than when she had left. The country had celebrated its independence on December 12, 1963, after three years of a gradual transition from British colonial rule to full self-determination. A democratically elected president was bringing hope to the country. A rising economic tide was lifting all boats. And an extraordinary young woman was ready to join the new order.

You Don't Need a Degree to Plant a Tree

When Maathai reported for her first day of work in January 1966, however, she was struck by the reality that, in many ways, Kenya had not changed at all. Men still ruled, nepotism was still rampant, and power still trumped laws. Although she held a letter giving her the job as research assistant, when she reported to work she was told that it had been filled already—awarded to a man from the supervisor's tribe. Despite her appeals to higher officials at the university, the decision stood. She lamented, "I realized then that the sky would not be my limit! Most likely, my gender and my ethnicity would be."[24]

Shaken, but not bowed, she spent months looking for a similar position while camping on friends' sofas. A visiting professor from Germany's University of Giessen, recruited to establish a department of anatomy in the University College of Nairobi's veterinary school, hired Maathai because of her experience preparing tissue samples back in Kansas City—the kind of merit-based hiring that Maathai had expected.

She thrived in the anatomy department, breaking gender barriers as she went. She learned to use an electron microscope, a rare skill for a man or a woman in Kenya. She taught classes, overturning the usual practice that only male faculty taught male students; she was a serious teacher who demanded—and got—respect in the classroom. Her supervisors sent her to the University of Giessen in 1967 to study electron microscopy and anatomy in greater detail; she stayed for twenty months. On her return to Kenya, she began work on her PhD, finishing in 1971 and becoming the first woman in East or Central Africa to hold a doctorate. Promotion followed promotion until she finally became the head of the Department of Veterinary Anatomy—once again, she was the first woman in the region to achieve such a high position.

Her personal life progressed in tandem with her academic career. She bridged the traditional and modern Kenyan lifestyles, enjoying the urban nightlife of the capital city while retaining a strong connection to her rural family. A succession of nieces and nephews migrated to Nairobi to live with her, and she started a small retail store to employ them. She became engaged to her future husband, Mwangi Mathai, also a beneficiary of the earlier Kennedy Airlift to the United States. While she was away studying in Germany, he looked after his fiancée's store—and built it into a thriving business. They married in 1969, holding both Kikuyu and Christian services. A son soon followed, joined later by two daughters. These were busy and happy years for Wangari—helping her husband, raising three children, and pursuing her academic career.

"Luckily, I enjoyed using my potential and I had a lot of energy. Then, I could move like a gazelle...."[25]

Her happiness evaporated, however, under the stress of bridging modern and traditional lifestyles. Although her husband often declared that he honored his wife's high levels of education and achievement, he constantly strove to outdo her success. He ran for Parliament, initially losing but eventually being elected. Although he supported Wangari publicly as his equal, both he and his constituents expected a more subservient, domestic kind of wife. He privately chafed that Wangari was "too educated, too strong, too successful, too stubborn, and too hard to control."[26] One day in 1977, she returned home to find the house empty—her husband had deserted her. She was shocked by his actions and their impact on her life, later observing that "nobody warned me—and it had never occurred to me—that in order for us to survive as a couple I should fake failure and deny any of my God-given talents."[27]

At the time, a Kenyan divorce required a court hearing. In the hearing, Mwangi falsely accused his wife of adultery, and the judge ruled hard against her. Mortified, she challenged the judge as being either ignorant or corrupt. The judge ordered her arrest for slander, and she was immediately hauled off to jail—her first of many experiences with imprisonment. She was released after three days, having provided a satisfactory apology to the court. Maathai saw this as a turning point in her understanding of how life unfolded in Kenya, and maybe everywhere:

Far from beating me down, however, this message gave me strength. I knew I'd done nothing wrong. I had not acted maliciously, arrogantly, or criminally. And look what had been done to me! Despite my wrenching experience, something positive may have come out of it for other women who faced divorce in future years. Because many men saw that I remained resolute in the face of the pressure put on me, they realized that if they wanted to divorce their wives it would be best, for themselves as well as for their children and families, if they did it fairly and respectfully.[28]

Wangari met this change in her life the same way she met all the conflicts and obstacles that lay ahead. "When pressure is applied to me unfairly," she wrote, "I tend to dig in my heels and stand my ground—precisely the opposite of what those applying the pressure hope or expect."[29] She could not keep her husband's name, but neither did she want to abandon the name by which she was widely known. In typical fashion, she found a unique solution. She added an extra "a" to Mathai, and became Wangari Muta Maathai, the spelling of her name by which we know her today.

Both during and after her marriage, Maathai was driven to succeed in her career and to contribute to her country's well-being. (She later remarked that "not having a husband had been a blessing, because she could not have accomplished all she had with a husband—at least not the one she had married."[30]) Because of her status as one of the most educated and successful women in Kenya, she was often asked to join civic organizations. She became a leader of the Kenya Association of University Women, the Kenya Red Cross, and—most importantly for her future—the National Council of Women of Kenya (NCWK). Her influence increased in 1973, when the United Nations established its new Environment Programme and headquartered it in Nairobi. A companion organization, the Environmental Liaison Centre, was also established in Nairobi to allow civil society organizations to collaborate with and advise the new UN agency. Most Liaison Centre board members, who came from around the world, chose a local alternate to serve in their place when they could not be present. Maurice Strong, a leading environmentalist from Canada, chose Maathai to represent him. From this position, she could now see the world in its entire breadth and depth, and the rest of the world could see her. She eventually became chairwoman of the board, a position she held for a decade.

Throughout this time, trees occupied an ever-increasing part of Maathai's life. While still married, she first implemented the idea of caring for trees as part of fulfilling her husband's campaign promise to provide jobs for local people. Although he abandoned the promise after being elected to Parliament in 1974 (it was a campaign promise, he said, so no one expected him to really do anything about it), her commitment to the poor and her entrepreneurial streak sparked an idea. She formed a private company, Envirocare, that employed workers to tend the lawns, shrubbery, and trees of the wealthy. The business struggled for some time before failing, the victim of her husband's disinterest, unmotivated workers, too few clients, and an extended drought.

Later, Maathai's university duties also stimulated her interest in trees. She ran a project that monitored tick-borne diseases of livestock; the project took her on extended journeys throughout rural Kenya. She was appalled at the living conditions she saw in the countryside. Rather than the healthy and prosperous communities of her youth, she saw destitute families racked by malnourishment and disease. Farmers had quit growing crops for their own food, instead converting their forests and fields into plantations of tea, pine, and other crops for export. Their food now came from the store, and their incomes were insufficient to pay for the nutritious diets their families needed.

At the same time, the conversion of native forests to plantations had devastated the environment. Fields had eroded, streams had dried, firewood was scarce, and much natural biodiversity had disappeared. Maathai felt the loss everywhere, but no more than in her home village. The fig tree that her family had held sacred was now gone, sacrificed to the long, straight rows of a tea plantation. In her Nobel acceptance speech, she took time to

> . . . reflect on my childhood experience when I would visit a stream next to our home to fetch water for my mother. I would drink water straight from the stream. Playing among the arrowroot leaves I tried in vain to pick up the strands of frogs' eggs, believing they were beads. But every time I put my little fingers under them they would break. Later, I saw thousands of tadpoles: black, energetic, and wriggling through the clear water against the background of the brown earth. This is the world I inherited from my parents. Today, over fifty years later, the stream has dried up, women walk long distances for water, which is not always clean, and children will never know what they have lost.[31]

Native forests were also being wrenched from the ground to be replanted with massive fields of exotic pines and eucalyptus. She remembered "seeing huge bonfires in the forests as the indigenous biodiversity was burned to make way for the commercial tree plantation."[32]

Maathai eventually put the pieces together. "I listened to rural women in Kenya listing their problems. I could see that all the challenges they had were rooted in a degraded rural environment."[33] She understood that the Kenyan people were "threatened by a deteriorating environment. . . . The connection between the symptoms of environmental degradation and their causes—deforestation, devegetation, unsustainable agriculture, and soil loss—were self-evident."[34]

And the solution seemed self-evident as well. "It just came to me," she recalled. "'Why not plant trees?'"[35] Planting a tree was a task that could be done by one person or a small group. It was tangible, and the benefits were obvious. "When you plant a tree and see it grow, something happens to you," she said. "You want to protect it, and you value it."[36] In Kenya, the rewards came quickly: a tree grew to maturity in just a few years, supplying fruit, wood, shade, and soil protection.

The idea of planting trees as civic engagement, however, was not immediately popular. After she was elected to the executive committee of the NCWK in 1977 and began chairing their environmental committee, Maathai suggested that the group take on tree planting as a project. She recounted the inspirational examples of green cities she had witnessed at a UN meeting in Vancouver the previous year, envisioning a similar restoration of the Kenyan countryside. Her fellow board members were skeptical, though, especially since they believed that planting trees needed the expertise of professional foresters. She presented an argument that became a staple for the movement: "You don't need a diploma to plant a tree."[37]

In the absence of any better suggestions, the council relented and endorsed the project. It was first called "Harambee," a Swahili word meaning "let us all pull together"; Maathai convinced them to expand the title to "Save the Land Harambee." The goal was to stop desertification and reestablish the forests of Kenya.[38]

Maathai and her colleagues planted their first trees in a Nairobi city park on June 5, 1977, the fifth anniversary of the first World Environment Day. Their early plantings all had themes, and the first theme honored seven fallen national heroes. Maathai stated that she "felt deeply that the leaders who had sacrificed so much on our behalf were part of our history, and that they deserved our respect and honor for their extremely significant and selfless contributions." Two of those original trees survived for at least forty years.[39]

The second tree planting came the following September, as part of the UN Conference on Desertification that was meeting in Nairobi. Not content with just a few trees this time, Maathai and her supporters planted rows of trees ("green belts") on the outskirts of Nairobi as a demonstration of how forests could slow soil loss and erosion. This planting received extensive publicity across Africa and the world. Requests flooded in from communities throughout Kenya, asking for help—where could they get seedlings, and how should they care for them? With the momentum of growing grassroots demand, the Council of Women was now fully behind Save the Land Harambee.

From the beginning, Maathai was the driving force behind the tree-planting effort. Without pay and without sanction or affiliation with other groups, she spent all her available time nurturing the plants and the program. She kept the focus on rural communities and the work that women could do to grow and plant trees where they lived. Originally, government tree nurseries agreed to supply their extra trees to Maathai, anticipating that the demand would always be small. Within a year, however, the movement's needs overtook the capacity of the state nurseries, and the government backed out. Undaunted, Maathai organized local tree nurseries run by women themselves. They gathered seeds from local trees, planted and cared for them, and eventually transplanted them into fields and forests.

At first, the program sought help and advice from the country's professional forestry staff. Behind Maathai's back, the officials scoffed at the program, convinced that only a trained forester could manage a tree nursery. They reluctantly ran seminars for the women, but their insistence on using technical language and complicated horticultural protocols soon wore out their welcome. "Then came the revolution," wrote Maathai. "The women decided to do away with the professional approach to forestry and instead use their common sense! After all, they had for a long time successfully cultivated various crops on their farms. What was so difficult about applying this knowledge to tree planting?"[40]

The women, she was sure, knew how to plant trees. She had a clear for-mula: "Here is the basic method: Take a pot, put in the soil, and put in the seeds. Put the pot in an elevated position so that the chickens and the goats don't come and eat the seedlings."[41]

For the next five years, Maathai balanced her university career and leadership of the tree planting activity, now organized as the Green Belt Movement. Its goal was simple: "to raise the consciousness of com-munity members to a level that would drive them to do what was right for the environment because their hearts had been touched and their minds convinced—popular opinion notwithstanding."[42] To stay true to the mission of helping rural communities, they produced all program materials in local languages, and they trained future participants in their home villages to make the training as convenient as possible.

Eventually, she and her staff formalized the program into a ten-step process. The first three steps helped local women form into a team, learn about the principles of tree care, and, most importantly, appreciate their own fundamental role in community development. The fourth step was establishment of a tree nursery, including finding and preparing the site, gathering seeds, planting the seeds, and caring for the seedlings. They grew only native trees, including fig, banana, citrus, papaya, avocado, mango, nandi flame, acacia, thorn, and cedar. Step five was regular data collection about the status of the seedlings and monthly reporting to the offices in Nairobi; often local men who could read and do basic math were given this role, assuring their buy-in to the projects. Steps six and seven were announcing the availability of seedlings, selecting places for them to be planted, and preparing the holes to accept the plants. In step eight, seedlings were distributed and planted. Step nine documented the survival of seedlings through the first few months, and step ten verified how many had survived at least six months. The Green Belt Movement then paid a small stipend to the community for each surviving seedling.[43]

In 1982, Maathai suffered another personal blow. She had decided to run for Parliament, sensing that she could contribute more to her country from an official position in government. However, because university employees could not run for public office, she resigned her university position. Then a technical discrepancy between her residence and her intended constituency made her ineligible to be a candidate. She returned to the university immediately to rescind her resignation,

but in an eerie coincidence with her first promised job, the department had refilled her position the same day she resigned. The following day, police evicted her from her university-supplied house. "I had no job and no salary," she recalled. "I had no pension and very few savings. I was about to be evicted from my house. Everything that I had hoped for and relied on was gone—in the space of three days. I was forty-one years old and for the first time in decades I had nothing to do. I was down to zero."[44]

What seemed bad for Maathai at the time turned out well for Kenya. She threw herself full time into being the volunteer director of the Green Belt Movement. She explained, "The rest, as they say, is history. I never looked for another job, since strengthening and expanding the Green Belt Movement as its coordinator became my work and my passion."[45]

The results have been inspirational. Trees survived and grew, providing food, fuel, and healthier environments. A successful campaign to open new nurseries led to reducing the travel distance for the women, giving many more an opportunity to participate. By the mid-1980s, Maathai reported, "nearly two thousand women's groups were managing nurseries and planting and tending trees, and more than a thousand green belts were being run by schools and students."[46] These numbers continued to swell; eventually there were more than 4,000 tree nurseries and more than 50 million trees planted. A goal thought to be impossible at the program's start—"one person, one tree"—has been surpassed by 10 million trees.[47]

But other changes were occurring as well, as Maathai described in her Nobel lecture:

> So, together, we have planted . . . trees that provide fuel, food, shelter, and income to support their children's education and household needs. The activity also creates employment and improves soils and watersheds. Through their involvement, women gain some degree of power over their lives, especially their social and economic position and relevance in the family. . . . Entire communities also come to understand that while it is necessary to hold their governments accountable, it is equally important that in their own relationship with each other, they exemplify

the leadership values they wish to see in their own leaders, namely justice, integrity, and trust. . . . Through the Green Belt Movement, thousands of ordinary citizens were mobilized and empowered to take action and effect change. They learned to overcome fear and a sense of helplessness and moved to defend democratic rights.[48]

Tree Planter to Green Crusader

Maathai's dedication to restoring and protecting the environment— implemented through the planting of trees—eventually put her in conflict with her government. At its core, the Green Belt Movement was about empowering average citizens, especially women. This concept was far from the agenda of President Daniel Moi, who was in power during the time (1978–2002) when Maathai was building the Green Belt Movement. Moi ruled with an iron hand, allowing only a single political party and muzzling the national media. The corruption that had plagued Kenya throughout the colonial period continued under Moi. There was no democracy, no investment in the people, no freedom of expression, and certainly no empowerment.

Maathai challenged all that when she learned about a massive project to be built inside Uhuru Park in downtown Nairobi in 1989. Uhuru— which means "freedom" in Swahili—is the Kenyan equivalent of New York City's Central Park. Only about thirty-five acres in size, it provided a green oasis amidst the towering buildings of the rapidly developing capital city. Small buildings and monuments had chipped away at the park's borders for decades, but this new project dwarfed all of those. President Moi proposed to build a sixty-two-story office building in the park, accompanied by a four-story statue of himself. Maathai was dismayed: "This building will cost 200 million dollars, which the ruling party—the *only* party—proposes to borrow mostly from foreign banks. We already have a debt crisis—we owe billions to foreign banks now. And the people are starving. They need food; they need medicine; they need education. They do not need a skyscraper to house the ruling party and a 24-hour TV station."[49]

Wishing to know more details about the plans, Maathai began writing letters to government officials. She received no responses, and fences went up in the park and construction equipment rolled in. She expanded her letter-writing campaign, now asking foreign embassies and the United Nations to intervene. Eventually the Western press began running the story—her polite inquiries had grown into an international issue.

The Kenyan government had power on its side, however, and they turned it full-force on Maathai. A meeting of Parliament on November 8, 1989, devolved into name calling. The Green Belt Movement was accused of being a bogus organization used by Maathai to promote her fame and line her pockets. Her plea for people to speak their mind about the project was "ugly and ominous" and deserving of court action. One member said, "I don't see the sense at all in a bunch of divorcees coming out to criticize such a complex."[50] Ground was broken for the project one week later.

Attacks on Maathai accelerated. President Moi gave a speech in Uhuru Park in which she remembered him "suggesting that if I was to be a proper woman 'in the African tradition'—I should respect men and be quiet."[51] A prominent women's group, under the thumb of the ruling party, denounced her. A public speech made by a party official led to public chants of "Remove her! Remove her!"[52] Friends began to avoid her, fearing reprisals. The government ordered an audit of the Green Belt Movement's books for the previous five years. Sure of her honesty, Maathai sent ten years of records. Of course, Maathai held her ground: "It was okay for me to be called crazy and told that I had insects in my head: That is the way people using their own mirror saw me. But I offered women a different mirror—my own. What is important, indeed necessary, is to hold up your own mirror to see yourself as you really are."[53]

The government evicted the Green Belt Movement from the dilapidated offices they occupied in a forgotten corner of the main police station—with just twenty-four hours' notice. The next day, police destroyed everything Maathai had been unable to move out. Unable to find space elsewhere (no one would take on this woman and her organization under such a cloud), Maathai had no other choice: she moved the Green Belt

Figure 7.3 In 1999, Wangari Maathai confronted armed guards at the entrance to Karura Forest in Nairobi, where she was protesting the illegal giveaway of public forestlands. (Reproduced courtesy SIMON MAINA/ AFP/Getty Images.)

Movement into her own house. Keeping two small bedrooms for herself and her children, she converted the other rooms and areas outside into offices for the staff of eighty. The driveway held filing cabinets. For the next seven years, the Green Belt Movement and Maathai lived together.

Persistence was one of Maathai's greatest traits. She seldom gave up on anything, and she never gave up on preserving Uhuru Park. "Fortunately, my skin is thick," she explained, "like an elephant's. The more they abused and ridiculed me, the more they hardened me. I know I was right, and they were wrong."[54] A year after the ground was broken, the government announced new plans for a smaller project. After another two years, in early 1992, the construction fences disappeared, and so did the project. Maathai and her supporters danced in victory, hanging a wreath "at the site to declare the project dead and buried."[55] Uhuru Park remains today a vibrant part of Nairobi's open space.

The battle for Uhuru Park elevated Maathai from the leader of a rural environmental group to a national political figure. People began calling her the Green Militant or the Green Crusader. She had become an advocate for freedom and rights, comparing her interests to the traditional three-legged African stool: "The first leg represents democratic space, where rights—whether human, women's, children's, or environmental—are respected. The second leg symbolizes the sustainable and accountable management of natural resources both for those living today and for those in the future, in a manner that is just and fair, including for people on the margins of society. The third leg stands for what I term 'cultures of peace'. These take the form of fairness, respect, compassion, forgiveness, recompense, and justice."[56]

The Green Belt Movement evolved along with Maathai. She used the tree-planting context to plant the seeds of democracy and freedom in rural communities. She "realized it was necessary to enlarge the Green Belt Movement's conception of conservation to include a recognition of cultural heritage and the consequences of its loss, how and why culture was important, and how its neglect manifested itself in the ways the public reacts to the environment, and even to life itself."[57] In seminars with rural women, she used her now-famous analogy to riding on a bus. If you get on the wrong bus, she told her listeners, you won't go where you want and you will encounter problems when you arrive. Rather than accepting that situation, when you are on the wrong bus, you need to get off and find a new bus. She believed her audience generally understood her message and agreed: "Individuals in the seminars are usually unanimous in their opinions: they *are* on the wrong bus."[58] Maathai encouraged them to question their leaders, acknowledge their own ability to change their circumstances, and join together for the common good.

But trees always remained central to her passion for a more democratic and free Kenya. In 1990, after a large rally for the pro-democracy Saba Saba movement led to a violent response by the government, Maathai and her supporters planted a grove of trees in Uhuru Park to memorialize the victims. Despite repeated attempts by the government to destroy the trees, they survived. "The rains would come and the sun would shine and before you knew it the trees would be throwing new leaves and shoots into the air. These trees, like Saba Saba, inspired me," she remembered. "They showed me that, no matter how much you try to destroy it, you can't stop the truth and justice from sprouting."[59]

Kenya remained deeply authoritarian, however, and Maathai was a hated enemy of the state. Friends begged her to stay in New York after a conference, because they feared she would be assassinated upon her return to Nairobi. Indeed, after she did return, the government targeted her and several colleagues who had formed a minority party. They scattered, and she remained underground for several days, moving among friends' homes to avoid detection. She eventually reached her own home, barricading herself behind the strong steel doors and iron-barred windows of the house. For three days, police laid siege, countered by hundreds of protesting citizens who had gathered to support Maathai. The police finally cut their way into the house with saws and bolt-cutters, and captured Maathai.

For the second time, she was arrested and this time charged with capital offenses of sedition and treason. She was held in a damp, cold cell without a blanket and sanitary facilities, where she was unable to sleep or eat. Long-term arthritis in her knees made her unable to walk to her court appearance, and after posting bail, she was taken by ambulance to the Nairobi hospital for care. Demoralized and wondering if she would ever walk again, her strength returned when she saw a banner held by supporters that declared, "Wangari, brave daughter of Kenya, you will never walk alone again!"[60] Beleaguered by worldwide criticism of her arrest, the government soon dropped all charges against her and her colleagues.

Maathai continued to challenge Kenya's authoritarian government throughout the early 1990s. On behalf of mothers whose sons were political prisoners, she organized a protest encampment in Uhuru Park. After several days, government forces moved in to disperse the crowd. Maathai was knocked unconscious and left bleeding from gashes in her head. Again, the protesters persevered, sleeping in a nearby church for more than a year; Maathai stayed with them. Eventually, with pressure from the world press, fifty-one sons of the mothers were released. Later, she intervened to stop a series of ethnic clashes in rural Kenya that were being fueled by the government. The Green Belt Movement held seminars for the conflicting communities, aimed at exposing the truth. Those efforts again made her an assassination target, labeled as an enemy of the state. She went underground for many months, moving from safe house to safe house, often transported in diplomatic cars in the dark of night. Police routinely showed up at her home to break up meetings, but a group of informers usually kept Maathai one step ahead of the authorities.

In the 1990s, the Green Belt Movement redirected its energies to focus on a severe environmental problem—forest protection and preservation. Planting new trees on private land was important, but even more crucial was maintaining and improving the forests that remained. Kenya's forests had declined from over 10 percent of the country's land area to less than 2 percent, the result of plantation agriculture and urban development.

Combatting this problem again put Maathai in harm's way. Embedded in government corruption was the practice of land-grabbing—giving away public lands, mainly forests, to wealthy political supporters of the regime. The Karura Forest, a 2,500-acre woodland just outside Nairobi, became a lucrative site for such landgrabs. Maathai and the Green Belt Movement protested at the forest gates repeatedly, usually by the peaceful action of planting trees to replace those cut by the new landowners. Standoffs with police and private security forces were common. Not to be dissuaded, Maathai used ingenious ways to enter the forest, including a trek through an unfenced, unguarded border that crossed a wetland. She recalled the event: "A group of about twenty—the women hitching up their dresses, the men rolling up their trousers, and all of us removing our shoes—stepped into the wet ground, using the footprints of our guide in front of us. I was armed with my watering can, and the press was with us, too."[61]

Their efforts at Karura Forest were eventually noticed. The headquarters of the UN Environment Programme was at the edge of the forest, and their staff took up the cause. Clashes continued, however, including a violent encounter in early 1999 that left Maathai clubbed and bleeding from a large laceration on her neck. Undaunted, as usual, she signed the police report with her own blood. And as usual, Maathai's perseverance won out, as the president announced that year the end of all public-land giveaways.

Figure 7.4 Wangari Maathai doing what she always did—planting a tree. Here, she planted a tree at United Nations headquarters in New York in 2005. (UN Photo/Evan Schneider.)

Always Forward

Wangari Maathai knew only one direction: forward. And she seldom fretted about where that forward motion might take her. "Throughout my life," she wrote, "I have never stopped to strategize about my next steps. I often just keep walking along, through whichever door opens. I have been on a journey and this journey has never stopped. When the journey is acknowledged and sustained by those I work with, they are the source of inspiration, energy, and encouragement. They are the reasons I kept walking, and will keep walking, as long as my knees hold out."[62]

Like other conservationists profiled in this book—Rachel Carson, John Muir—Maathai had not intended to follow the path of an environmental and societal reformer. "I never saw myself as an activist," she conceded. "When all this began I was a very decent professor at the

University of Nairobi. I was a good girl. But once I started I realized activism was a necessity. As we moved further and deep into it we kept finding doors closed, so we had to force those doors open."[63]

As the century turned over, many new doors opened. By then, the Green Belt Movement and Maathai were internationally famous. Awards from around the world kept arriving, hardly missing a year from 1990 onwards.[64] As a consequence, the government continued to soften its views toward Maathai. At last, she was now being honored, rather than demonized, in her own country.

Maathai ran for Parliament in 2002—and was elected overwhelmingly, with 98 percent of the vote. Soon after, she was appointed an assistant minister for environment, natural resources, and wildlife. Her political career, however, had mixed results. She hoped to advance the role of tree planting for the country and to reestablish respect for traditional values and cultures, but she often met resistance. "I know what the ministry should do," she admitted, "but I can't say it. The minister has to buy that idea, and do it and say it. I try to be persuasive, but [things are] not moving as fast as I would have liked."[65] Her political independence also led to conflict with the existing political parties and the president, who expected loyalty to their common Kikuyu heritage, regardless of whether she agreed with their policies or practices. She resigned from her ministerial position in 2005 and lost her parliamentary reelection bid in 2007, with little progress made.

Receiving the Nobel Peace Prize in 2004 was, of course, the honor of a lifetime. The best outcome was that it gave her a platform for expressing her profound understanding of the need to sustain the earth. Columnist John Vidal for the *Guardian* newspaper remembered one interaction: "Her fierce denunciation of the rich North, that day, was shocking: 'The top of the pyramid is blinded by insatiable appetites backed by scientific knowledge, industrial advancement, the need to acquire, accumulate, and over-consume. The rights of those at the bottom are violated every day by those at the top.'"[66]

Maathai believed, therefore, that Africa needed to take command of its future. "Africa has been on her knees for too long," she wrote, "whether during the dehumanizing slave trade, under the colonial yoke, begging for aid from the international community, paying now-illegitimate debts, or praying for miracles."[67] She believed that Africa needed to modernize in order to control its economy rather than just ship raw materials to other countries, which made products and then shipped them back at higher prices. And was there a trade-off between environment and development? "I always say no. We need and must have both; what is important is a good balance between the two."[68]

Vidal also noted how she worried that notoriety would take her away from her passion to be with the women of rural Kenya. "She was wary of ping-ponging around the world to give inspirational talks to presidents and parliaments. She knew she was in danger of being captured by the very elites she worked so hard to overthrow, but, she said, there was no other way to effect change."[69]

Not notoriety, but cancer took her away on September 25, 2011. "Sometimes you don't have enough time," she wrote in 2010, "and too much needs to be done. I have come to accept that you cannot do everything, and no one should expect you to—including yourself."[70]

She needn't have worried that fame would take her away from her roots. Seldom has a world leader been as grounded as Wangari Maathai. Her *New York Times* obituary stated, "Dr. Maathai was as comfortable in the gritty streets of Nairobi's slums or the muddy hillsides of central Kenya as she was hobnobbing with heads of state."[71] She recognized "that she earned only a tenth of what she could earn on the international market," but commitment to her fellow Kenyans came first.[72] Her entire life was spent working in the soil, surrounded by the women whom she loved and who loved her. The proof is planted all over Kenya and throughout Africa—and in the lives of more than 900,000 rural women who have benefited from the Green Belt Movement. As one of those women said, "I am so thankful for the knowledge of the Green Belt Movement. I alone could not make it. Because of the knowledge I have gained from the Green Belt Movement, I am now able to dress well, sleep well, eat well, and to do anything."[73]

Perhaps the best proof of what Wangari Maathai did accomplish was symbolized in 2004, just after learning that she had been chosen to receive the Nobel Peace Prize. She was driving between stops in

Kenya, en route to a local hotel for the evening. News of her selection had preceded her arrival, and a crowd of admirers had gathered. She greeted the applauding crowd with a request—for a shovel. And she planted a tree.

Figure 8.1 Gro Harlem Brundtland, b. 1939. (Reproduced courtesy of Colorado State University, photograph by John Eisele.)

Chapter 8

Gro Harlem Brundtland

Godmother of Sustainable Development

The party had been a great success. A lovely wedding, good friends, delicious food, excellent red wine, and, for a time, a welcome Friday evening pause in the hectic life of a minister of the environment. April in Norway could be beautiful, and this particular evening glowed with the promise of spring.

Until 11:55 p.m., that is, when a messenger approached with a serious look: "Telephone for Gro."[1] An unexpected call at midnight strikes fear into the heart of a mother—or a cabinet minister. Fortunately, the children were fine. Unfortunately, the North Sea was not.

An offshore oil-drilling platform—the *Ekofisk Bravo*—had malfunctioned. Oil and gas were spewing high into the air, just like in old movies about Texas wildcatters. Gro Harlem Brundtland immediately switched gears, from relaxed wedding guest to focused leader. "I was concentrating so intently. . . . I recognized the feeling from my days as a doctor when I could be awoken in the middle of the night to deal with a serious accident or a patient suddenly entering crisis."[2]

Two hours later, details began to emerge. The blowout was raging uncontrolled. Miraculously, no explosions or fire had occurred, and all 115 workers on the platform had escaped without injury. The problem was a safety device that had been installed upside down, causing it to malfunction when a "kick"—an unexpected entry of gas or fluid into a well—rocketed up the pipe. The platform was 200 miles offshore, so there was no immediate threat to the coast, but high seas were hampering efforts to stop the rupture or contain the spill.[3]

Saturday morning passed in a flurry of intense activity—continuous updates from the oil field, conversations with other cabinet officials and the prime minister, notifications to other North Sea nations, establishment of a local action team, briefings with the owner of the platform and licensee for the Ekofisk oil field, Phillips Petroleum. In the afternoon, she flew with the prime minister to the site.

Brundtland took control, as usual, making decisions with the confidence of a medical doctor and the aplomb of a politician. Yes, of course, she would take all questions from the press. Yes, Phillips Petroleum needed to prepare to drill relief wells, regardless of the cost. No, they would not be allowed to use chemical dispersants. No, Norway was not going to stop offshore oil drilling in the North Sea. One journalist, normally a critic of Brundtland's party, admiringly summed up her demeanor: "Look at her as she takes her place before the cameras, completely at ease and relaxed, lovely as a jewel, nerves and brain cells under complete control. She speaks concisely, always to the point, seriously, but unsentimentally, and yet with a tough optimism that many of her male colleagues from the world of politics might envy her, instead of indulging themselves in a mixture of hysteria and opportunistic point-scoring."[4]

On April 22, 1977, a generation before the *Deepwater Horizon* oil spill made history in the US waters of the Gulf of Mexico, Norway had experienced its first marine oil spill. In the next few days, the blowout would become the largest ever in the North Sea and, at the time, the largest-ever marine spill in the world. The actions of Minister of the Environment Gro Harlem Brundtland ended the disaster quickly: she brought in the famous American oil-well firefighter Red Adair to help—and he succeeded in short order, reportedly telling the minister, "Don't worry, baby. I'll fix it."[5] The success planted Brundtland firmly in the hearts of her fellow Norwegians as the leader of environmental sustainability. She was someone who could be trusted to do the right thing, the right way.

As one journalist described, she was a "Viking warrior incarnate, smiting others down not with the sword but with the strength of her beliefs."[6]

Brundtland's reputation for environmental stewardship grew continuously over the coming years, until not just Norwegians but people across the world saw her as a beacon for hope. Along the way, she earned a number of affectionate labels that expressed the world's trust, admiration, and confidence in her—the Green Goddess, Earth Mother, Mrs. Green, and Godmother of Sustainable Development. In Norway, she became the nation's Landsmoderen—Mother of the Nation. But mostly, everyone just calls her Gro.[7]

Gro Growing Up

The question goes unresolved whether nature or nurture has more influence on how a child develops. In Gro Harlem Brundtland's case, the question is moot. Both her genes and her environment shouted the same prediction: she was going to be a rabble-rouser.

Gro—pronounced "Grew"—came from generations of strong activist, socialist stock. She was born on April 20, 1939, just a few months after the marriage of her parents, Inga Brynolf and Gudmund Harlem. Inga was a firebrand: "a radical, a socialist who dreams of a coming era of justice and equality."[8] Gudmund had similar liberal inclinations. He was a medical student when he met Inga, but also the local leader of an international organization that pursued a socialist and pacifist agenda.

Soon after their marriage the Harlems set up housekeeping in Oslo, but it was hardly a traditional home. They purchased an apartment at Camilla Collett's Way, No. 2, in the neighborhood of the royal palace. The address rapidly became known throughout the community of young radicals as "CC2," a place where they could find both a free bed and politically charged discussion. The Harlems subdivided the large, formerly elegant rooms into seven small bedrooms, providing sleeping space for a constant stream of visitors. "People came and went," Gro remembers. "Strangers often stayed overnight."[9]

Nazi Germany invaded Norway just before Gro's first birthday. Oslo changed virtually overnight from an open, welcoming community into a dangerous place, especially for radical socialists. Her mother gathered up baby Gro and hid in a delivery truck that secreted them out of Oslo to a rural hideaway. From there, they journeyed carefully on to Sweden, where Gro waited out the war with her grandmother.

With Gro safe in Sweden, her mother returned to Oslo and worked beside her husband in the underground anti-Nazi resistance. Nazi rule grew steadily harsher and more dangerous. In 1942, the Gestapo came to arrest her father, who fled the apartment and ran down a fire escape just ahead of his pursuers. It was clearly time to leave. The Harlems made their way by a treacherous and circuitous route to Stockholm, where they were reunited with Gro and her grandmother.

As soon as the war ended, the family returned to Oslo and their home at CC2. Needing to support a family that now included Gro and two younger brothers, Gudmund reestablished his medical practice. CC2 rapidly regained its earlier status as a refuge that liberal thinkers could also call home. The circle enlarged to include a broader range of intellectuals, radicals, socialists, and artists. "On the bookshelves at home, classics like Marx stood next to Karl Evang's *Sexual Education* and the *Workers' Lexicon*," Brundtland remembers. "There were history books, polemical tracts, party literature."[10] The Harlems were particularly interested in the plight of workers, and hence Gudmund Harlem, although far from meeting the definition of "worker," became a leader in the Norwegian Labour Party.

This liberal environment nurtured every part of Gro's early life. She recalls being "proud of my father for voting Labour because it's right, even though he doesn't benefit from it."[11] Dinner conversation was about politics and human rights, and Gro "was always the one asking why the government could not do more to help its citizens."[12] Gro and her siblings took up their parents' causes, helping out by spreading pamphlets and posting announcements for speeches, meetings, and protest actions. "Throughout my childhood the workers' movement and the ideals of social democracy had influenced me," she recalls.[13] "I was . . . lucky to be brought up in a family of strong convictions, deeply held values of solidarity, justice, and equality."[14]

The Harlems lived what they preached. They shunned luxuries even though a physician's income could afford them. Gro's clothes were simple and few, and she learned to sew her own dresses from plain cotton fabric: "Simplicity pattern, Mamma's sewing machine, Singer thread."[15] An exasperated aunt once commented, "Look at you, Gro, you're dressed like a domestic missionary!"[16]

The entire family loved being outdoors. Their socialist youth organization emphasized the value of outdoor activities, like camping and hiking, that discouraged competition in favor of cooperation. Cross-country skiing was a particular favorite, perhaps because it also permitted freedom, "where nature was for everyone and you could just fasten your skis and set off in any direction you liked."[17]

Gro was always a good student, but so independent as a thinker that she often ended up on the short side of classroom opinion. When a teacher asked her class whether they thought it better to have a king or a president, everyone shouted support for their popular king. Except Gro. She raised her hand and said, "President, because that way you can choose, and if you don't like it you can change it."[18] Being in the minority was never a problem for Gro. "I liked to obey my impulses, and I wasn't afraid of others' opinions. I had a lot of energy to use up, a lot of limits to test."[19]

Despite her political upbringing and activities, politics as a career had never crossed her mind. Science was much more attractive. "Law, economics, and engineering were attractive to me, but medicine had never been far from my thoughts since I was a little girl. . . ."[20] She had learned the linkage between poverty and illness from her father, and she was compelled to follow his footsteps as a physician. After graduating from high school, she entered medical school at the University of Oslo.

Once again, however, she was hardly the traditional medical student, entirely consumed by the demanding disciplines of chemistry and biology. Her classmates and their perspectives were as important as her classes. "We had heated discussions about sex education, sexual equality, and abortion; about Christianity and religion; about religious fundamentalism and hell. I was always an active participant, curious to discover the strength and variety of other people's views."[21]

If, as the saying goes, politics makes strange bedfellows, this was proven by Gro Harlem. A devoted liberal and socialist, she fell in love with Arne Olav Brundtland, an equally devoted conservative student from the Institute of Political Science. She was attracted not to the content of his ideas, but to his willingness to speak and act on them. "He had a bold, open way about him that I liked. . . . He certainly wasn't afraid of me."[22]

Rumors were flying, and her friends were incredulous. Olav was a fine fellow, they admitted, but this was treasonous! On the street one day, she met the wife of the prime minister, a family friend. "What's this I hear, Gro?" she asked, "Are you going out with a Conservative?"[23] Her father was equally doubtful, asking her "to think deeply about whether [she] was making the right choice."[24] In typical Brundtland fashion, these rebukes just stiffened her resolve: "I felt a growing sense of defiance. This wasn't right. I was a free woman, after all. The Labour Party didn't own me. I was still Gro, and Olav was Olav. That was equality, if you like—and this was life in a free, modern country."[25]

Gro and Olav married on December 9, 1960, in a home ceremony at CC2. For the next several years, she was fully occupied as a medical student, wife, and, soon, mother. "Nothing can compare with the moment when your first child passes through you and separates from you. The sense of wonder when you can feel the shape, the shoulders, and even the arms along the sides of the little body."[26]

Medical school and motherhood don't always get along well, but Brundtland thrived at both with the help of her husband and mother. She nursed her children, so mother and child needed to come together regularly during the day. She reports that her mother "wheeled Knut down to the national hospital where I was studying in the reading room, sometimes twice a day. I nursed him in the ladies' cloakroom."[27] Olav was equally helpful with the baby and other duties, a role he gladly performed. He was a good sport—press photographs in later years often showed him in the background holding her purse—but he did demand that he run the household his way, not hers. Less fastidious than his physician wife, he hung a sign in their home's hallway: "A House Must Be Clean Enough to Be Healthy and Dirty Enough to Be Happy."[28] Within a few years, the children numbered four—three boys and a girl, all born within an eight-year span. Just as in her childhood home, mother and father shared the chores—except one. After a year or so, Brundtland lamented that "Olav had acquired an extraordinary ability to not hear the children at night. It is a talent he has preserved."[29]

Figure 8.2 Even as a medical student and young mother, Brundtland was actively involved in social welfare and politics; she is seen here marching in a Labour Party parade on May 1, 1960. (Reproduced courtesy of the Labour Movement Archives and Library in Norway.)

With medical school behind them, the family journeyed to the United States. Olav had been invited to study with Henry Kissinger at the Harvard Center for International Affairs, and Brundtland entered Harvard's public health program. They lived in International House, where they made friends from across the globe. The time in Boston had a deep effect on Brundtland: "The most important part of our trip was the inspiration we received from all the new people we met, both teachers and fellow students. . . . Each day we learned about the poverty, population trends, food resources, and health problems that affected different parts of the world."[30]

Her immersion in public health issues fueled a new academic interest—ecology. Always interested in nature, she was now making the connection between the human condition and the environment, spurred by the new ideas that swirled around her. During a visit by her father, she remembers, they were "talking with great enthusiasm about ecology, about how important it was to work toward a condition in which people lived in harmony with nature."[31] She was shocked that her father knew nothing of the concept, and she couldn't "understand why ecology was not universally viewed as a crucial issue."[32]

Once back in Norway, Brundtland began her medical practice, but always in a public health setting. She worked for the Oslo Board of Health as a school doctor and at the Municipal Health Center for Mother and Child; one night each week, she doctored at a hostel for homeless men. As a young physician, she "was preoccupied by medicine's role in society, by the need to educate people, by how best to improve public health, safety, equality, and dignity of treatment in the broadest sense."[33] As a public health doctor, she sat on a committee that judged, on a case-by-case basis, whether needy women would be allowed to have publicly supported abortions. The experience moved her deeply. "This was an area, like so many others, in which those with the fewest resources found it most difficult to tell their stories and to explain their point of view."[34]

When the abortion issue heated up in Norway, Brundtland waded into the battle. "As a professional, as a woman, and as a politically active person, Gro became infuriated by the anti-abortion activities of the Conservative Party in the 1970s and launched a press campaign that made her name well known."[35] With a colleague, she wrote a series of articles for newspapers and journals. "I wrote about real cases I had dealt with on the abortion committee. . . . In general, the abortion debate was being conducted over the heads of most people; it lacked a recognizable human dimension. . . . I felt I had a duty to fight for women."[36]

And when, in August 1974, she received a summons to meet with the nation's prime minister, she assumed that the topic would be her role in the abortion issue. She was wrong.

Minister of the Environment

Getting a personal call from the president or prime minister would shock most of us, but not a member of the Brundtland family. The Brundtlands brushed shoulders with the nation's leaders regularly. Gro's father had risen to chief physician for the Norwegian Research Institute and, thus, had been the personal physician for a string of prime ministers. His prominence in the Labour Party also led to government appointments; over a ten-year period he served first as minister of social affairs and then minister of defense. Contact with the prime minister was just part of everyday life.

But Brundtland was not prepared for what she heard that day from the prime minister. He didn't want to discuss her role in women's issues. He didn't want to discuss her father's work. He wanted her to join his cabinet as minister of the environment. As she remembers, "Well, you know when I was thirty-five . . . the prime minister of this country surprised me very much by calling me to his office without saying why. . . . But then he said, 'I ask you to enter the cabinet,' and I was completely surprised. . . ."[37] She sought the advice of her husband and father, both of whom encouraged her to accept the job. Gro had been raised for public service, but not in this role. "I never planned to become a politician, although I always had a political interest, always was engaged in political debates and thinking; I never saw myself as a politician before I was asked to become one."[38] Nevertheless, she accepted, and Norway—and the world—had its first female environmental minister.

Minister of the environment was not an easy job. The ministry was in its infancy, and it had churned through four leaders in its brief two-year existence. Without a track record that might have helped define the ministry's mission, much of what she was asked to do would be new—and probably controversial. "Immediately, in 1974, the new minister of the environment began doing things that angered industrialists."[39] She addressed acid rain, fishing rights, nature preservation, and fees for pollution. Brundtland found all of this exhilarating. "It was an incredible time of challenge and inspiration, one which I spent in the company of talented and committed people. Together we formed an unstoppable team, which succeeded in bringing our field right into the center of the political debate."[40]

Business-as-usual was not her style, especially not political business-as-usual. She was analytic rather than intuitive, objective rather than emotional, practical rather than dogmatic. "From the time I started in politics my instinct has always been to stick to the facts and avoid being too emotional. The arguments for environmental protection, to give one example, are strong enough to stand by themselves."[41] As a social democrat, she sought consensus and solidarity, empowering her staff and advisors to speak their minds. Once the facts were clear, however, she stood by them. "*Decisive* was an adjective that well fitted Brundtland. . . ."[42] She was famous for her work ethic, her days often stretching into the early morning hours. She traveled often, both around Norway and throughout the world. "Nature," she says, "could not afford any indifference."[43]

Her passion, however, came with drawbacks. She was direct, a trait that some observers saw as willful and arrogant. She had a temper that she usually controlled, but occasionally it flared. "Her detractors . . . pointed to an easily aroused temper, self-important air, and often aggressive style."[44] One journalist called her the "minister from the sunny side of the street," referring to her easy rise to high office, helped by being a member of a prominent Norwegian family.[45] Brundtland answered the criticism with the conviction she had learned as a child, stating, "If you are born strong, with parents who give you the best, you have an even stronger responsibility for the people who didn't get the same start."[46]

Her tenure as environmental minister lasted five years, and was punctuated by two significant events. First was the *Ekofisk* oil platform disaster in April 1977, as described earlier.

Second was her effort to protect the Hardangervidda wilderness. The Hardangervidda is a high mountain plain in southern Norway, bisecting the country and drained by two unspoiled rivers. Divergent plans for the area arose in the early 1970s—one called for protecting it as a national park; the other called for damming the two rivers to create hydroelectric power. Brundtland was warned not to come out too strongly for protection, but rather promote a compromise of damming one river and protecting the other. Compromise, she believed, was not the right decision in this case. "I don't have a choice," she said. "The issue is too important. . . . I cannot in all conscience do anything but go all the way with this."[47] Through repeated rounds of government, Labour Party, parliamentary, and public debates, she held her ground, once stating publicly, "I have no doubt that there is no other area in southern Norway which is in greater need of our protection than the Hardangervidda wilderness."[48] Her viewpoint prevailed, and eventually, in 1981, the area was designated a national park.

She understood that the love of a healthy environment was at the core of being Norwegian. The day after the *Ekofisk* rupture was resolved, she traveled to Bergen for the annual May Day celebration. Norwegian flags flew everywhere, the bright blue cross on a vivid red background complemented by a clear blue sky. She remembers: "There was applause for the procession, something I had never experienced before. The town square was jam-packed. The public listened attentively. I spoke about quality of life, about our environment and our children, about the Hardangervidda wilderness, to thunderous applause. This was about more than our own oil crisis."[49]

Brundtland was maturing as a politician at the same time she was becoming the nation's environmental leader. In 1975, just a year after her appointment as minister, the Labour Party asked her to accept the position of deputy leader. At first she declined, believing she was too junior to hold such a post, but she finally accepted with the encouragement of other women politicians. Two years later, she ran successfully for Parliament. (In Norway, cabinet officials can hold a seat in Parliament, but must be represented by a surrogate while still in office.[50])

In 1979, the Labour Party was suffering from internal disagreements and declining popularity; municipal elections (Americans call these "midterm elections") were disastrous. Changes were needed, in the form of shuffling the deck of cabinet and parliamentary roles. At the party's direction, Brundtland left her ministerial position; she recalls that "it seems to me now that [the party leader] found the political struggle between development and conservation burdensome."[51] In positioning the party on these topics, the leadership "thought of me as tough, someone who knew her stuff a little too well for comfort. I had become a heavyweight opponent."[52]

Now able to take her seat in Parliament, she used her time to gain experience and contacts in the political trenches. She made friends in other political parties, learning their personalities and motivations. "You

Figure 8.3 Early in her term as minister of the environment, Brundtland confronted the largest oil spill in Norwegian history when an offshore oil platform ruptured in April 1977. (Reproduced courtesy of the Labour Movement Archives and Library in Norway.)

get to know the way they think and the way they like to present themselves—two things that are sometimes quite contradictory!"[53] Her party was grooming her for higher office; as one newspaper reported, "Gro goes to Prime Minister's School."[54]

Her schooling came just in time. In early 1981, the prime minister resigned for health reasons. Out of a frenzy of internal Labour Party squabbles, Brundtland emerged as the leading candidate, and the king of Norway formally appointed her prime minister on February 1, 1981. "Certainly we made Norwegian political history that evening. I would be the first woman prime minister, and the youngest."[55]

Putting a woman in the prime minister's chair was revolutionary. She immediately expanded the number of women in the cabinet from two to four; throughout her political career, she continued to strive for parity in her appointments. She was committed to teamwork, communication, and openness. Her secretary described the new working environment: "Gro was something completely new at the prime minister's office. It was not only that she is a woman. She was glowing with a fighting spirit and willingness to work. . . . The heavy atmosphere had been lifted. Behind the desk sat Gro, smiling with her whole body. She put out her arms and exclaimed, 'This will all be fun.'"[56]

It might have been fun, but it was certainly short-lived. The Labour Party lost national elections that fall, and Brundtland was out as prime minister after a short eight months. Once again, she returned to Parliament, this time also as the unchallenged leader of her party. Her place as a world leader had been won, however, and her influence gradually spread beyond Norway's borders.

A keystone experience for her was serving on a new kind of international commission. In 1980, the United Nations asked Olof Palme, former prime minister of Sweden, to form and lead the Independent Commission on Disarmament and Security Issues, in order to address the threat of nuclear weapons. Composed of respected world leaders, the commission had freedom to operate outside the constraints of representing specific nations or organizations like the United Nations or World Bank. Brundtland served on this commission, and her respect for Olof Palme was unbounded. They became close colleagues, united by their common experience of the ups and downs of high political office. Palme was assassinated in 1986, a crime that remains unsolved. Brundtland was devastated at the loss of her close friend and an exceptional world leader. She recalls his legacy: "What was it that made him so extraordinary? It was his personal qualities. But it was also his ability to inspire trust in the ideals of Northern Europe and the United Nations, trust that fueled his restless drive toward bettering the lot of the underprivileged. He was genuinely the world's symbol of hope for a better and more just future."[57]

Brundtland looked to Palme for her inspiration. Soon people across the world looked to her for theirs.

World Commission on Environment and Development

This time the invitation came not from Norway, but from the United Nations, and it was less of a surprise. In December 1983, UN Secretary-

General Perez de Cuellar approached Brundtland to chair an initiative to address the state of the world's environment as the new century was approaching. Why me? she asked, but she knew the answer: "No other political leader had become prime minister with a background of several years of political struggle, nationally and internationally, as an environment minister."[58]

The concept for an environmental commission had been brewing for some time. In 1972, the UN had created an environmental unit, the United Nations Environment Programme (UNEP), in response to the awakening of a worldwide environmental movement. Since then, a series of meetings had addressed individual environmental issues in isolation—air pollution, perhaps, or excessive fish harvests, or accelerating human population growth. Accompanying each of those problems, however, was the elephant in the room—the fundamental linkages among environment, the economy, and the condition of the human race. Something more was needed—a comprehensive, global consideration of how those issues were connected and how they affected one another. The UN General Assembly again chose an independent commission, one modeled after the Palme Commission. "This was a chance to choose an interdisciplinary approach to environment and development which did not fit into the mandate of any UN institution."[59]

Brundtland said yes without much hesitation, encouraged by family and colleagues. "In the final analysis," she writes, "I decided to accept the challenge. The challenge of facing the future, and of safeguarding the interests of coming generations. For it was abundantly clear: We needed a mandate for change."[60] Just before Christmas in 1983, de Cuellar announced the new World Commission on Environment and Development (WCED) with Gro Harlem Brundtland as its chair.

She approached a respected Canadian environmental diplomat, Jim MacNeill, to take the full-time position as the commission's secretary-general. At first he was skeptical, put off by a task he thought was doomed to fail; the mandate was not only too idealistic but was also riddled with back doors for waffling and compromise. Brundtland told him, "So we will write our own mandate."[61] Eventually he succumbed to Brundtland's charm and persistence, "convinced that, with a bit of luck, a lot of hard work, a simple mandate, and about US$8 million in voluntary contributions, the impossible was doable."[62] MacNeill matched Brundtland in conviction, independence, and backbone; they were going to drive this effort as they saw fit, period. She reflects: "I had deliberately chosen a strong person. Jim MacNeill could be obstinate, and there were occasional conflicts with other colleagues, but he had an extremely tidy mind and an enormous capacity for work. . . ."[63]

They also agreed that writing a report was just step one; step two was promoting the report's recommendations. An explicit commitment to blanketing the world with their conclusions was needed to motivate the reforms they sought. That commitment, MacNeill said, "enabled a huge initial outreach by the commission, which was crucial, in my view, to the ultimate impact of our report."[64]

They next chose the twenty-three individuals who would comprise the commission. Brundtland received a great deal of advice regarding the membership (Jane Fonda would be perfect, some believed), but "she made choices based primarily on her personal knowledge of people or of recommendations by people she trusted."[65] She avoided environmental zealots, instead favoring experienced, realistic proponents of environmental improvement. She was particularly conscious to balance the North-South, rich-poor dichotomy. "No previous international commission had reflected the international spectrum as we did. A clear majority of our members were from developing countries."[66]

Assembling a diverse team had its problems. She hoped for gender balance, but few women were recommended or, finally, appointed. But differing politics was the biggest threat to agreement. MacNeill remembered that "taken together, we represented almost every shade of ideology extant in the Cold War world of the '80s. . . . Although we served in a personal capacity, national, cultural, and group loyalties were very strong, always below the surface and sometimes above."[67] And such group loyalties weren't necessarily going to be overcome easily. "One of our commissioners was a distinguished scientist from the Soviet Union," MacNeill recalled, "and he was accompanied to all of our meetings by a friendly KGB minder."[68]

Corralling this team was an effort, but one that Brundtland managed with her usual diplomacy. Regarding just one issue—human population—she reflected in the commission's report that "the differences of perspectives seemed at the outset to be unbridgeable, and they required a lot of thought and willingness to communicate across the divides of cultures, religions, and regions."[69] Her lifelong fearlessness in addressing a diversity of opinion served her well. "All commission members . . . agreed that her skills at moderating discussions, encouraging both debate and compromise, were essential to the success of the commission. It was also, in the words of one commissioner, 'really a joyful experience to work with her.'"[70]

The commission did not necessarily seek a joyful outcome to match the joyful experience, but it knew that a realistic, positive, forward-looking outcome was essential. While the commission was at work, the world was shocked by a series of environmental calamities—long-term drought in Ethiopia, massive forest fires in Borneo, a chemical-plant explosion in Bhopal, an expanding ozone hole over the Antarctic, and nuclear catastrophe in Chernobyl—that colored the anticipation of their conclusions. Observers worried that, against this backdrop, the commission's report would either be another gloom-and-doom downer or else a rosy scenario based on impractical and politically unrealistic ideals. Brundtland and MacNeill understood the dilemma, and they had another solution. "We were quick to make our basic view known: It is possible to construct an economically sounder and fairer future based upon policies and behavior that can secure our ecological foundation."[71] People needed hope, and they needed a blueprint. "We cannot give up," Brundtland demanded. "Passivity and pessimism have never helped the earth to advance."[72]

But a positive future required changes in the way the world saw environment and development. One essential paradigm shift underscored the work of the commission. Whereas environmental concerns had been seen primarily as a task of cleaning up the mess left over after development, from that moment forward environment and development had to be seen as conjoined twins. The question wasn't how to clean up the environment, it was how to sustain it. As MacNeill stated the problem: "The environmental protection agenda that nations adopted . . . only tackled the *symptoms* of environmental degradation; it completely ignored the *sources*. The sources were not to be found in the air, soils, and waters that were the focus of the environmental protection agenda; but rather, they were, and still are, to be found in a whole range of perverse public policies, especially our dominant fiscal and tax policies, our energy policies, and also our trade, agricultural, industrial, and other policies."[73] A commission to achieve this transformation needed to be different, and Brundtland made sure that it was. To compel the members beyond the usual "think-tank" activities—"commission expert papers, engage the best consultants, establish high-level panels, invite distinguished people"[74]—they needed a different set of experiences. So, first, rather than convening only in the elegant historic headquarters in Geneva, provided by the Swiss government, they traveled around the world. Over a three-year period, from 1984 through 1987, the commission met eight times—in Switzerland, Indonesia, Norway, Brazil, Canada, Zimbabwe and Kenya, the Soviet Union, and, finally, Tokyo. They went to where the problems were happening.

Second, they added a unique aspect to their meetings—public hearings. From the beginning, Brundtland and MacNeill insisted that they "hold public hearings on every continent and visit sites in the field that would demonstrate the issues and dilemmas we were addressing."[75] MacNeill believed that "the hearings went on to become our hallmark and, in my view, the primary source of the eventual consensus."[76] Brundtland recalls the crowds in Brazil: "The hearings in São Paulo turned into the most enthusiastic affair. The newly acquired freedom of expression and the Latin temperament brought things to a boil. When the hearings were officially over, some of the participants climbed up on the stage and proclaimed that proceedings must go on. . . . There were thousands of people there. . . . Things quieted down gradually, but it was a profound experience."[77]

The hearings, and the field excursions that accompanied them, gave the commissioners a shared and vivid experience. "By providing commissioners with a common base of—sometimes demanding—experience they created trust and bonding, which would eventually be crucial for finding consensus on critical issues of the report."[78] They had come to the commission as individuals, but they left it as a unanimous body of forceful advocates for change.

Agreeing to principles was one thing; agreeing to the specific words that expressed those principles was another. The task of writing a report that commissioners from twenty-two countries could endorse was a long, arduous process. Of their final meeting in Tokyo—"the decisive meeting"—Brundtland has said, "We had to review every sentence in the report and create the feeling of joint responsibility necessary to position the report squarely on the international agenda."[79]

The commission issued its report in a book called *Our Common Future*, published on March 20, 1987. As intended from the beginning, it was comprehensive. Sections of the report cover specific issues—human population growth, food security, ecosystem protection, energy, industrial production, and the urban environment—but the overall message is integrative. This essential perspective is reflected, for example, in the section on species and ecosystems:

> The link between conservation and development and the need to attack the problem at the sources can be seen clearly in the case of tropical forests. Sometimes it is government policy, not economic necessity, that drives the overexploitation and destruction of these resources. The direct economic and fiscal costs of this over-exploitation—in addition to those of species extinction—are huge. The result has been wasteful exploitation of the tropical forests, the sacrifice of most of their timber and non-timber values, enormous losses of potential revenue to the government, and the destruction of rich biological resources.[80]

Underlying these specific analyses was one foundational concept that sought to redefine the world's priorities: sustainable development. The commissioners developed "a compelling sense of the urgency of the issues and a recognition that the approaches to environmental management then in place were both seriously limited and deeply flawed, a recognition that grew into a strong conviction as our work progressed."[81] Eventually, "sustainable development" became the catchphrase for the report. Likewise, the commission's definition of sustainable development has become the standard. *Our Common Future* declares: "Humanity has the ability to make development sustainable—to ensure that it meets the needs of the present without compromising the ability of future generations to meet their own needs."[82]

The fate of an international commission's work is uncertain. After the initial publicity dies down, a report is typically acknowledged, applauded, criticized, and then forgotten. Brundtland and MacNeill were not about to let that happen to *Our Common Future*, but the start was rocky. They originally planned to release the report officially in Washington, DC, for maximum press exposure. But President Reagan, who had never endorsed the commission, refused to meet Brundtland, and the release was canceled. The public launch shifted to London on April 27, 1987, and a formal presentation was made to the UN General Assembly in New York on October 19, 1987. Once again, they expected widespread press coverage. Once again, they were disappointed—the US stock market crashed that very morning, causing a mass migration of the press from UN headquarters to Wall Street, and the report got little coverage.

Undaunted, the pair kept on. In April 1988, they encouraged a colleague to start a new organization—the Centre for Our Common Future—specifically to promote the report and its recommendations. It worked. As Jim MacNeill reported,

> Within a year . . . , our recommendations were endorsed by the UN systems and by ASEAN, OECD, the Commonwealth and other regional bodies, as well as the World Bank and all of the regional banks. Within two years, they began to reshape curricula in universities and graduate schools and became a preoccupation of a growing number of leading companies worldwide. Within three years, the G-7 summits were producing long declarations devoted to sustainable development. Within five years, our recommendation for an international conference for a global transition to more sustainable forms of development was realized, at least in part, through the '92 Earth summit in Rio. . . . *Our Common Future* went on to become the most widely read UN report in history, available in over twenty languages.[83]

The impact of *Our Common Future* was monumental in effecting change, the kind of change that Brundtland had envisioned. Robert Mugabe, then president of Zimbabwe, said the report was "a breath of

Figure 8.4 Gro Harlem Brundtland, while serving as Norway's prime minister, presents the findings of the World Commission on Environment and Development to the United Nations, October 19, 1987. (UN Photo/Milton Grant.)

fresh air in a world polluted by poverty, hunger, disease, racism, industrial waste, and the threat of nuclear annihilation."[84] Reagan's successor, George H. W. Bush, "declared his intention to include environmental consideration into all policy decisions."[85] Today, although the report itself is rarely read, it lives on impressively through its offspring—a series of global environmental conferences starting from the Rio Earth Summit in 1992 to the Millennium Development Goals of 2000, as well as the Rio+20 conference in 2012 and continuing, presumably, forever.

Our Common Future also lives on with a legacy closely associated with its chair. Universally, WCED is now known as the "Brundtland Commission," and *Our Common Future* is known as the "Brundtland Report." And the world's prevailing definition of sustainability is likewise known as the "Brundtland Definition." So universal is the phrase "sustainable development" that a Google search can turn up tens of millions of hits. Sustainable development has, as Jim MacNeill said, "become part of the common everyday lexicon of humankind."[86]

Beyond the Commission

Authoring the world's predominant expression of environmental stewardship might be a big enough accomplishment for any one lifetime, but it hasn't been enough for Gro Harlem Brundtland. Chairing the WCED was, after all, just a part-time job for Brundtland; her full-time job remained Norwegian politics. After her 1981 ouster as prime minister, she immediately reclaimed her seat in Parliament and her leadership of the Labour Party. Norway was reeling at this time, the economy faltering as the oil market collapsed and three minority parties swapped control of the government.

She heard from the Royal Palace again in the spring of 1986. Once again, the king asked her to form a new government and become the nation's prime minister. "This time," she reported, "we spoke only briefly. My answer was yes."[87]

Some skeptics questioned her ability to be both prime minister and chair of WCED at the same time, but she proved them wrong, becoming a masterful and forceful leader for Norway. Inheriting "a government that leaves the dirty dishes for others once the meal is over,"[88] she deftly eased the country out of its economic crisis. She publicly opposed Ronald Reagan's positions on space and chemical weapons, and she chastened the Soviet Union on its response to the Chernobyl nuclear disaster. She upheld the rights of commercial fishermen against the demands of the European Union for access to Norwegian fishing grounds. Norway is a fiercely independent country, and such positions resonated with her constituents. She installed eight women in her cabinet, earning it the sobriquet of "the government of women."

Despite Brundtland's popularity, Norwegian politics at the time remained decidedly unstable. Her Labour Party lost control of government in the 1989 elections, and she was out as prime minister after a three-year term. The chair barely had time to grow cold, however, before the government turned over again, and she returned as prime minister within a year, this time serving for six more years, until the fall of 1996.

The essence of Brundtland's leadership is illustrated by her actions on an issue that spanned her career—regulation of fishing and whaling. Norway and fishing are almost synonymous. "Norway's fish industry has enormous emotional resonance for Norwegians and is a central component of Norwegians' self-image."[89] Whaling, too, has always been a part of Norwegian life, so much so that the country was among the world's leaders in whaling up to World War II. When large-scale industrial whaling expanded after the war, however, Norway's prominence as a whaling nation declined. But rural fishing communities continued to hunt abundant Minke whales, despite growing concern—environmental and moral—over the treatment of whales. Norwegian harvest of whales came to a head in 1982, when the International Whaling Commission, of which Norway was a member, declared a worldwide moratorium on commercial whaling. Norway, as allowed by the rules, objected to the moratorium and, therefore, continued whaling without violating the treaty.

This action, of course, incensed the environmental community worldwide. How could a nation—and a prime minister—so dedicated to the environment condone whaling? Brundtland stood her ground. Whales, she reasoned, were renewable resources that could be managed sustainably—the exploitation rates just needed to be correct. She also believed that Norway managed its coastal whale resources better than other nations around the world that were criticizing her country.

But, when scientists began to question the validity of Norwegian data in 1987, Brundtland responded as she always had—analytically, not politically. She has said, "My credo is this: Build on and strengthen the Evidence, share the Evidence, and act upon the Evidence."[90] So she temporarily suspended whaling and appointed a four-person scientific team to get the data right. Then, in 1993, when Norwegian research showed that Minke whales were both abundant and sustainably harvestable, she announced that Norway would resume commercial whaling. She believed that "after years of a moratorium and subsequently only small quotas for research purposes, this was great news for coastal Norway. This was Norway's attitude to the resources in the oceans—long-term management built on a scientific basis."[91]

The environmental world fumed. Norway was accused of "pirate-whaling";[92] the International Whaling Commission adopted "hate-resolutions" against Norway;[93] the United States threatened economic sanctions. Brundtland and her minister of foreign affairs personally made the decision, based on the data and on her belief that "it simply was not *right* for outsiders, considered to have no understanding of the issue, to decide the question."[94] The Norwegian people and their major environmental organizations agreed: Norway was right, the rest of the world was wrong. And when the question was put to the Parliament, "there was not one single vote against this move."[95]

Brundtland began her retreat from Norwegian politics when personal tragedy struck in 1992. Her youngest son committed suicide, unable to cope with a bipolar condition that had spun out of control. That November, she resigned as leader of the Labour Party, too overcome by grief to continue such a demanding political role. She remained as prime minister, however, and some believe that the need to escape her loss spurred her on when her natural energy had begun to wane. She declined to stand for election again in 1996, believing it was just the right time to depart, even though the party and the country loved her. A Norwegian business newspaper editor stated, "Not for fifty years has Norway had a prime minister with such wide support from all sections of society," and opinion polls showed approval ratings as high as 90 percent.[96] As she left her office for the last time, Olav waited patiently at the curb, as he had always done. The car was packed for a weekend at their forest cabin: "He had filled it up with clothes, tools, and a case of light beer."[97]

Her respite was brief, however, as her leadership was still sought and needed. In 1998, Brundtland again assumed a major international role, this time as director-general of the World Health Organization. She was perfectly prepared to lead the WHO. She was a physician (a required qualification for the job), but equally important were her political and environmental experiences. "I have had to ask myself this question again and again," she admits. "Am I a doctor or a politician?"[98] Both were essential for the task before her. The WHO's reputation had fallen in the eyes of the world—its programs were seen as ineffective, its staff lazy, perhaps even corrupt; it needed aggressive leadership, focused on results and comfortable with change. Brundtland saw and accepted the challenge:

> In my opening address, I said it was my prime responsibility to maintain and further develop the technical excellence of the WHO. But I was also convinced that I needed to bring a political dimension to the WHO's leadership, a greater awareness of a changing world, a better sense of interaction with the countries and populations we were there to serve, a better grasp of the key economic and technological issues that shape the global development agenda of which health is a critical component.[99]

Her fundamental view of the world did not need to change to lead the WHO. Health, environment, and the alleviation of poverty all were part of a greater whole in her mind. "WHO's focus on sustainable development," she contends, "is within the context of healthy environments and the impact of development on human health. It is also on human health as a prerequisite for and generator of sustainable development."[100] Everything was connected, she understood, and solutions depended just as much on human health as they did on a clean environment. "As a doctor and public health specialist, I learnt to always look for the close and near as well as the far away, the small as well as the large—through a multifaceted, holistic lens."[101]

Brundtland identified a small number of critical human-health challenges for the coming century. Communicable diseases needed to be controlled, and she established that "the WHO's goal is the vaccination of every child."[102] She believed that tobacco use was a pressing public health issue, and she campaigned vigorously for its suppression: "Tobacco should not be advertised, subsidized, or glamorized."[103] At the heart of the matter, however, was poverty, and the solution to poverty was the education and empowerment of women. Progress meant "investing in women. I believe the next increment of global growth could come from the full economic empowerment of women. Half of humankind's collective intelligence and capacity is a resource we can no longer afford to lose out on!"[104]

She chose not to seek a second term at the WHO in 2003, but she has continued to act on behalf of the world's people. For three years she served as the UN secretary-general's special envoy on climate change, a topic that has figured largely in her career, even before others were paying close attention. The Brundtland Commission called for control of greenhouse gases in their final report, and their recommendations led to the 1992 Framework Convention on Climate Change, which in turn produced the Kyoto Protocol and subsequent efforts to control greenhouse gases. Along with the prime minister of Canada, she called for a "global 'law of the air'" as early as 1988, stating that "the impact of world climate change may be greater than any challenge mankind has faced, with the exception of preventing nuclear war."[105] Under Brundtland's leadership, Norway was among the first countries to recognize the need to control carbon emissions. She remembers, "In 1990, my government instituted a carbon dioxide tax. I had all the oil-producing countries of the world lining up against me. I explained there is no other way to deal with climate change than to do something about the price of carbon."[106]

Brundtland's agenda seems hardly changed since the formative years when she first linked health, ecology, and economics in a student apartment in Boston. The constancy isn't surprising, because the problems she has always sought to tackle are the most difficult, persistent, and intertwined of our civilization. But we have made great advances toward a better world because of her efforts. And, thus, we should let her have the final word:

George Bernard Shaw said that "The worst sin toward our fellow creatures is not to hate them but to be indifferent to them." Let us fight the indifference which has prevailed in the past and move towards that equilibrium between people, consumption, and the carrying capacity of our earth which we call sustainable development. Let us listen to the voice of unborn generations and make the earth the hospitable place that any human being deserves.[107]

Notes

Introduction

1. John F. Kennedy, *Profiles in Courage*, Memorial Edition (New York: Harper & Row, 1964). Although the book lists the author as John F. Kennedy, it is now widely acknowledged that Ted Sorensen contributed substantially to all aspects of the book's research, writing, and editing.

2. Ibid., 18.

3. Wangari Maathai, Nobel lecture; available at: http://www.nobelprize .org/nobel_prizes/peace/laureates/2004/maathai-lecture-text.html.

4. Trova Heffernan, *Where the Salmon Run: The Life and Legacy of Billy Frank Jr.* (Seattle, WA: University of Washington Press, 2012), 206.

5. Lyrics to "The Garden Song," made famous by Pete Seeger and written in 1975 by David Mallett.

Chapter 1

1. John Muir, *The Mountains of California* (New York: The Century Company, 1894), ch. 10 ("A Windstorm in the Forests").

2. Ibid.

3. Ibid.

4. Anonymous, quoted in: *America's Wilderness: The Photographs of Ansel Adams with the Writings of John Muir* (Philadelphia: Running Press, 1997), 75.

5. Linnie Marsh Wolfe, *Son of the Wilderness: The Life of John Muir* (Madison, WI: University of Wisconsin Press, 1945), 55.

6. Donald Worster, *A Passion for Nature: The Life of John Muir* (New York: Oxford University Press, 2008), 29.

7. Ibid., 27.

8. Ibid., 52.

9. Stephen Fox, *The American Conservation Movement: John Muir and His Legacy* (Madison, WI: University of Wisconsin Press, 1981), 14.

10. John Muir, quoted in: *America's Wilderness*, 116.

11. Muir, quoted in Wolfe, 55.

12. Ibid., 57.

13. Wolfe, 67.

14. Muir, quoted in Fox, 43.

15. Ibid., 104.

16. Ibid., 105.

17. Ibid., 110.

18. Muir, quoted in Wolfe, 110.

19. John Muir, *A Thousand-Mile Walk to the Gulf* (Boston: Houghton Mifflin, 1916), 30.

20. John Muir, "The Treasures of the Yosemite," *Century Magazine* XL, no. 4 (August 1890).

21. Ibid.

22. US Senate Bill 203, June 30, 1864.

23. Muir, quoted in Fox, 11.

24. Muir, quoted in Wolfe, 144.

25. Yelverton, quoted in Fox, 15–16.

26. Muir, quoted in Wolfe, 167.

27. Quoted in Fox, 78.

28. The term "a proper cultivated plant" shows up in many places, but is the chapter title from Fox, 54.

29. The partnership between Muir and Johnson is described in both Worster and Wolfe, but Johnson also wrote about it himself in his autobiography, *Remembered Yesterdays* (Boston: Little, Brown and Company, 1923). Muir is covered in pages 278–316.

30. The description of mugwumps in relationship to Muir comes from: Dennis C. Williams, *God's Wilds: John Muir's Vision of Nature* (College Station, TX: Texas A&M University Press, 2002), 165.

31. Muir, "The Treasures of the Yosemite."

32. John Muir, "Features of the Proposed Yosemite National Park," *Century Magazine* XL, no. 9 (September 1890).

33. Robert Underwood Johnson, "John Muir as I Knew Him," *Sierra Club Bulletin*, John Muir Memorial Number, January 1916.

34. Muir, quoted in Wolfe, 274.

35. Muir, quoted in Fox, 126.

36. Muir, quoted in Johnson, *Remembered Yesterdays*, 292.

37. Muir, quoted in Williams, 187.

38. Muir, quoted in Worster, 424.

39. Muir, quoted in Williams, 161.

40. Johnson "John Muir as I Knew Him," 316.

Chapter 2

1. The Des Moines newspaper was called the *Register and Leader* when Darling joined their staff, but became the *Des Moines Register* in 1915.

2. David L. Lendt, *Ding: The Life of Jay Norwood Darling*, 4th ed. (Mount Pleasant, SC: Maecenas Press, 2001), 133. (Although Maecenas Press is the publisher, the book is available primarily through the Ding Darling Foundation, Sanibel Island, Florida.)

3. Ibid., 8.

4. Quotes from dictation made by Darling, entitled "On Conservation," February 9, 1959 (University of Iowa archives).

5. Ibid.

6. Darling, quoted in Lendt, 12.

7. Darling, quoted in: Patricia Byrnes, *Environmental Pioneers* (Minneapolis, MN: Oliver Press, 1998), 40.

8. Darling, quoted in Lendt, 6.

9. Ibid., 16.

10. Ibid., 17.

11. William B. Friedricks, *Covering Iowa: The History of the Des Moines Register and Tribune Company* (Ames, IA: Iowa State University Press, 2000), 61–63.

12. Quoted in: Laurence F. Jonson, *Federal Duck Stamp Story: Fifty Years of Excellence* (Davenport, IA: Alexander & Company, 1984), 188–89.

13. J. N. Darling, letter to Jack Bender, November 8, 1961 (University of Iowa archives).

14. J. N. Darling, "Why I Wouldn't Trade Des Moines for New York," *American Magazine* 88 (July 1919): 37–38 and 120.

15. Darling, quoted in: Gene Byrnes, ed., *Commercial Art: A Complete Guide to Drawing, Illustration, Cartooning, and Printing* (New York: Simon & Schuster, 1952), 133–34.

16. J. N. Darling, letter to Jack Bender, November 8, 1961 (University of Iowa archives).

17. Quotes and related information from a dictation by Darling, "The Long, Long Trail," made on January 26, 1955 (University of Iowa archives).

18. Jay N. Darling, *As Ding Saw Herbert Hoover* (Ames, IA: Iowa State University Press, 1954), 16 and 17.

19. Darling, quoted in Lendt, 10.

20. Jay N. Darling, *Poverty or Conservation: Your National Problem* (Washington, DC: National Wildlife Federation, 1944), 6–7.

21. Official charge is quoted from the *Iowa Register* for 1931–32.

22. Jacob L. Crane Jr. and George Wheeler Olcott, "Report on the Iowa Twenty-Five-Year Conservation Plan," Iowa Board of Conservation and Iowa Fish and Game Commission, 1933, 1–2.

23. Lendt, 65.

24. Darling, *As Ding Saw Herbert Hoover*, 10.

25. Darling, quoted in Lendt, 79.

26. Darling, quoted in: George Laycock, *The Sign of the Flying Goose: The Story of the National Wildlife Refuges* (Garden City, NY: Anchor Press/ Doubleday, 1973), 6.

27. The most complete version of this event is from: Jon Farrar, "The Federal," *NEBRASKAland*, undated.

28. Franklin Roosevelt, quoted in Lendt, 77.

29. Several versions of this event exist. The one described here is from page 190 of Laurence Jonson's book about the duck stamp (complete citation above, note 12). Jonson's description seems most authentic, with details not reported elsewhere. A much different description is provided by Patricia Byrnes, who says (on page 48 of her book, complete citation above, note 7) that Darling drew it on a paper lunch bag in the office cafeteria.

30. Ding's sobriquet as "the best friend a duck ever had" can be found repeatedly in the literature, but never with attribution of the original use of the phrase. Several sources indicate that he had earned the name while he was chief of the US Biological Survey.

31. Darling, quoted in Lendt, 50.

32. Ibid., 86.

33. Darling, quote from dictation labeled "autobiographical," January 26, 1955 (University of Iowa archives).

34. Darling, quoted in Lendt, 142.

35. Darling, quoted in Lendt, 109.

36. Ibid., 107.

37. Ibid.

38. Ibid., 120.

39. Jay N. Darling, "Conservation Education," speech dated September 15, 1950 (University of Iowa archives).

40. Darling, quoted in Lendt, 141.

41. Ibid., 158.

42. Ibid., 157.

43. Ibid., 165.

Chapter 3

1. Aldo Leopold, cited in: Curt Meine, *Aldo Leopold: His Life and Work*, 2nd ed. (Madison, WI: University of Wisconsin Press, 2010), 484–85.

2. Leopold, cited in: Julianne Lutz Newton, *Aldo Leopold's Odyssey: Rediscovering the Author of* A Sand County Almanac (Washington, DC: Island Press, 2006), 264.

3. Frederic Leopold, quoted in Meine, 20.

4. Ibid., 17.

5. Frederic Leopold, quoted in: Thomas Tanner, ed., *Aldo Leopold: The Man and His Legacy* (Ankeny, IA: Soil Conservation Society of America, 1987), 78.

6. Aldo Leopold, quoted in Meine, 23.

7. Ibid., 70.

8. Ibid., 41.

9. Ibid., 52.

10. Ibid., 58.

11. Ibid., 65.

12. Ibid., 81.

13. Ibid., 82.

14. Aldo Leopold, *A Sand County Almanac*, special commemorative edition (New York: Oxford University Press, 1989; first published, 1949), 134.

15. Aldo Leopold, quoted in Meine, 94.

16. Leopold, quoted in: Susan L. Flader, *Thinking Like a Mountain: Aldo Leopold and the Evolution of an Ecological Attitude toward Deer, Wolves, and Forests* (Madison, WI: University of Wisconsin Press, 1994), 53.

17. Leopold, quoted in Meine, 97.

18. Ibid., 95.

19. Ibid., 116.

20. Leopold, quoted in Tanner, 130.

21. Leopold, quoted in Meine, 130.

22. Ibid., 119.

23. Ibid., 106.

24. Ibid., 109.

25. Ibid., 152.

26. Ibid., 137.

27. Ibid., 146.

28. Flader, *Thinking Like a Mountain*, 12.

29. Leopold, quoted in Meine, 188.

30. Leopold, quoted in: Craig W. Allin, "The Leopold Legacy and American Wilderness," in Tanner, 29.

31. Leopold, quoted in Meine, 196.

32. Ibid., 183.

33. Ibid., 196.

34. Leopold, quoted in Newton, 14.

35. Meine, 234.

36. Robert A. McCabe, *Aldo Leopold: The Professor* (Amherst, WI: Palmer Publications, 1987), 134.

37. Estella Leopold, quoted in Tanner, 165–66.

38. Flader, *Thinking Like a Mountain*, 4.

39. Data from Flader, *Thinking Like a Mountain*, 21.

40. Leopold, quoted in Newton, 111.

41. Meine, 279.

42. Flader, *Thinking Like a Mountain*, 22.

43. Leopold, quoted in Meine, 277.

44. Leopold, quoted in Meine, 298.

45. Leopold, quoted in Newton, 271.

46. Leopold, quoted in: Curt Meine, "The Farmer as Conservationist: Leopold on Agriculture," in Tanner, 39.

47. Ibid., 46.

48. Aldo Leopold, *Game Management* (Madison, WI: University of Wisconsin Press, 1986; first published, 1933), xxxi.

49. Cited in Newton, 275.

50. McCabe, 4.

51. Leopold, quoted in McCabe, 16.

52. Ibid., 57.

53. Cited in Meine, 397.

54. Details in this and the previous paragraph are drawn from: Susan Flader, "Aldo Leopold's Sand County," in J. Baird Callicott, ed., *Companion to A Sand County Almanac* (Madison, WI: University of Wisconsin Press, 1987).

55. Ibid., 53.

56. Nina Leopold to Estella Leopold, in Tanner, 169–70.

57. McCabe, 94.

58. Leopold, quoted in Newton, 182.

59. Leopold, quoted in Meine, 394.

60. Ibid., 383.

61. Leopold, quoted in Flader, *Thinking Like a Mountain*, 330.

62. Meine, 405.

63. P. S. Lovejoy, quoted in Meine, 407.

64. Ibid.

65. Leopold, *A Sand County Almanac*, 224–25.

66. Leopold, quoted in: H. Albert Hochbaum, in Robert A. McCabe, *Aldo Leopold: Mentor, Department of Wildlife Ecology* (Madison, WI: University of Wisconsin Press, 1988), 63.

67. Flader, *Thinking Like a Mountain*, 138.

68. Quoted in Flader, *Thinking Like a Mountain*, 202.

69. Leopold, quoted in Flader, *Thinking Like a Mountain*, 260.

70. Letter from Estella Leopold to her sister, Nina, dated April 26, 1948, included in McCabe, *Aldo Leopold: The Professor*, 143–44.

71. Roderick Nash, "Aldo Leopold and the Limits of American Liberalism," in Tanner, 78.

Chapter 4

1. The listing for the house is at http://www.nationalregisterofhistoric places.com/md/Montgomery/state.html.

2. William O. Douglas, quoted in: Linda Lear, *Rachel Carson: Witness for Nature* (New York: Henry Holt and Company, 1997), 419.

3. Quoted in Lear, *Rachel Carson*, 174.

4. Rachel Carson, quoted in: Mark Hamilton Lytle, *The Gentle Subversive: Rachel Carson, Silent Spring, and the Rise of the Environment Movement* (New York: Oxford University Press, 2007), 15.

5. Ibid.

6. Rachel Carson, *The Sense of Wonder* (New York: Harper & Row, 1985), 45.

7. Carson, quoted in Lear, *Rachel Carson*, 42.

8. Carson, quoted in: Ginger Wadsworth, *Rachel Carson: Voice for the Earth* (Minneapolis, MN: Lernere Publications Company, 1992), 24.

9. Alfred, Lord Tennyson, "Locksley Hall," ll. 192–94. In *The Norton Anthology of English Literature*, 3rd ed., vol. 2 (New York: W. W. Norton & Co., 1974).

10. Carson, quoted in Lear, *Rachel Carson*, 40.

11. Ibid., 60.

12. Elmer Higgins, quoted in Wadsworth, 33.

13. Excerpt from *The Edge of the Sea*, reprinted in: Paul Brooks, *Rachel Carson at Work: The House of Life* (Boston: G. K. Hall & Company, 1985), 165.

14. This description of the transformation of "Undersea" from a failed government draft to a successful national magazine article comes from Lear, *Rachel Carson*, 81–88.

15. Carson, quoted in Lear, *Rachel Carson*, 88.

16. Value of royalties from Lear, *Rachel Carson*, 105. Sources give different figures for the initial sales of *Under the Sea Wind*, depending on the date chosen to report sales, but all agree that the total sales were far less than the original printing of 2,000 copies.

17. Carson, quoted in Wadsworth, 40.

18. Briggs, quoted in Lear, *Rachel Carson*, 133.

19. Carson, quoted in Lear, *Rachel Carson*, 145.

20. Sources differ on how long the book was in first place on the best-seller list. The *New York Times*, which should be the authoritative source for its own listings, in its obituary of Rachel Carson on April 15, 1964, stated that it was number one for thirty-nine weeks.

21. Cited in Wadsworth, 58.

22. Carson, quoted in Lear, *Rachel Carson*, 233.

23. Ibid., 134.

24. Ibid., 245.

25. Ibid., 160.

26. Carson, quoted in Wadsworth, 60.

27. Carson, quoted in Lear, *Rachel Carson*, 238.

28. Carson, quoted in Lytle, 118.

29. Carson, quoted in Wadsworth, 45.

30. Carson, quoted in: Linda Lear, ed., *Lost Woods: The Discovered Writing of Rachel Carson* (Boston: Beacon Press, 1998), 228.

31. Huckins, quoted in Lear, *Rachel Carson*, 315.

32. Carson, quoted in Lear, *Rachel Carson*, 362.

33. Ibid., 361–62.

34. Ibid., 340.

35. Ibid., 338.

36. Ibid., 336.

37. Discussion of the titling process for *Silent Spring* can be found in Lear, *Rachel Carson*, 389, and in Lytle, 157.

38. Rachel Carson, *Silent Spring* (New York: Crest Book edition, 1964; first published by Houghton Mifflin, 1962), 13–15.

39. President Kennedy, in an August 1962 press conference, was asked if the government was concerned about pesticides. He responded that it was, "particularly since the publication of Miss Carson's book." (Quoted in Lytle, 176.)

40. Carson, *Silent Spring*, 22.

41. Quoted in Lear, *Rachel Carson*, 409.

42. Quoted in Lytle, 178.

43. "The Desolate Year" (pamphlet issued by the Monsanto Company, 1963), quoted in: Priscilla Coit Murphy, *What a Book Can Do: The Publication and Reception of* Silent Spring (Amherst, MA: University of Massachusetts Press, 2005), 100.

44. Quoted in the *New York Times* obituary of Rachel Carson, April 15, 1964. Accounts differ about the role of White-Stevens, whether he was employed by the industry or not, whether he was paid for his efforts or not.

45. The CBS program is discussed in Lytle, 179–83, and in Lear, *Rachel Carson*, 143–50.

46. Robert White-Stevens, quoted in Lear, *Rachel Carson*, 449.

47. Carson, quoted in Lear, *Rachel Carson*, 450.

48. Eric Sevareid, quoted in Lear, *Rachel Carson*, 452.

49. Abraham Ribicoff, quoted in Lytle, 187.

50. The exact number of copies of *Silent Spring* that have been sold is not public information.

51. Excerpt from an essay Rachel Carson wrote to accompany a bibliography for the National Council of Teachers of English, which appeared in 1956. The section included here is quoted in Lear, *Lost Woods*, 165–66.

52. Carson, quoted in Lear, *Rachel Carson*, 442.

53. Carson, letter to Dorothy Freeman, quoted in Lear, *Lost Woods*, 247.

Chapter 5

1. Gomercindo Rodrigues, *Walking the Forest with Chico Mendes: The Struggle for Justice in the Amazon* (Austin, TX: University of Texas Press, 2007), 20. Rodrigues went by the nickname "Goma," but Mendes always called him "Guma."

2. Andrew Revkin, *The Burning Season: The Murder of Chico Mendes and the Fight for the Amazon Rain Forest* (Washington, DC: Island Press, 2004), xv.

3. "White gold" reference from: Felipe Milanez, interview with Gomercindo Rodrigues, *Chico Vive* (blog), December 22, 2013, http://www.chicovive .org/node/59.

4. Information about rubber trees from: Alex Shoumatoff, *The World Is Burning* (Boston: Little, Brown and Company, 1990).

5. Revkin, 43.

6. Information about Acre's rubber production from: Anthony Hall, "Did Chico Mendes Die in Vain? Brazilian Rubber Tappers in the 1990s," in Helen Collinson, ed., *Green Guerrillas: Environmental Conflicts and Initiatives in Latin America and the Caribbean* (London: Latin American Bureau, 1996), 93–102.

7. Rodrigues, 65.

8. Mendes, in: Miranda Smith, *Voice of the Amazon* (film), 1989.

9. Chico Mendes, *Fight for the Forest: Chico Mendes in His Own Words* (London: Latin American Bureau, 1989), 17.

10. Augusta Dwyer, *Into the Amazon: Chico Mendes and the Struggle for the Rain Forest* (Toronto: Key Porter Books, 1990), 10.

11. Quoted in Revkin, 75.

12. Mendes, *Fight for the Forest*, 17.

13. Rodrigues, 126.

14. Mendes, *Fight for the Forest*, 18.

15. Ibid., 19.

16. Mendes, quoted in: Bjorn Maybury-Lewis, *The Politics of the Possible: The Brazilian Rural Workers' Trade Union Movement, 1964–1985* (Philadelphia: Temple University Press, 1994), 223.

17. Mendes, in Smith film.

18. Euclides Tavora, quoted in Dwyer, 19.

19. Mendes, *Fight for the Forest*, 21.

20. Tavora, quoted in Dwyer, 19.

21. Mendes, quoted in Maybury-Lewis, 224.

22. Reported in Dwyer, 5.

23. Smith film.

24. Mendes, *Fight for the Forest*, 22.

25. Smith film.

26. Data about land speculation from Revkin, 135.

27. Mendes, in Dwyer, 21.

28. Mendes in Rodrigues, 148.

29. Mendes, in Revkin, 5.

30. Ilsamar Mendes, quoted in Revkin, 212.

31. Mendes, *Fight for the Forest*, 22.

32. Mendes, quoted in Maybury-Lewis, 224.

33. Milanez.

34. Mendes, quoted in Dwyer, 22.

35. Ilsamar Mendes, quoted in Shoumatoff, 76.

36. Mendes, *Fight for the Forest*, 2.

37. Mendes, quoted in Shoumatoff, 29.

38. Quoted in Dwyer, 4.

39. Ilsamar Mendes in Smith film.

40. Revkin, 8.

41. Mendes, *Fight for the Forest*, 72.

42. Ibid., 37.

43. Mendes, quoted in Dwyer, 10.

44. Mendes, quoted in Shoumatoff, 28.

45. Quoted in Shoumatoff, 100.

46. Mary Allegretti, quoted in Revkin, 180.

47. Quoted in Revkin, 203.

48. Mendes, quoted in Maybury-Lewis, 228.

49. Revkin, 177.

50. Mendes, quoted in Dwyer, 11.

51. Mendes, *Fight for the Forest*, 43.

52. Revkin, 219.

53. Mendes, *Fight for the Forest*, 63.

54. Goma Rodrigues in Smith film.

55. Steven Schwartzman, *EDF's Schwartzman Remembers Chico Mendes* (blog), 2008, http://blogs.edf.org/climatetalks/2008/edfs-schwartzman-remembers -chico-mendes/.

56. Mendes, quoted in Maybury-Lewis, 230.

57. Mendes, *Fight for the Forest*, 51.

58. Milanez.

59. Mendes in Smith film.

60. Mendes, quoted in Maybury-Lewis, 229.

61. Moacyr Grechi, quoted in Shoumatoff, 72.

62. Steven Schwartzman, quoted in Shoumatoff, 88.

63. Collinson, 2.

64. Mendes, quoted in Rodrigues, 151.

65. Mendes, quoted in Maybury-Lewis, 226.

66. Shoumatoff, 90.

67. Mendes, quoted in Maybury-Lewis, 227.

68. Mendes in Smith film.

69. Quoted in Shoumatoff, 91.

70. Quoted in Revkin, 227.

71. Mendes, quoted in Revkin, 268.

72. Mendes, quoted in Maybury-Lewis, 234.

73. Darly Alves da Silva, quoted in Revkin, 266.

74. For information on extractive reserves from Unidades de Conser-vação, see: http://uc.socioambiental.org/en/uso-sustent%C3%A1velextractive -reserve.

75. Milanez.

76. Al Gore in Smith film.

77. Luiz Inácio Lula da Silva, quoted in: "Brazil Salutes Chico Mendes 25 Years after His Murder," *Guardian*, December 20, 2013, http://www.the-guardian.com/world/2013/dec/20/brazil-salutes-chico-mendes-25-years -after-his-murder.

78. Marina Silva, quoted in Rodrigues, xi.

Chapter 6

1. Trova Heffernan, *Where the Salmon Run: The Life and Legacy of Billy Frank Jr.* (Seattle, WA: University of Washington Press, 2012).

2. Charles Wilkinson, *Messages from Frank's Landing: A Story of Salmon, Treaties, and the Indian Way* (Seattle, WA: University of Seattle Press, 2000), 6.

3. Billy Frank Jr., "Message from the Chairman," Northwest Indian Fish-eries Commission (NWIFC) website, May 22, 2013, http://nwifc.org/.

4. Frank, quoted in Heffernan, *Where the Salmon Run*, 33.

5. Billy Frank Jr., *Tell the Truth: The Collected Columns of Billy Frank Jr.* (Olympia, WA: Northwest Indian Fisheries Commission, 2015), 152.

6. Frank, quoted in Heffernan, *Where the Salmon Run*, 35–36.

7. Ibid., 35.

8. Ibid., 33.

9. Willie Frank in the film documentary *As Long as the Rivers Run*, produced in 1971 by filmmaker Carol Burns. The film is now owned by and available from Salmon Defense. It can be accessed at http://salmondefense .org/projects/as-long-as-the-rivers-run/.

10. Frank, quoted in Wilkinson, 21.

11. Frank, quoted in Heffernan, *Where the Salmon Run*, 33.

12. Frank, quoted in Wilkinson, 3.

13. This is perhaps the most often told story used to illustrate the early life of Billy Frank Jr. It is recited in Wilkinson, 4, and Heffernan, 44.

14. Much of the information in this section is drawn from: Richard Kluger, *The Bitter Waters of Medicine Creek: A Tragic Clash between White and Native America* (New York: Alfred A. Knopf, 2011). The other major source is a booklet: Maria Pascualy and Cecilia Carpenter, "Remembering Medicine Creek" (Madison, WI: Fireweed Press, 2005). This booklet accompanied an exhibit at the Washington State History Museum, Tacoma.

15. Kluger, 57–61.

16. Ibid., 35.

17. The phrase "Young Man in a Hurry" is the subtitle of the definitive biography of Stevens, Kent Richards's *Isaac I. Stevens: Young Man in a Hurry*, WSU Press Reprint Series (Pullman, WA: Washington State University Press, 1993), described by Kluger, 3.

18. The entire treaty is reproduced verbatim in Pascualy and Carpenter, 28–30. The sixty-two Indian signers are listed in Pascualy and Carpenter, 22.

19. Willie Frank, quoted in Heffernan, *Where the Salmon Run*, 29.

20. Billy Frank Jr., "Letter from the Chairman," *2012 State of Our Watersheds Report*, NWIFC, 3.

21. Tom Keefe, quoted in Heffernan, *Where the Salmon Run*, 62.

22. Wilkinson, 31.

23. Frank, quoted in Wilkinson, 32.

24. Quoted in Heffernan, *Where the Salmon Run*, 46.

25. Reports differ somewhat on the timing and duration of Frank's struggle with alcohol and the specific events that led him to rehabilitation and eventual sobriety. The important point is that, despite fears of family members and friends that he would relapse during several emotionally trying episodes, he remained sober for the rest of his life.

26. Frank, quoted in Heffernan, *Where the Salmon Run*, 82.

27. Frank, quoted in Wilkinson, 34.

28. Frank, quoted in Heffernan, *Where the Salmon Run*, 80.

29. Ibid., 62.

30. Ibid.

31. Wilkinson, 38.

32. Frank, quoted in Wilkinson, 43. The phrase "I was a getting-arrested guy" is repeated in several accounts.

33. Willie Frank III, quoted in Wilkinson, 8.

34. Dan Evans, quoted in Heffernan, *Where the Salmon Run*, 72.

35. Much of the information for this section comes from the edited volume of Hank Adams's writings: David E. Wilkins, ed., *The Hank Adams Reader: An Exemplary Native Activist and the Unleashing of Indigenous Sovereignty* (Golden, CO: Fulcrum Publishing, 2011). The compilation begins with a substantial biographical introduction by Wilkins.

36. Marlon Brando, quoted in Heffernan, *Where the Salmon Run*, 74.

37. Hank Adams's contributions to Carol Burns's film, *As Long as the Rivers Run*, are credited differently in various sources. Sometimes he is credited with convincing her to do the film, sometimes he is listed as a coproducer, but I believe the most accurate description of his role is content advisor.

38. Wilkinson, 46.

39. Trova Heffernan, "The Most Important Indian," Legacy Project, Washington Secretary of State, 2012, http://www.sos.wa.gov/legacyproject/oral histories/BillyFrankJr/pdf/HankAdams.pdf.

40. Wilkins, 1.

41. Jack Anderson, quoted in Wilkins, 13.

42. Suzan Shown Harjo, "Hank Adams: An Unassuming Visionary," *Indian Country News*, January 11, 2006.

43. Adams, quoted in Heffernan, "The Most Important Indian."

44. Harjo.

45. Ibid., vii.

46. Heffernan, "The Most Important Indian."

47. Janet McCloud, quoted in Heffernan, *Where the Salmon Run*, 69.

48. United States Code, Title 4, Chapter 1, Section 8 a (the "Flag Code"); it describes the only condition under which an American flag can be flown with the blue field of stars at the bottom.

49. Maiselle Bridges, quoted in Heffernan, *Where the Salmon Run*, 116.

50. Frank, *Tell the Truth*, 190.

51. Alison Bridges, quoted in Heffernan, *Where the Salmon Run*, 117.

52. Frank, *Tell the Truth*, 189.

53. Frank, quoted in Heffernan, *Where the Salmon Run*, 129.

54. Wilkinson, 51.

55. Ibid., 61.

56. Information is from Yelm History Project, Part VI—The Boldt Decision (1974–1979), Yelm Community Schools, Yelm, Washington.

57. Wilkinson, 62.

58. Yelm History Project.

59. Heffernan, *Where the Salmon Run*, 148.

60. Frank, quoted in Heffernan, *Where the Salmon Run*, 139.

61. Adams, quoted in Wilkins, 27.

62. Frank, *Tell the Truth*, 176.

63. From the preamble to the NWIFC Constitution, available on the NWIFC website at: http://nwifc.org/w/wp-content/uploads/downloads/2016/01/NWIFC-annual-report-1.pdf.

64. Adams, quoted in Heffernan, *Where the Salmon Run*, 157.

65. Frank, quoted in Heffernan, *Where the Salmon Run*, 156.

66. Bill Wilkerson, quoted in Heffernan, *Where the Salmon Run*, 186.

67. Ibid., 188.

68. Frank, *Tell the Truth*, 141.

69. "How Tribes and State Co-manage Salmon and Steelhead," Washington Department of Fish and Wildlife, 2016, http://wdfw.wa.gov/conservation/salmon/co-management.

70. Wilkerson, quoted in Heffernan, *Where the Salmon Run*, 203.

71. Heffernan, *Where the Salmon Run*, 206.

72. Frank, quoted in Wilkinson, 80.

73. William Yardley, "Billy Frank Jr., 83, Defiant Fighter for Native Fishing Rights," *New York Times*, May 9, 2014.

74. Jim Adams, "Billy Frank Jr., American Indian Visionary 2004," *Indian Country Today*, January 5, 2004, http://indiancountrytodaymedianetwork.com/2004/01/05/billy-frank-jr-american-indian-visionary-2004-89785.

75. Heffernan, *Where the Salmon Run*, 282.

76. Shaunna McCovery, "River Revolutionary: Billy Frank Jr. Is the Conscience of Salmon Country," *Edible Portland*, Fall 2012, 28–37.

77. Billy Frank Jr., reported in *NWIFC News*, Summer 2014, 5.

78. Jeff Shaw, ibid., 8.

Chapter 7

1. This quote and the quote in the preceding paragraph are from the press release of the Norwegian Nobel Committee announcing the awarding of

the 2004 Peace Prize to Maathai; see: http://www.nobelprize.org/nobel_prizes /peace/laureates/2004/press.html.

2. Wangari Maathai, *The Challenge for Africa* (New York: Anchor Books, 2009), 21.

3. Wangari Maathai, Nobel lecture, 2004, http://www.nobelprize.org /nobel_prizes/peace/laureates/2004/maathai-lecture.html.

4. Wangari Maathai, *The Green Belt Movement: Sharing the Approach and the Experience* (New York: Lantern Books, 1985), xiii.

5. Wangari Maathai, *Unbowed: A Memoir* (New York: Anchor Books, 2007), 4.

6. Wangari Maathai, *Replenishing the Earth: Spiritual Values for Healing Ourselves and the World* (New York: Doubleday, 2010), 78.

7. Maathai, *Unbowed*, 4.

8. Ibid., 8–9.

9. Ibid., 11.

10. Ibid., 13.

11. Ibid., 16.

12. Ibid., 44.

13. Ibid., 38.

14. Ibid., 39.

15. Ibid., 41.

16. Ibid., 72.

17. Ibid.

18. John F. Kennedy, quoted in "JFK and the Student Airlift" (undated webpage), John F. Kennedy Presidential Library and Museum, http://www .jfklibrary.org/JFK/JFK-in-History/JFK-and-the-Student-Airlift.aspx.

19. Maathai, *Unbowed*, 74.

20. Ibid., 74.

21. Ibid., 87.

22. Ibid., 92.

23. Ibid., 95.

24. Ibid., 101.

25. Ibid., 133.

26. Priscilla Sears, "Wangari Maathai: 'You Strike the Woman . . . ,'" originally appearing in *Making It Happen* (Context Institute, spring 1991), available at: http://www.context.org/icilib/ic28/sears/.

27. Maathai, *Unbowed*, 140.

28. Ibid., 151.

29. Ibid., 158.

30. Mary Jo Breton, *Women Pioneers for the Environment* (Boston: North-eastern University Press, 1998), 17.

31. Maathai, Nobel lecture.

32. Maathai, *The Challenge for Africa*, 244.

33. Maathai, *Replenishing the Earth*, 25.

34. Maathai, *Unbowed*, 124–25.

35. Ibid., 125.

36. Kerry Kennedy Cuomo, *Speak Truth to Power: Human Rights Defenders Who Are Changing Our World* (New York: Crown Publishers, 2000), 40.

37. Maathai, *Unbowed*, 138.

38. Maathai, *The Green Belt Movement*, ch. 2.

39. Ibid., 22.

40. Ibid., 27.

41. Maathai, quoted in Cuomo, 40.

42. Maathai, *The Green Belt Movement*, 33.

43. Ibid., ch. 3.

44. Maathai, *Unbowed*, 163.

45. Ibid., 168.

46. Ibid., 175.

47. Data about the program are drawn from the annual reports of the Green Belt Movement; see: http://www.greenbeltmovement.org/sites/green beltmovement.org/files/2012%20Annual%20Report.pdf.

48. Maathai, Nobel lecture.

49. Maathai, quoted in Sears.

50. Maathai, *Unbowed*, 191.

51. Ibid., 196.

52. Ibid., 196.

53. Ibid., 197.

54. Maathai, quoted in Cuomo, 42–43.

55. Maathai, *Unbowed*, 203.

56. Maathai, *The Challenge for Africa*, 56–57.

57. Ibid., 167.

58. Ibid., 169.

59. Maathai, *Unbowed*, 207.

60. Ibid., 215.

61. Ibid., 265.

62. Ibid., 286.

63. Maathai, quoted in: Nicola Graydon, "From Tiny Seeds . . . ," *Ecologist* 35, no. 2 (2005): 36–39.

64. The Green Belt Movement provides a comprehensive list of Maathai's honors and awards; see: http://www.greenbeltmovement.org/wangari -maathai/biography.

65. Maathai, *The Green Belt Movement*, 128.

66. John Vidal, "Wangari Maathai, the Woman I Knew," *Guardian*, September 26, 2011.

67. Maathai, *The Challenge for Africa*, 20.

68. Ibid., 230.

69. Vidal, "Wangari Maathai, the Woman I Knew."

70. Maathai, *Replenishing the Earth*, 191.

71. Jeffrey Gettleman, "Wangari Maathai, Nobel Peace Prize Laureate, Dies at 71," *New York Times*, September 27, 2011.

72. Anita Price Davis and Marla J. Selvidge, *Women Nobel Peace Prize Winners* (Jefferson, NC: McFarland & Company, 2006), 198.

73. Lisa Merton and Alan Dater, *Planting Hope: Wangari Maathai & the Green Belt Movement*, video, Marlboro Productions, Marlboro, VT, 2009.

Chapter 8

1. Gro Harlem Brundtland, *Madam Prime Minister: A Life in Power and Politics* (New York: Farrar, Straus and Giroux, 2002), 92.

2. Ibid., 93.

3. Robin J. Law, "The *Ekofisk Bravo* Blowout, 1977," pp. 1107–8 in Mervin F. Fingas, ed., *Oil Spill Science and Technology: Prevention, Response, and Cleanup* (Burlington, MA: Elsevier, 2011).

4. Ibid., 100.

5. Brundtland, *Madam Prime Minister*, 101.

6. Sarah L. Henderson, "Gro Harlem Brundtland of Norway," pp. 43–79 in M. A. Genovese and J. S. Steckenrider, eds., *Women as Political Leaders: Studies in Gender and Governing* (New York: Routledge, 2013), 43.

7. References to Brundtland's nicknames have been widely reported, in many sources.

8. Brundtland, *Madam Prime Minister*, 3.

9. Ibid., 7.

10. Ibid., 26.

11. Ibid., 14.

12. Joan Axelrod-Contrada, *Women Who Led Nations* (Minneapolis, MN: Oliver Press, 1999), 122.

13. Brundtland, *Madam Prime Minister*, 26.

14. Gro Harlem Brundtland, acceptance speech for Catalonia Award, United Nations Foundation, June 22, 2014; available at: http://www.unfounda tion.org/news-and-media/publications-and-speeches/catalonia-award -ceremony.html?referrer=https://www.google.co.uk/.

15. Brundtland, *Madam Prime Minister*, 26.

16. Ibid., 23.

17. Ibid., 18.

18. Ibid., 19.

19. Ibid., 14.

20. Ibid., 20.

21. Ibid., 28.

22. Ibid., 32.

23. Ibid., 32.

24. Ibid., 32.

25. Ibid., 32–33.

26. Ibid., 37.

27. Ibid., 39.

28. Axelrod-Contrada, 123.

29. Brundtland, *Madam Prime Minister*, 40.

30. Ibid., 45.

31. Ibid., 47.

32. Ibid., 47–48.

33. Ibid., 40.

34. Ibid., 59.

35. Olga S. Opfell, *Women Prime Ministers and Presidents* (Jefferson, NC: McFarland & Company, 1993), 104.

36. Brundtland, *Madam Prime Minister*, 60.

37. Brundtland, quoted in: Laura Liswood, *Women World Leaders: Fifteen Great Politicians Tell Their Stories* (London: Pandora, 1995), 51.

38. Ibid., 51.

39. Opfell, 105.

40. Brundtland, *Madam Prime Minister*, 69.

41. Ibid., 100.

42. Opfell, 105.

43. Brundtland, *Madam Prime Minister*, 90.

44. Opfell, 106.

45. Brundtland, *Madam Prime Minister*, 84.

46. Nancy Gibbs, "Norway's Radical Daughter," *Time* magazine, June 24, 2001, http://content.time.com/time/magazine/article/0,9171,152609,00.html.

47. Brundtland, *Madam Prime Minister*, 105.

48. Ibid., 104.

49. Ibid., 102.

50. A concise description of how parliamentary seats are won in Norway is available in Liswood, 113.

51. Brundtland, *Madam Prime Minister*, 115.

52. Ibid., 115.

53. Ibid., 116.

54. Ibid.

55. Ibid., 133–34.

56. Ibid., 138–39.

57. Ibid., 190.

58. Brundtland, quoted in: Mary Joy Breton, *Women Pioneers for the Environment* (Boston: Northeastern University Press, 1998), 188.

59. Iris Borowy, *Defining Sustainable Development for Our Common Future: A History of the World Commission on Environment and Development (Brundtland Commission)* (Abingdon, England: Routledge, 2014), 55.

60. Brundtland, in "Chairman's Foreword" to: World Commission on Environment and Development, *Our Common Future* (Oxford: Oxford University Press, 1987), x. (*Our Common Future* is also known as "The Brundtland Report.")

61. Brundtland, *Madam Prime Minister*, 195.

62. Jim MacNeill, "From Controversy to Consensus—Building Global Agreement for Change," *Environmental Policy and Law* 37, no. 2 (2007): 243.

63. Brundtland, *Madam Prime Minister*, 195.

64. MacNeill, "From Controversy to Consensus," 245.

65. Borowy, 57.

66. Brundtland, *Madam Prime Minister*, 197.

67. MacNeill, "From Controversy to Consensus," 245.

68. Jim MacNeill, "Brundtland+25; Rio+20," *Environmental Policy and Law* 44, nos. 1–2 (2014): 28.

69. Brundtland, quoted in Borowy, 58.

70. Ibid.

71. Brundtland, *Madam Prime Minister*, 197.

72. Ibid., 199.

73. MacNeill, "Brundtland+25; Rio+20," 28.

74. MacNeill, "From Controversy to Consensus," 244.

75. Ibid.

76. Ibid.

77. Brundtland, *Madam Prime Minister*, 202.

78. Borowy, 69.

79. Brundtland, *Madam Prime Minister*, 213.

80. *Our Common Future*, 157.

81. MacNeill, "From Controversy to Consensus," 245.

82. *Our Common Future*, 8.

83. MacNeill, "From Controversy to Consensus," 246.

84. Robert Mugabe, quoted in Borowy, 159.

85. Borowy, 169.

86. MacNeill, "Brundtland+25; Rio+20," 29. Other estimates of the number of Google hits for sustainable development range widely; suffice it to say that the phrase gets a lot of hits.

87. Brundtland, *Madam Prime Minister*, 237.

88. Ibid., 241.

89. Henderson, 52.

90. Brundtland, acceptance speech for Catalonia Award.

91. Brundtland, *Madam Prime Minister*, 308.

92. Axelrod-Contrada, 134.

93. Steiner Andresen, "Whaling: Peace at Home, War Abroad," pp. 41–63 in J. B. Skjaerseth, ed., *International Regimes and Norway's Environmental Policy: Crossfire and Coherence* (Aldershot, England: Ashgate Publishing, 2004), 50.

94. Ibid.

95. Ibid., 51.

96. Roy Hattersley, "The Observer Profile: Earth Mother Gro Harlem Brundtland, the UN's New Hope," *The Observer*, January 1, 2011. Reference for approval rating is Henderson, 63–64.

97. Brundtland, *Madam Prime Minister*, 427.

98. Ibid., 471.

99. Ibid., 457.

100. H. C. Bugge and L. Watters, "A Perspective on Sustainable Development after Johannesburg on the Fifteenth Anniversary of *Our Common Future*: An Interview with Gro Harlem Brundtland," *Georgetown International Law Review* 15 (2003): 364.

101. Brundtland, acceptance speech for Catalonia Award.

102. Brundtland, *Madam Prime Minister*, 464.

103. Ibid., 462–63.

104. Gro Harlem Brundtland, "Rio+20 Report Card and Our Common Future" (acceptance speech for Huntington Environmental Prize, Woods Hole Research Center, MA, February 7, 2013; available at: http://whrc.org/wp-content/uploads/2015/05/Bruntland_HuntingtonPrize_Speech.pdf).

105. Philip Shabecoff, "Norway and Canada Call for Pact to Protect Atmosphere," *New York Times*, June 28, 1988.

106. Andrew C. Revkin, "20 Years Later, Again Assigned to Fight Climate Change," *New York Times*, May 8, 2007.

107. Gro Harlem Brundtland, "On Population, Environment, and Development," *Population and Development Review* 19, no. 4 (1993): 899.

About the Author

Larry A. Nielsen is Professor of Natural Resources at North Carolina State University. He has worked in land grant universities—including earlier tenures at Virginia Tech and Penn State—for forty years, as a faculty member and administrator, eventually becoming provost of North Carolina State University before returning to teaching and writing in 2009. He is a Fellow and Past President of the American Fisheries Society. He is author, coauthor, or coeditor of six books, including *Ecosystem Management*, published by Island Press, and *Provost*, a memoir and an analysis of university administration. Among many professional service roles, he served on the board of directors of the National Council for Science and the Environment for more than a decade. With Sharon, his wife of forty-six years, he lives in Raleigh, North Carolina.

Index

Page numbers followed by "f" indicate illustrations and photographs.